LIVING THE QUESTIONS

Living
the
Questions

THE WISDOM OF
PROGRESSIVE CHRISTIANITY

David M. Felten and
Jeff Procter-Murphy

HarperOne
An Imprint of HarperCollins*Publishers*

HarperOne

HarperCollins books may be purchased for educational,
business, or sales promotional use. For information, please e-mail
the Special Markets Department at SPsales@harpercollins.com.

HarperCollins website: http://www.harpercollins.com

HarperCollins®, 🏠®, and HarperOne™ are
trademarks of HarperCollins Publishers.

FIRST EDITION

Designed by Greta D. Sibley

Library of Congress Cataloging-in-Publication Data
Felten, David M.
Living the questions : the wisdom of progressive Christianity /
David M. Felten and Jeff Procter-Murphy. — 1st ed.
p. cm.
Includes bibliographical references.
ISBN 978–0–06–210936–1
1. Liberalism (Religion) I. Procter-Murphy, Jeff. II. Title.
BR1615.F45 2012
230'.046 — dc23
2012004793

17 18 19 20 RRD(H) 16 15 14 13 12 11 10 9 8

To
Nathaniel, Mattie, and Samuel,
Rachel and Claire,
for the gift of being your dads.

CONTENTS

SECTION THREE   Transformation

The beginning of true wisdom is asking the questions for which there are no answers.

—Harrell Beck

Preface

A religion is as much a progressive unlearning of
false ideas concerning God as it is the
learning of the true ideas concerning God.

—Rabbi Mordecai Kaplan, founder of the
Reconstructionist movement of Judaism

It was early in the fall and the group settled in for its first session of the Bible study. In introducing the Genesis material for discussion, the facilitator referred to Adam and Eve as metaphors and not historic individuals. The participants' reactions were swift—and representative of what might occur in many churches. There was anger: "How dare you question the Bible? I just knew you were one of those damned liberals who dismantle everything to suit your political agenda!" There was panic: "Why are you trying to destroy my faith? What else do I believe that isn't true?" There was confusion: "You mean there are *two* Creation stories in Genesis? How come I've never seen this before? What else have I missed?" And there were tears.

But there was also relief. There were some who looked at the facilitator as though she had opened a door they'd been peeking through for years. One participant said, "Thank you, thank you, thank you. I've known in my heart there was more to these stories, that reading them as a literal account didn't make sense. But I never said anything because I was afraid it would make me a heretic."

And these are the people who were interested enough to commit to a Bible study! A lot of people just don't care anymore. They stopped going to church long ago because nothing they heard or experienced resonated with them. Despite claims by church-growth gurus, the fields are not "ripe for harvest." Far from it. As one Christian pollster noted, the large numbers of people not involved in faith communities are not just waiting to be invited to church. They are passionately disinterested in the church.

The graying and abandonment of so-called old-line churches is but one symptom of this disinterest and dissatisfaction with the way churches do religion. Many speak of being "spiritual" rather than "religious," honest rather than hypocritical. Evangelical and fundamentalist leaders attribute the atrophy of the old-line church's influence and its ever-decreasing numbers to those churches having failed to proclaim the "true" gospel. Meanwhile, superficial arguments over issues like the preference of music styles and levels of formality in worship only continue to serve as a distraction from the real problem: people are dissatisfied with the core message, dogma, and practice of the Christian faith in today's world.

The fields are *not* filled with faithless people in need of the gospel. They are filled with people of deep spiritual integrity who simply cannot suffer the shallow message of the churches of their birth any longer. These people have an intuitive sense that there is more to Christianity than the rigid rules and theological constructs of the past. As philosopher Sam Keen reminds us, "History is littered with the remains of civilizations that chose to die rather than change their organizing myth."[1] Without a reevaluation of the organizing myths of Christianity, the church seems poised to pass into the same irrelevance as so many religions of the past.

But there is another conversation going on, and it's been going for a long time.

As pastors, we became concerned that there were very few resources available for lay people that approached the depth and breadth of theological reflection that we encountered in seminary. What we needed was a practical tool to bring together, reeducate, and equip thinking Christians to wrestle with the latest scholarship and how it affects the way disciples engage with the realities of the twenty-first century. It soon became clear that if we wanted it, we would have to produce it ourselves.

Tapping video footage of some of the most provocative and authoritative voices of Christianity, the result was the *Living the Questions* DVD series. Envisioned as a way to expose lay people to the best of contemporary theological thought, the format combined in-class video segments, written material, and open-ended discussion questions that gave people permission to wrestle with many of the questions that are too often ignored or avoided by many churches.

This book is an effort to expand the conversation even further. Although the church might have been the obvious place for these questions in the past, a growing segment of the population stopped taking the church seriously a long time ago. What hasn't gone away is people's longing for meaning—our very human need to work through what theologian Paul Tillich called issues of "ultimate concern." With fewer and fewer people looking to church-sponsored studies or a person in a pulpit for guidance, it made sense to us to make the resources of the DVD series available in another format.

In the pages that follow you'll find much of the written material from the *Living the Questions 2.0* guidebook, combined with the words of the great thinkers and practitioners featured in the DVDs—people like John Dominic Crossan, Sister Helen Prejean, and Brian McLaren. You'll also hear from writers and thinkers who wrestled with these questions centuries ago. These are voices that have inspired and encouraged us as we've waded through our own questions and doubts, and we think you'll find them hopeful companions along your path.

Much of the original written material was first developed as we collaborated on sermons in our local churches. To that end we owe a great deal of thanks to teachers and mentors like Harrell Beck, Ted Loder, Mark Trotter, and DeWane Zimmerman, all of whom contributed to our thinking and approach. You'll also find the wisdom of colleague Rev. Cynthia Langston Kirk, whose poetry was originally published as part of a devotional supplement to the *LtQ2* participant guide.

The result of all this collaboration is a lively presentation of ideas and controversies and theological perspectives that we hope will expose readers to the ideas and concepts that have been taught and discussed for generations in our seminaries, ideas that for a host of reasons don't get taught or discussed in our churches. *Living the Questions* is for those who are yearning for something more than the shallow platitudes that too often pass for theology in our churches. It's for those who are looking for a faith conversation that encourages questions and open dialogue. *Living the Questions* doesn't offer a "systematic theology," but is more of a thematic overview borne of day-to-day conversation and questions raised both in—and outside—the local parish.

Living the Questions is divided into three sections, each with seven chapters. Each section delves deeper into the wisdom of what has been being discussed for generations but what is today called "progressive" Christianity. Using the metaphor of journey for life in the Spirit, we start with Section One: Journey, which serves as a general overview of progressive Christianity. Section Two: Reconciliation concerns the healing of relationships between God and self, humanity, and our relationship with the earth. Section Three: Transformation seeks to uncover renewed meaning in some of what have become threadbare concepts at the heart of popular Christianity. Altogether, we think the concepts of Journey, Reconciliation, and Transformation offer a path toward new life in the Spirit and for the future of the faith. In the back of this book you'll find a reader's guide to help facilitate individual reflection and small group discussion.

Many of us know that at its core, Christianity has something good to offer the human race. At the same time, we have a sense that the version of Christianity we see in the media, or hear about in political debates, or read about in the news, isn't the kind of faith we can embrace. Many feel like there's no place in organized religion for deep thought, doubt, or questions that challenge the status quo.

Living the Questions is meant to create that place for you. It's an invitation for those who seek to go beyond the stagnant clichés of faith and pursue the questions that deepen your understanding as you make your way through a lifelong spiritual journey.

There is a revolutionary re-visioning of Christianity emerging in the world. It is our hope that this book will be a resource for you in joining with those who are discovering a faith that is relevant and meaningful in the twenty-first century.

—Rev. David M. Felten and Rev. Jeff Procter-Murphy
    Phoenix, Arizona

Unless otherwise indicated, all quotations (including block quotes) are taken from *Living the Questions 2.0: An Introduction to Progressive Christianity*, a DVD and internet-based program created by David M. Felten and Jeff Procter-Murphy. Group and home editions are available at www.livingthequestions.com.

SECTION ONE

Journey

1

An Invitation to Journey

Live the questions now. Perhaps then, someday far
in the future, you will gradually, without even
noticing it, live your way into the answer.[1]

—Rainer Maria Rilke

There's an old joke about a man talking to his rabbi. He asks, "Why is it that rabbis always answer a question with another question?" The rabbi answers, "So what's wrong with a question?"

Jesus was typical of the rabbis of his day. According to the canonical Gospels, Jesus rarely gave a straight answer to a question. Instead, he put his questioners in a position of having to think for themselves. Rather than offer his disciples answers to life's most perplexing problems, Jesus introduced them to deeper and deeper levels of ambiguity.

Clearly Jesus knew what mystics and the wisest of spiritual guides have known all along: that answers can provide a false sense of security and pride that can stand in the way of a deeper awareness of the Divine.

And yet our twenty-first-century Western culture revels in instant gratification—the easy fix. We want our answers, our entertainment, and our sense of personal fulfillment and we want it now! The idea that something worthwhile might require careful thought or take a long time to develop is not only uncomfortable for some, but often condemned as suspicious or morally questionable by those who like to think they have all the answers.

This consumer mentality bleeds over into religion and spirituality. We want salvation or fulfillment in a simple, easy-to-understand, instantly accessible formula. Rooted in our primal fascination with all things magic (just say this prayer/incantation and you're all set!), many churches have warped Jesus's life-transforming call to "follow me" into a smorgasbord of methods for achieving wealth, health, and victory in a few painless and mindlessly easy steps.

Take, for example, the way many churches use the phrase "born again" to indicate that a person is a Christian. Even though a whole religious culture has risen up around the phrase, the concept of being born again is essentially based on a mistranslation.

The phrase comes from John 3:3. And while some biblical translations have Jesus telling Nicodemus that he must be "born again," the more accurate translation has Jesus telling Nicodemus that he must be born "from above" (*anothen* in Greek). Nicodemus misunderstands and asks, "How can anyone be born after having grown old?"

This mistranslation has led to two very different approaches to the spiritual life. Being born again has come to mean a once-and-for-all experience of God's grace and love. Insofar as it can be the first step in a life's journey of faith, being born again can be a helpful experience and concept. But Jesus never said you have to be born again. He said you have to be born "from above." Being born from above implies a journey, a process, an orientation, a way of life.

Consider the words of John Shelby Spong, who says:

> The Christian life is a journey and people ought to enjoy it. The people that think they have arrived are the ones that always get us in trouble. Anytime somebody thinks the journey is over and they have finally achieved the truth, they always put their wagons in a circle and begin to defend their truth against all comers and

in the process they kill one another. There is nothing about the Christian life that says it ever is complete. It is ultimately a journey into the mystery of God. Now, there are some things about the journey that I think are important: One is you can't start anywhere. You've got to start somewhere in particular. You cannot just say, "Well I'll go out here into the wild blue yonder." The way you start a journey into the mystery of God, I believe, is in the faith tradition, which is native to you. For you and me this would be the Christian tradition. Jesus becomes the doorway, the point of entry; so you enter into the journey through the tradition with which you are familiar and then you begin to walk into and journey toward the mystery.

EVOLUTIONARY, NOT REVOLUTIONARY

The author Maya Angelou speaks to the lifelong journey of faith. She says, "I'm startled or taken aback when people walk up to me and tell me they are Christians. My first response is the question 'Already?'"[2] Arriving at some point of spiritual completion is unlikely for most of us. Besides making us totally insufferable, this view prevents us from examining ourselves critically, learning from other faith traditions, or even opening up the Bible and looking at it again with the openness, thoughtfulness, and the critical thought necessary to help us along the way.

Each denomination has developed its own particular formula for salvation. Some churches view salvation as a once-and-for-all decision, while others see it as a lifelong process of transformation. In the Methodist tradition, the moment that some would compare to being born again is called "justification"—a revolutionary experience for many. But then, as one practices the faith, the evolutionary work of "sanctification" begins and one works toward becoming more whole as life goes on. A person doesn't become complete by simply reciting the Jesus prayer or claiming Jesus as Lord and Savior.

Churches who hold to the evolutionary perspective on faith might be characterized by their desire to draw the circle wider in an effort to stay open to new ideas and experiences in which the Divine might be revealed. When fundamentalism rules the day, new information becomes a threat. There can be no latitude as to belief and practice. Those who believe that they alone possess the once-and-for-all truth are much more likely to oppose differences of opinion and seek the ouster of their opponents—by legislative or other, more violent, means. John Dominic Crossan warns, "Every religion today must take responsibility for its own fundamentalism—because religious fundamentalism is probably the most dangerous thing in the world at the moment. Christian or Muslim. I am not making any distinction."

Reverend Mel White explains it this way:

> When people begin to become fundamentalist, it becomes a real challenge to the church to maintain the Spirit of Christ. What happens is people get defensive about their faith because they're insecure and this is a very insecure time for the world. Fundamentalism says we know the answers; therefore, we should superimpose them on anybody who doesn't agree with us. And along comes the organization of fundamentalists into a political bloc that not only takes over their churches but takes over (or attempts to take over) the governments of their countries, whether you're a fundamentalist Muslim or a fundamentalist Jew or a fundamentalist Christian, the spirit is about all the same.

Those who slip into fundamentalism can develop what Crossan calls a "genocidal germ" that too often manifests itself in oppression of anyone who disagrees with their perspective. In some cases, that oppression happens at the church level—certain groups of people are not allowed to receive communion or become members of the church. Sometimes it happens at the government level—churches support political candidates or legislation that limits personal freedoms based on a particular moral perspective. And sometimes, that oppression becomes violent. The bombings of abortion clinics by radical pro-life proponents or the torture and murder of Matthew Shepherd, a young gay man attacked by those who considered his sexuality an abomination, are just two examples of the way in which, in the words of Crossan, "the trajectory of human violence escalates almost inevitably from the ideological through the rhetorical to the physical."[3]

The push for certainty has led to dangerous, terrible places. Yet for most of us, the cost is far more subtle. Absolute certainty keeps us separated from God and our neighbors by claiming that what we know is the whole truth and that there's no room for others' experience or input. When we're not open to ambiguity and different ways of looking at things, we risk becoming stagnant, stuck in a cul-de-sac rather than being out on the adventure and open to the mystery of the Divine. To say you ascribe, without question, to a dogmatic set of beliefs that were developed and set in stone by someone else is easy. The bigger challenge is to follow a story that is always evolving, one in which the ending is not yet written. Like Jesus, we can opt for a story that demands thought, raises questions, and often runs counter to conventional wisdom. Perhaps real "faith" involves seeing ambiguity not as an enemy, but as a vital part of the journey.

THE BEGINNING OF WISDOM

When Billie Holiday sang: "Thems that got shall get, thems that not shall lose…God Bless the child that's got his own, that's got his own," she was tapping into a profound truth about life — and spirituality. Relying solely on doctrines and dogma passed on from others has seldom been a satisfying exercise for those longing for something deeper spiritually or thought-provoking theologically. To not ask questions is tantamount to forfeiting one's own spiritual birthright and allowing other people's experience of the Divine to define your experience.

Wrestling with life's injustices, resisting the urge to be satisfied with the way the world is, and asking difficult questions are all at the heart of theological integrity and spiritual growth. Excessive certitude can become a substitute for God and cripple an otherwise dynamic relationship with the Spirit. In short, being satisfied with easy answers is a cop-out.

A far richer, and perhaps more faithful, alternative is to wrestle with the questions. Emilie Townes of Yale Divinity School says, "I would hate to think that there would be a point in time in life where we would actually think we've arrived at the fullness of what faith can be for ourselves as people molded into the Christian tradition. That tradition is still alive and growing. I take the revelation of God very seriously as being one that is ongoing. I would think that in order to be attuned to that, our faith would have to be ongoing."

Every question we ask without receiving a satisfactory answer makes us more adept at honing our questions. Every ambiguity with which we wrestle strengthens us for dealing with life's ever-increasing complexities. The Center for Progressive Christianity's "8 Points of Progressive Christianity" suggests there is more grace in the search for meaning than in absolute certainty, in the questions than in the answers.[4] It's in living the questions that we find direction in life.

Retired UCC minister Culver "Bill" Nelson remembers a conversation with theologian Paul Tillich in which Tillich pointed out that, "Everyone seeks answers, mostly to questions that are not very important. The great concern in life should be to discover which are the right questions. Then, even if you rarely get answers, you are at least journeying in the right direction."

On any authentic spiritual journey, asking the hard questions is not only permitted, but necessary! What we learn along the way, through difficulties and disequilibrium, mistakes and challenges, discoveries and unlearnings, is that the process is what's important. The unanswerable questions asked in the company of fellow seekers along the way become a central part of the process of the deepening quest, the broadening understanding, and the journey beyond our otherwise limited horizons.

—⟋⟍⟍—

STRIPPED BY GOD

What would happen if I pursued God—
If I filled my pockets with openness,
Grabbed a thermos half full of fortitude,
And crawled into the cave of the Almighty
Nose first, eyes peeled, heart hesitantly following
Until I was face to face
With the raw, pulsing beat of Mystery?

What if I entered and it looked different
Than anyone ever described?
What if the cave was too large to be fully known,
Far too extensive to be comprehended by
    one person or group,
Too vast for one dogma or doctrine?

Would I shatter at such a thought?
Perish from paradox or puzzle?
Shrink and shrivel before the power?
Would God be diminished if I lived a question
Rather than a statement?
Would I lose my faith
As I discovered the magnitude of Grace?

O, for the willingness to explore
To leave my tiny vocabulary at the entrance
And stand before you naked
Stripped of pretenses and rigidity,
Disrobed of self righteousness and tidy packages,

Stripped of all that holds me at a distance from you
And your world.

Strip me, O God,
Then clothe me in curiosity and courage.

—Cynthia Langston Kirk

2

Taking the Bible Seriously

The unexamined Bible is not worth reading.[1]
—N. T. Wright

Author and sociologist Tex Sample tells a story of his childhood in Mississippi. He says:

> My Sunday school teacher in the fifth grade was a man that I'll call Mr. Archon. Mr. A was the wealthiest, most important man in our town. And he was a terrific Sunday school teacher, in the sense that he knew how to talk to us fifth grade boys. He knew things we were interested in and he just knew how to say 'em. And he had what Max Weber called *charisma*. At the same time it seemed that about once a month he would teach us that Black people were inferior, that they were sub-human, that slavery had been right, that it was biblical, and that we southern boys should defend segregation with our very lives. He told us that we especially had to protect southern white girls.
>
> It just so happened that in that same church we had a retired missionary named Miss Hattie Bowie. She'd been a missionary in Korea for thirty years. I never remember a direct confrontation

between her and Mr. Archon, but it seemed like every time Mr. Archon would say some of those terrible things, she had some way of countering it.

She would take us to her house and she had wonderful artifacts out of Korea. She had small houses that Korean people had made. She had wonderful paintings with a kind of a peculiar method that they had used. She had of course Korean dolls and Korean toys that we so enjoyed. It was my first experience with a culture radically different from my own. She also taught us songs. She taught us that song, "Jesus Loves the Little Children, all the Children of the World . . . Red and Yellow, Black and White, they are precious in his sight." And she taught us "Jesus Loves Me" in Korean. I still remember it:

> Nal sa-rang ha-shim,
> Nal sa-rang ha-shim,
> Nal sa-rang ha-shim,
> Sung-kyung-ae Seo-it-nae.

That's been a long time ago, but what I remember is that Mr. Archon took the racist story and put God's story in it to support the racist story. Miss Hattie Bowie took the racist story, put it into God's story and *dismantled* it. I have wondered so very many times, what would have happened to me if it had not been for Miss Hattie Bowie.

Any way you slice it, it turns out to be true: how a Christian reads the Bible and the authority she places in its words plays a critical role in the reader's worldview and understanding of a life of faith. But even if you *never* read the Bible, its influence on the world, for good and for ill, is hard to deny.

The Bible has been quoted and misquoted, used and abused, appealed to and discredited. Pastors and politicians, songwriters and poets, have employed its images to inspire and motivate, to encourage and comfort. But it has also been used as a tool by those who have sought to oppress women, support slavery, justify wars, breed cults, and promote violence, racism, and terror.

It seems ridiculous to have to say it, but the Bible itself defies being defined as a single book with a clear-cut message to the masses. It's not a collection of handy quotes to be randomly plucked out as support for this point or that ideology. It is instead a complex, often confounding collection of strange and wonderful stories cobbled together over thousands of years. In fact, as a record of various peoples' experience of God's faithfulness and human infidelities, the Bible is full of colorful characters, lying, cheating, sex, hate, war, sex, betrayal, murder, sex, letters, poetry, history, sex, great ideas, lousy ideas, and more sex.

Those who read closely find a variety of theological voices. Sometimes those voices are harmonious, other times they create a cacophony of contradiction. For example, many people don't realize that there are two flood stories in Genesis: the familiar one where God has Noah collect two of each animal (Gen. 7:14), and the other where he is to collect seven pairs of each animal (Gen. 7:2). Perhaps we only hear about the two-by-two story because the seven-by-seven version would clutter up the illustrations in children's books and murals.

It's this sort of puzzling storytelling that leads many Bible readers to conclude that they simply cannot hold a literalist view of scripture. There are just too many inconsistencies for them to take every word as historically accurate eyewitness accounts. Jesus scholar Marcus Borg says of this issue:

> There are many Christians in North America who are bothered by any suggestion that the Bible might be anything less than a divine product. There are also millions of people in North America and in Europe who simply cannot be biblical literalists. And my passion, my vocation, my mission even, if you will, is talking to the people who can't be literalists. And what I want to say to

conservative Christians who are upset by this other approach to the Bible is, "What do we say to the people who can't be literalists? Do we say, 'Sorry. Only literalists can be Christians.'? Or, do we say, 'Sorry. God accepts only literalists.'? Now, if you are a literalist and your literalism isn't getting in your way and you're not using it to beat up on other people, I have no problem with it whatsoever. God can work through literalism or nonliteralism. But again, what do we say to the people who can't be literalists? And here, my argument is that a more historical and metaphorical approach to the Gospels, to the story of Jesus, and to the Bible as a whole provides a way for nonliteralists to be Christian.

At issue is the authority of scripture. We have to ask ourselves how we determine the level of trust we place in any written material, including the Bible. As perhaps the bestselling least-read book of all time, the Bible—and our relationship with it—needs to be reexamined.

A SERIOUS RELATIONSHIP

In his bestseller, *Meeting Jesus Again for the First Time*, Borg writes, "the Christian life is not primarily about believing the right things or even being good. The Christian life is about being in a relationship with God which transforms us into more and more compassionate beings, 'into the likeness of Christ.'"[2] Likewise, having a relationship with the biblical text, a serious relationship that grows and evolves, has the potential to be transformative as well. Such a relationship might be said to have more spiritual and intellectual integrity than performing the mental gymnastics necessary to cling to the notion of the Bible as a literal, perfect document unaffected by human influence.

Yet many people are afraid that if they admit that there are contradictions in the Bible then the whole thing has to be dismissed as a worthless lie. While the rift between literalists and nonliteralists has heated up in recent years, it is not a new conflict.

In the early part of the twentieth century, there was a popular pamphlet about the fundamentals of Christianity making its way through the American church. It spawned a whole movement committed to the inerrancy of scripture and other supposedly bedrock doctrines. Defenders of these fundamentals pointed to one verse in the New Testament, 2 Timothy 3:16, which reads, "All scripture is inspired by God and is useful for teaching, for reproof, for correction, and for training in righteousness." This led to a kind of circular argument, in which it was said that because the Bible is without error or inconsistency, it must be the work of God, and because it is the work of God, it must be without error or inconsistency. It doesn't matter which proposition comes first, the other is argued to follow.

In the 1920s, a highly publicized controversy flared up between the mainstream church and what had become known as the Fundamentalists. The so-called Scopes Monkey Trial was front-page news in national newspapers. For the Fundamentalists, this court case represented the battle for the soul of America. On the other side of that battle were the mainline churches. In an effort to stir people to action, one of America's great preachers, Harry Emerson Fosdick, preached a sermon called, "Shall the Fundamentalists Win?" in which he argued for a nonliteral interpretation of the Bible. He was worried that if the mainline church didn't do more to educate its people about the metaphorical and mythological origins of scripture, it would lose its brightest and best young people. The general disinterest in Christianity and the dwindling numbers in today's mainline churches suggest that he was right.

There are a variety of reasons people are dissatisfied with the church today. But this issue of biblical literalism is one of the most significant. Increasingly, Christians look at the way they are asked to read the Bible and ask themselves why this book calls for a whole different category of reading. Why, they wonder, are they expected to suspend disbelief and not think through what they are reading the way they would with any other book, issue, or situation? Why are they discouraged from asking questions of this text upon which they are being asked to base their lives?

Biblical scholar Amy-Jill Levine explains the situation:

> In some churches today, there's a problem: people are hesitant to voice questions, to say, "This doesn't quite cohere. In Matthew, Mark, and Luke, the Last Supper is a Passover meal. But in the Gospel of John, it's not. Did something go wrong? Did Jesus cleanse the temple at the beginning of his ministry? That's John. Did he do it at the beginning of the Passion like in Matthew and Mark? Did he do it twice? Didn't it take the first time? What did he say when he did it?" Jesus didn't ask people to give up their minds. He asked for one's heart. Jesus expands on Deuteronomy in the Great Commandment: "Love the Lord your God with all your heart, with all your soul, with all your mind, with all your strength." It doesn't say, "Give up your intelligence, that good intelligence that God gave you." I think if one's faith is so fragile that the very mention of a possible discrepancy threatens to topple the whole thing, then that faith requires reconsideration.

A FOURTH MEMBER OF THE TRINITY?

Hebrew scripture scholar Harrell Beck used to stir up people with the exclamation: "The Bible is *not* the Word of God—but the Word of God is in the Bible."[3] Beck's point was to remind people that the Bible is not God. For too many faith communities, the Bible serves as an object to be venerated. Instead of seeking the God of the Bible, they almost seem to worship the Bible itself, fearing any suggestion that it is anything other than holy and infallible. According to sociologist of religion Nancy Ammerman, it's a form of idolatry that in many traditions makes the Bible a "fourth member of the Trinity."

That kind of bibliolatry fails to take into account the human element involved in the creation of the Bible. Many people cling to the unspoken cultural belief that scripture is the result of a series of supernatural events. Tongue firmly planted in cheek, Harrell Beck imagines the scene: "Long ago, a shepherd boy in Palestine was startled by an ungodly clap of thunder and the King James Version of the Bible floated out of a cloud and settled at his feet. Having an uncanny appreciation for the value of an ancient text in Elizabethan English, the boy immediately took it to the religious authorities for distribution. Voila!"[4]

In reality, the sixty-six separate books crammed together in a not-always-logical arrangement came together in very human ways. With all the haggling and bickering you'd expect from a committee, the Catholic Council of Carthage pulled together one of the first official collections in 397 CE—nearly 400 years after the time of Jesus. What we call the Old Testament is concerned with Yahweh, the God of the Hebrews, and a history of the early Israelites. The New Testament is the work of early Christians and reflects their beliefs about Jesus. The Old Testament consists of thirty-nine books, many of which had multiple authors. The New Testament has twenty-seven books, many of which are an accumulation of traditions or of uncertain authorship. Catholic Bibles include an additional twelve books known as the Apocrypha.

The composition of the various books began before 1000 BCE and continued for more than 1,000 years. It included oral material that was repeated from generation to generation, revised over and over again, and then put into written form by various redactors. These editors worked in different locations and in different time periods and with very different socioeconomic, philosophical, theological, and spiritual worldviews. They were most certainly unaware of each other and it is highly unlikely that any of them foresaw their work being included in a cohesive collection of sacred texts. Their work was intended for local use.

The four Gospels, Matthew, Mark, Luke, and John, are examples of books that did not carry the names of their actual authors. Their present names were assigned long after the books were written and circulated anonymously. Despite the witness of the Gospels themselves, biblical scholars are now almost unanimously agreed—based on evidence within the books themselves—that none of the Gospel authors was a disciple of Jesus or an eyewitness to his ministry.

There are no extant or original manuscripts of these ancient texts. Our current versions of these texts are probably not anything like their original forms. There are countless differences between the oldest surviving copies and the most recent manuscripts. These differences indicate that additions and alterations were made to the originals by various copyists and editors. Scholars give precedence to the oldest texts as they are likely to be most like the originals.

This tangled process is the reason there are stories in the Bible that don't sync—the two creation stories in Genesis, two flood stories, and what scholars believe might be four separate versions of the exodus lurking in the book we call Exodus. While there are four canonical Gospels, the narratives of Jesus's birth appear in only Matthew and Luke (and they don't have the same characters, timeline, or story emphasis). It also accounts for the occasional mishmash of cultural myths and beliefs that find their way into the Bible. Imagine the surprise of Victorian scholars who discovered that story elements in the Genesis flood story had been lifted from *The Epic of Gilgamesh*!

None of this is meant to suggest that we dispense with the Bible or relegate it to a dusty bookshelf along with all the other ancient texts. It's exactly these kinds of inconsistencies in scripture that have led careful readers of the Bible to be curious about what was going on. These people aren't folks looking to discredit the Bible. Far from it! They are people who have dedicated their lives to understanding scripture through and through.

For scholars and practitioners such as Reverend Winnie Varghese of the Episcopal Church, this careful biblical criticism is an essential part of the long history of the Christian faith. Varghese points out:

> Some of these narratives are poetry, some are collective memories, some are prophecy. They're different genres of text that exist together and from them we discern where God has been revealed

in those communities and where God is revealed to us. So we discern the workings of God in this time through the lens of this text as we gain increasing knowledge about them. Our increasing knowledge of archeology and literary criticism and the social sciences and the humanities takes us to different places with these texts than we would have been even fifty years ago, in some ways, much more accurate places. In some ways, much more complicated places. I believe that we are called to engage that. If we take the text seriously, we have to take the work around it seriously.

Acknowledging the literary challenges the Bible presents is a more honest, faith-filled endeavor than living in denial over its clashing stories and contradictions. In the words of theologian Walter Brueggemann, "The Bible is an act of faithful imagination. It is not a package of certitudes. It is an act of imagination that invites our faithful imagination that makes it possible to live faithfully."

A WINDOW ON THE DIVINE

Author Frederick Buechner uses the metaphor of a window to illustrate how we can hold on to our belief in both the need for questions and the relevance of scripture. He notes that when we look through a window, we don't worship the window. We simply look through it to get a glimpse of the Divine on the other side. Just because there are smudges, swatted flies, and hairline cracks obstructing our view, we don't throw the window out. We learn to distinguish between what is part of the window and what is beyond it.[5] Even though one can point to countless examples of political and theological spin that are anything but holy, the Bible has nonetheless established itself in our culture as a source of inspired (not dictated) guidance and observations. Although a flawed and imperfect window, it was fashioned by people of faith who have helped generations of seekers catch a glimpse of the mystery beyond.

The Bible is many things to many people. It's what people make of it and what they let it make of them over the course of time. Even if we all read the same translation of the Bible — and there are many different translations, each with its own interpretative slant — it has been said that there are as many Bibles as there are readers of the Bible. We all bring our assumptions, presuppositions, prejudices, and experiences to bear on the text. As William Blake wrote, "Both read the Bible day and night but thou readst black where I read white."[6] Acknowledging that the history of interpreting scripture is itself in process is one of the first steps in establishing a personal, life-long journey with the biblical text — a sometimes frustrating, often rewarding, and always surprising relationship.

In an effort to explain one of the shifts we need to make on our journey of faith, Marcus Borg speaks of the various stages people pass through as they develop an appreciation of the Bible as metaphor. As young children we interpret the Bible with what Borg calls a "pre-critical naïveté." In this stage we believe what we are told and don't give it another thought. As we get older, we move into a stage of critical thinking in which we unpack our understanding of the world and toss out what we recognize as false, such as the tooth fairy or the idea that you can break your mother's back by stepping on a crack.

While many get stuck in the stage of "critical thinking," there's a third stage that Borg calls "post-critical naïveté" that is demonstrated by the capacity to recognize the truth in the biblical stories, "even as you know that their truth does not depend upon their factuality. And even as you are pretty darn sure that many of them are not historically factual." Using the Christmas story as an example, he explains:

These stories use ancient archetypal language with one of their central affirmations being, "Jesus is the light of the world," the true light that enlightens every person, was even then coming into the world. That's the star, the radiant glory of God, and the angels in the night sky. It's the ability to hear the birth stories as true stories even though you know the star is not an astronomical object of history but probably the exegetical creation of Matthew as he interprets the 60th chapter of Isaiah. It's a literary creation. Even as you know that Jesus was probably born in Nazareth and not in Bethlehem. And even as you know that Herod the Great never ordered the slaying of all male babies in Bethlehem under age two, but rather that's the use of the story of the birth of Moses in the time of Pharaoh when Pharaoh issued a similar order. The author of Matthew is saying the story of Jesus is about the story of the true king coming into the world whom the evil kings seek to swallow up. This is the story of the Exodus all over again. This is the story of the conflict between the Lordship of God known in Christ and the Lordship of Pharaoh and the rulers of this world. And the rulers of this world always try to swallow up the one who is of God. Post-critical naïveté is the ability to hear that as a true story.

As people are given permission to think critically about the Bible and are resourced with a broad understanding of the history, culture, and political intrigues that originally drove the content, story lines, and theologies of the canon, the text can become less of a stuffy rulebook and more of a lens through which one's spiritual seeking and life journey comes into focus.

The re-visioning of Christianity that is already emerging in the world is motivated in part by taking the Bible seriously and not literally. The core message, dogma, and practices of the Christian faith in today's world are being reevaluated with a love for and relationship with scripture at its center.

3

Thinking Theologically

We must get away from this theistic supernatural
God that imperils our humanity and come back
to a God who permeates life so deeply that our
humanity becomes the very means through
which we experience the Divine Presence.

— John Shelby Spong

Alice Walker's *The Color Purple* is an account of a journey of faith. The sojourner, named Celie, discovers new ways of understanding religion and of imaging the Divine. In one of her letters to her sister, Nettie, Celie writes about a conversation she's had with her friend/lover Shug: "She say, 'My first step from the old white man was trees. Then air. Then birds. Then other people. But one day when I was sitting quiet and feeling like a motherless child, which I was, it come to me: that feeling of being a part of everything, not separate at all. I knew that if I cut a tree, my arm would bleed.'"[1]

To think theologically is to ask the questions of how the Divine is intertwined with the world: How do we understand the unfathomable mystery that we've come to call God? Is there a God whose character and ways of relating to the world can be explained in ways that make sense? As Culver "Bill" Nelson has suggested, even the word "God" itself is a "very slender word that simply covers our shivering ignorance." Exploring these and other questions and concepts is at the heart of thinking theologically—a practice in which we all engage, whether we know it or not.

Reading the Bible closely, it becomes clear that there's no one way of understanding who God is and how God relates to the world. Hebrew scripture scholar Rolf Knierim opens his *The Task of Old Testament Theology* by stating that, "The Old Testament contains a plurality of theologies."[2] The Bible is the witness of generations of faithful people recording their own understandings of the divine in their particular time, place, and culture. This theological pluralism reveals changing, developing, and sometimes conflicting ideas about God.

The challenge of thinking theologically is about maintaining a creative tension between various perspectives—an exercise that generates dialogue, not absolute certainty. At its best, thinking theologically is not about facts, but about wrestling with often abstract ideas and concepts.

Winnie Varghese puts it this way:

> I think a theological framework keeps us with the perspective that what God desires for us is much greater than what we can imagine amongst ourselves. The gift of theological thinking is that it can give us a freedom to hope for much more than seems practical. It should make us seem a bit foolish, I think, what we dream of as justice, what we dream of for our families, what we dream of for our nation and for the world, because we are supposed to be trying to view the world with God's vision and not just with what we can imagine. From the beginning, our imaginations about who we can be are just far too small.

Traditional understandings of Christology, Atonement, and the Incarnation are all in flux. In fact, many people find these concepts to be irrelevant to contemporary spirituality. Yet thinking theologically creates a disequilibrium that makes us continually rethink our beliefs in light of our changing understanding and ongoing experiences. In many ways, this entire book is an exercise in thinking theologically.

To demonstrate how thinking theologically helps us make sense of the often confusing or contradictory ideas of the Bible, we'll spend this chapter looking at two of the major ideas that create conflict among people of faith. The first is the language we use for the Divine. The second is the notion of "omnipotence."

SPEAKING OF GOD

Many of us get in a rut with our language about or image of God. We find that our view of God is narrow and constricting. As our life experience broadens our understanding, some of us become conflicted over whether we can believe at all. Maya Angelou relates how in her twenties in San Francisco she "became a sophisticate and an acting agnostic." She says, "It wasn't that I stopped believing in God; it's just that God didn't seem to be around the neighborhoods I frequented."[3] Harry Emerson Fosdick was fond of telling the story of a distraught student who exclaimed, "I don't believe in God!" Fosdick replied, "Tell me about this God you don't believe in; chances are I don't believe in that God either."[4]

Mystics, theological thinkers, and the Bible itself have shown that there are as many images and ideas to express the Divine as there are experiences of God. The biblical writers use a rich pallet of metaphors and poetic language to point toward what is ultimately a mystery. The Divine is described as a potter, a cup (of cool water), a path, a safe place, a rock, a burning bush, an eagle, and a whirlwind — all wonderful metaphors that help us assign a variety of attributes to the Divine without being the exclusive last word.

One of the most common ways of imaging God is as a father. Listening to many prayers and liturgies, one might think it was the *only* image of God in scripture. However, God is also imaged as a mother in Deuteronomy 32:18: "You forgot the God who gave you birth"; as a woman in labor in Isaiah 42:14; and as a comforting mother in Isaiah 66:13. Is God a mother? Yes. A father? Yes. A rock? Yes. A wind? Yes. Everything we use to refer to God is simply a limited, human effort to explain the unexplainable. To be aware of our language and its implications is a great exercise in thinking theologically—remembering that the language we use to describe the Divine will directly influence how we relate to the Divine.

This is not a minor question. A person's—or faith community's—view of God shapes everything else about it. New Testament authority John Dominic Crossan suggests four questions for today's Christians:

1. *What is the character of your God?* When you think about God what are you imagining?
2. *What is the content of your faith?* We can't imagine any longer that the person says, "I have faith," and you say, "That's great." There are certain faith-based initiatives that aren't very great. Al Qaeda is a faith-based initiative. So I want to ask, What is the content of your faith? What do you believe in? If you tell me you believe, what do you believe in?
3. *What is the function of your church?* What are you coming together for? And if you tell me you come to gather to worship God then I will repeat the question.
4. *What is the purpose of your worship?* In case you've said you are going to worship God in that preceding one, how does God want to be worshipped? Does God simply want prayers said—or is God more interested in prayers that lead to a life? And then of course, it goes back to, What is the character of your God? It is a

circular exercise where each question flows into the next. These are the questions we have to face.

The ideas we hold about the nature of God and the language we use to describe God play out in small ways—how or even whether we pray, how we think about our purpose in life, how we relate to those who do not share our beliefs. But they also influence how we see the world and, ultimately, God's role in that world.

WHAT KIND OF POWER?

When remembering the old elementary school riddles like, If God is all-powerful, can God create a rock too heavy for God to lift? or, Can God create a square circle?, it doesn't take much life experience to realize just how silly and shallow such questions are. Does that rock really matter when you've lost a loved one, when you can't feed your family, or disease has compromised your health? When you're unemployed or divorcing or lonely? Yet the theological construct of "omnipotence," as questionable a concept as it is, has stuck around for centuries. There is something about the idea of an all-powerful God that continues to be compelling for many Christians.

Thomas Aquinas formulated our modern idea of omnipotence in the thirteenth century. He reckoned that in order for God to be God, God must hold more power than any earthly ruler. The highest conceivable form of power must be the Divine power. So the biblical term "Almighty" became all-powerful or omnipotent. What exactly does the highest conceivable form of power look like? Aquinas wasn't very clear on this.

However, many people operate with the understanding that the highest conceivable form of power is the power to determine every detail of what happens in the world. But there's the rub: when unexplainable catastrophe strikes, God is left wide open for people to ask, Why did God do this to me? or to cover for God by ascribing mysterious, Divine intentions behind even the worst catastrophes.

The road that follows a belief in an omnipotent God is a muddy one to say the least. If God has all the power, shouldn't everything be good? What about evil and those times when we choose the lesser good? Does God underwrite evil for the sake of letting us have free will? Does God permit sin in order to delude us into thinking we have the final decision? It's a road that gets God mixed up with some pretty shady business — up to and including natural disasters that can't be attributed to human freedom — even insurance companies call them "acts of God." What does it say about a Deity who has all the power and still allows horrible diseases, accidents, and natural disasters to occur?

Some might object to questioning anything but the pure and complete sovereignty of God, but there are lots of other ways to think of God than as one who rules over everything. In fact, the biblical witness makes it clear that this royal model of all-powerful kingship is just one feeble attempt to grasp a concept that is impossible for our minds to comprehend. What is clear is that the idea that God is in possession of all the power turns life and all of creation into a really bad puppet show.

Theologian John B. Cobb Jr. explains it like this:

First of all, the doctrine of omnipotence is not a biblical doctrine, so this is not an argument that should go to the heart of our faith. But from maybe the second century on and perhaps earlier, people thought, "Well, God is powerful. Certainly the God of the Bible is powerful and if we're really going to say the best things we can about God then we have to say, 'God has *all* the power.'" But the irony is that if you say God has all the power then that means he has no power at all because power is a relational term. And if I can influence the behavior of another human being, that's exercising significant power. If I can lift a piece of paper, that's not really such a marvelous demonstration of enormous power. Relational power is really the only kind of significant power there is. But the notion of omnipotence tends to focus on coercion.

The way we think and speak about God ripples into every aspect of our theological thinking. That's why it's worthwhile to step back from our language and ask questions about why we say what we do about God and what those words and images might mean. The Bible offers a multitude of images and ideas about the Divine. On their own, not one of them is right. Taken all together, they testify to the liveliness of theological thinking over the ages and the wisdom of the biblical compilers in including them all. If all we ever do is ask questions of these images and ideas, then we've gone a long way toward the practice of thinking theologically that will see us through to another level of understanding the Divine.

The practice of Christianity is rife with a variety of theological problems and concepts that cripple its relevance in the minds of many twenty-first-century people. But one of the most notable characteristics of the Judeo-Christian tradition has been its amazing flexibility in withstanding the changes and adaptations brought to them by cultures they encounter. The Bible itself is witness to the same event or idea being represented in a variety of theological interpretations, each of which was included in the canon of scripture despite obvious differences. Wrestling with those differences has always played a significant role in the history of both Jewish and Christian concepts of the Divine—and can again play a part in rethinking many of the staid theological ideas that have become stagnant and unhelpful in the twenty-first century.

—ᴪ—

BEYOND THE SIXTH GRADE

Graduated from theology
In the sixth grade
No need for Sunday School again
Too much struggle for mom and dad
To plead that young soul into a classroom
One more Sabbath.

Others finished with biblical studies
Just after clergy words and hands
Confirmed the journey.

For few remaining
Or handful brought later by a party
Simple answers served.
Just when spicy foods and rich meals
Could be appreciated,
Peanut butter and jelly fare, crust off,
Served cut in half
As to a preschooler.
As school encouraged wrestling with Plato and heavy weights
Church promoted "simply believe."

No one would conceive of youth departing
Chemistry, government, orchestra and basketball
Because knowledge and skills sufficient.
No memo to sit this one out
Concerning race relations and global affairs.
No teacher would convey the theory
That the universe would crack,
All knowledge shatter

If questioned, tugged, and manipulated
This way and that.

Monday-through-Friday learner she became
So did he.
Absorbing the mysteries of the galaxies,
Reveling in literature,
Practicing cello and backstroke,
Pondering ancient philosophies of the wise ones.
Delighted by discoveries within and beyond self,
Thrilled in the land of accomplishments
And meaningful living.

All the while religious education—
Perfect attendance awards
With Bible school art
Tucked in a scrapbook on a top shelf.
Journey with the Creator deemed complete
In an "all I need to know I learned by sixth grade" approach.

Is it any wonder that it is both stunning and refreshing
To consider divine study—
The kind where head and heart muscle grow
As we grapple with God?
Areas atrophied and places newly discovered
Surprised that Holy Mystery can withstand
Questions, fears, disillusionment, prods, and amazement—
As can our faith.

—Cynthia Langston Kirk

4

Stories of Creation

Think you know the story of creation? Then have a listen to theologian and storyteller Megan McKenna's version of the story of humanity's beginning:

> So God said, "Let there be light." What's the light? Consciousness? Understanding? The Jews say that it is the soul and the spirit of every human being since the beginning of time to the end. If you know the Jewish tradition every one of us is a shaft or a shard of light that has been shattered, broken, and scattered throughout the world. To collect all of those and put them together is *tikkun olam*, repairing the world, putting everything back together again the way it should be. So this is literally the creation of every single human being *ever*. That ought to blow your mind for a start. But this is the tradition of the Jews.

The ancient Hebrews who composed what we now know as Genesis were brilliant storytellers—and although their writings have for generations been thought to explain the "how" of what happened historically, their stories are much deeper and richer when they are properly understood metaphorically as wrestling with the "whys" of human life.

When we delve into these ancient stories through the practice of thinking theologically, we catch a glimpse of people seeking to answer the eternal question, "What's the meaning of life?" Their solution is to suggest a good place to start—that we are made in the image of the Divine, the one who brings order out of chaos and finds joy in the act of creating.

CREATION AS STORY

In the beginning, God may have created the heavens and the earth, but not even the Bible is daring enough to claim exactly how it happened. In fact, Genesis begins with two distinctive creation stories that are impossible to synthesize or string together into consecutive events with any integrity. Neither one was ever meant to give a scientific account of how creation happened. Instead, they offer theological claims about the characteristics of the creator and poetic explanations as to why human beings are the way we are.

Theologian Matthew Fox says:

There are hundreds of other creation stories in the Bible. The oldest creation story is not Genesis, it's Psalm 104. If you go back to Psalm 104, it's very evolutionary: it goes through all the creatures that are created and humans come way at the end. The Book of Wisdom has a creation story, too. The Song of Songs is a creation story about the recreation of the Garden of Eden through human love. And of course the New Testament has several creation stories—the first chapter of John is a creation story, the infancy narratives are creation stories. It's as if we never get enough creation stories. And, that's true! The creation story is so primal to any human tribe's survival. After all, this is what indigenous people around the world taught their children: where they come from, the creation story.

Now from science we have a new creation story, which is very alluring and very exciting. It's not about deposing all the other wisdom stories about creation that humanity has gathered, but it certainly supplements it. It offers a real universal view because it's beyond any particular religion, ethnicity, nation and so forth. As we're struggling as a species to come together as a tribe, it provides us our basic framework, because it's from creation stories that ethics derive. Today's creation story from science is that we come from 14 billion years of an organic unfolding of the universe and are connected physiologically with every being in the universe. We all share the same atoms and the same molecules. That's truly significant and important at this time in history. We're all kin, we're all interdependent. And that's the basis of compassion, which was Jesus's ultimate teaching.

The two creation stories at the beginning of Genesis grew out of different eras and reflect the purposes of two different "schools" or authors. Genesis 1 is the product of authors that scholars have dubbed the "Priestly" writers. Their rhythmic liturgical order of creation grew out of their experience in Babylonian exile some time after 586 BCE. As a product of the exile and the apparent defeat of Yahweh by the Babylonian Marduk, it has even been suggested that Genesis 1 is a kind of "resistance literature" created to claim Yahweh's superiority over all of creation. The second story, beginning with Genesis 2:4, is believed to have its roots in much older folk stories of creation. The editors of this story refer to the creator with the name "Yahweh," the distinctive Hebrew name for the Divine. As such they have since come to be known collectively as the "Yahwist."

The two sources present the story in totally different styles. Where the Priestly author is interested in how things are organized and presents the origin of all things with a structured list, the Yahwist is a wonderful storyteller, often emphasizing humor and relationships as a vehicle for making theological points. Overall, the authors never intended to answer the analytical Greco-Roman question of How? but instead, in typical rabbinic fashion, set out to address the much more important question of Why?

Because they have become foundational stories in the Christian faith, it's worth spending some time looking at the questions raised by a deeper understanding of the two creation accounts in Genesis.

GENESIS 1

Far from everything being created out of "nothing" (ex nihilo), creation begins with a torrential midnight hurricane at sea. The "formless void," *tohu wabohu* in Hebrew, literally means an unordered chaos, here described as an unending storm of violent wind on dark waters. When reading Genesis 1, keep in mind that ancient Jews perceived the sea as a symbol of chaos and distance from God. The sea in Genesis 1 is a metaphor for the chaos out of which God brings order. You might recall that Jonah was so determined to get away from God, he actually went to sea and eventually jumped in—clear acts of desperation to hearers who understood the sea as separation from the Divine. This cosmology is picked up at the end of the biblical canon in Revelation 21:1. One of the characteristics of God's "new heaven and new earth" is that the sea—chaos—will be no more.

The Priestly authors' rhythmic unfolding of creation is not without its theological digs. At a time when the surrounding cultures worshipped the sun, moon, and stars as gods, to claim that your God had *created* the sun, moon, and stars was not so veiled theological one-upmanship. Growing out of the experience of exile and intending to offer hope to a despairing people, this propaganda piece had as its essence the message that our God is better than your god. Not only were these other gods cast as the creations of the God of the Hebrews, but they were also gutted of their basic functions. The sun, for instance, doesn't actually provide light. Light has already been around for three days before the sun comes on the scene. This, of course, also throws a wrench into the literal interpretation of twenty-four-hour days. We've already had three "days" pass and the sun hasn't even been created yet.

One of the clearest conflicts between the two stories is in the creation of human beings. In Genesis 1, human beings are created male and female at the same time. The story of woman being created from man with all of its patriarchal implications is a story element used in Genesis 2.

Genesis 2:4–25 reserves the highest order of creation being left for last. Shabbat, to rest, is the crowning glory of creation, a day of holiness separating humans from their animal roots — a tradition unique to Jewish culture in the ancient world. It's not surprising that the "Priestly" authors would make the Sabbath, the event that would keep them in business, the pinnacle of creation.

GENESIS 2

Where Genesis 1 presents the maritime nightmare of too much water, Genesis 2 begins with the agricultural nightmare of drought. From the very beginning, the feel and style of Genesis 2 is different from that of Genesis 1. The Yahwist is a consummate storyteller who portrays Yahweh anthropomorphically — like a human being — in relationship with his creation: interacting with it, in conversation with the man and the woman, and taking a walk in the garden. One of the most obvious differences is that while Genesis 1 moves from wet to dry, Genesis 2 moves from dry to wet.

One of the Yahwist's many wordplays that's lost in the translation from Hebrew is in the creation of the first human being. In order for the ground to be tilled, God formed the farmer, *ha adam*, which means "the earth creature" in Hebrew. "Earth" or ground in Hebrew is *adamah*. So *ha adam* was formed from the *adamah*—words that take on a poetic flair when chanted in Hebrew. The character we call Adam is unnamed. English translators dropped "ha" (the definite article) and capitalized "adam" (a plural noun) and gave us Adam.

It's interesting to note that Jewish folklore suggests that God created a woman who was brought before Adam like the other creatures. However, there was conflict between Adam and his "first wife." In some stories, Adam didn't even acknowledge her with a name, let alone call her "mate." In others (*Alphabet of Ben Sira*, 23a–b), she was created from the dirt as Adam's equal and refused to be dominated by him. Either way, she was cast out of the garden. The tradition gave her the name Lilith and she came to be portrayed as a she-demon, the jealous queen of the underworld, and was said to be responsible for the deaths of babies, men straying from their wives, and any other circumstance that brought grief to families. In some traditions, she became identified as Satan's lover and mother to demons.

Keeping in mind that no self-respecting Jewish family would name their daughter Lilith (it would be like Christians naming their son "Lucifer"), the writers of the television show *Cheers* had the character Frasier Crane marry a Jewish woman named Lilith. Frasier being married to the queen of the underworld is an inside joke lost on the show's gentile viewers.

As you can see in the following table,[1] one of the most obvious differences between the two creation stories in Genesis is their order of events. The differing order excludes the possibilities of their describing the same events from different perspectives or their being sequential. They are simply different stories from different sources that were both important enough to the Jewish sense of identity to be included in the canon.

	Creation 1 (Priestly Source) (from wet to dry)	Creation 2 (Yahwist) (from dry to wet)
STAGE 1:	Light	A mist goes up
STAGE 2:	Firmament separated from water	Farmer "ha adam" created
STAGE 3:	Land	Garden created
STAGE 4:	Inhabitants of firmament	The one commandment
STAGE 5:	Inhabitants of sea & air	Critters all created
STAGE 6:	Inhabitants of earth	Woman created
STAGE 7:	God rests	Everybody out!

It is a disservice to the richness of the individual stories to try to synthesize them or make their two divergent story lines consecutive. Amy-Jill Levine says:

Genesis Chapter 1 is marvelous poetry. "When in the beginning God created the heaven and the earth and the earth was without form and void…" and then get "day one" and "day two" and it was good. It's all very clean and very neat. And we get the animals and we get male and female: "Created He, him, male and female created He them." Man and woman together are told to be fruitful and multiply. Splendid! Then we get to Genesis 2 and 3, and it gets a little bit more messy. Suddenly we find that a human being is created, but the animals are created later. And then Eve, the woman, is created after the animals. What's going on? We seem to have a discrepancy. The names of God are different, the style is different, the cadence is different. In effect, we've got two creation narratives. Is this a problem? Well, it's only a problem if we think there has to be only one creation narrative—if the world can be imaged in only one way.

For many, failing to recognize the two separate stories is simply a matter of having not read the stories since childhood Sunday school. But many Christians, bent on maintaining an inerrant Bible, manage to do the mental gymnastics necessary to ignore the blatantly obvious. In some circles, belief in a literal seven-day Creation has become a litmus test for being a "true" Christian. Those who claim the Bible as inerrant and interpret everything they can in a literal fashion are even now promoting the newest form of creation science, "intelligent design," to be taught in public schools across the United States.

What one thinks of the creation stories is not only critical to the way one looks at the Bible, but to one's worldview as well. What is at issue is no less than the way people think, who controls our schools, and who controls our culture. Reading the Bible metaphorically opens one to meanings that go deeper than literal interpretations allow. Unbending readings of the text have led to the alleged biblical endorsement of all kinds of social ills from slavery to the subjugation of women to the demonization of gays and lesbians. But reading the text in a way that is alert to meanings that transcend the literal paves the way for deeper understandings—including an appreciation of scientific advancements.

New Testament professor Barbara Rossing says:

Creation and evolution are really important topics for Christians to talk about and I believe in both of them. At the seminary where I teach we have what's called the Zygon Center for Religion and Science where we bring in top scientists from the University of Chicago. In a course called "The Epic of Creation" they talk about the world being created through the big bang. They talk about recent science like stem cell research. And then they lay those findings alongside the biblical text and the best in theology and try to help students see that there is no conflict between creation and evolution. God created the world; one can say that and still absolutely believe in evolution. I was trained as a geologist. I love to go to the Grand Canyon and see those layers. It's so exciting to think of all the species that have lived here and the complexity of earth's history. One can hold all of that and also believe in God and in creation. We've gotten sidetracked into this ridiculous sort of creationism versus evolution and now with the new sort of iteration on creationism, intelligent design, it's ridiculous. What we need to do is use the best of science and theology to figure out how to care for this earth before we create a disaster.

The church has often been slow to embrace advances in science. Galileo was condemned in 1633 because his teaching that the earth revolved around the sun contradicted traditional readings of scripture. It only took the Vatican until 1992 (359 years later) to admit Galileo might have been right.

Although the seminary-trained Charles Darwin died a professed agnostic, he didn't completely divorce his religious understanding from his passion for science. In letters edited by his son, Francis, we learn that Darwin considered the theory of evolution to be "quite compatible with the belief in a God; but that you must remember that different persons have different definitions of what they mean by God."[2]

The time is long past when a literal interpretation of the creation stories has any scientific, intellectual, or spiritual merit. They remain, however, a tribute to the wisdom of the compilers who believed that the inclusion of two different creation stories allowed for enough wiggle room to create space for people with different ideas about God and the purposes of creation.

5

Lives of Jesus

Truth be told, there are as many Jesuses as there are disciples of this remarkable first-century figure. Regardless of how faithful one is to the portrayals of Jesus by any particular denomination or tradition, no two people understand or relate to Jesus in exactly the same way. This is one of the reasons the Bible includes four different versions of the story of Jesus's life and why Second and Third Baptist Churches spun off from the First Baptist Church.

From apocalyptic firebrand to mystical faith healer to political insurrectionist, the various images of Jesus are celebrated and defended by true believers of every theological and political stripe. Walk into the narthex of any number of Protestant churches and you're likely to find the sentimental blue-eyed, pink-skinned Jesus of artist Warner Sallman gazing beatifically upon your comings and goings. Enter the neighboring Catholic church and you'll probably find the image of a beaten, bleeding, emaciated man suffering on a cross.

Beginning with Gospels themselves, Jesus has been the subject of considerable spin over the ages. Each tradition puts its own emphasis on this remarkable figure. For many middle-class Americans, the ideal Jesus is the gentle, upstanding, right-thinking (and often somewhat androgynous) suburbanite with good posture. The notion that Jesus might have been a short, dark, Middle-Eastern peasant rabble-rouser is beyond comprehension. A blond-haired, blue-eyed Jesus, meek and mild, is such a stalwart icon of Western culture that to suggest anything contrary or corrective to that image is tantamount to heresy.

A Discovery Channel special utilizing the latest in forensic technology — mosaic representations and the actual skull of a first-century Jew — reconstructed what Jesus might have looked like. The result fomented an outcry from commentators far and wide with accusations of revisionism and political correctness run amuck. Columnist Kathleen Parker was so distraught that she fretted that the Jesus she knew as a child was being replaced by "the kind of guy who wouldn't make it through airport security." She goes on to say, "Given the tendency of academic research to steer conclusions away from anything that might be construed as Aryan or, heaven forbid, Falwellian, it's easy to imagine that biblical revisionists won't be satisfied until they discover that Jesus was really a bisexual, cross-dressing, whale-saving, tobacco-hating vegetarian African Queen who actually went to the temple to lobby for women's rights."[1]

Non-Caucasian Christians have long been dissatisfied with the Aryan Jesus. Be it Asian, African, South American, or Native American, cultures all over the world have represented Jesus metaphorically as one of them. On the cover of John Shelby Spong's *Liberating the Gospels,* Douglas Andelin renders Jesus as a disheveled Jewish peasant. *The National Catholic Reporter* awarded Janet MacKenzie's "Jesus of the People" — an image of Jesus modeled on an African American woman — the winner of the Jesus 2000 International Art Competition.

The portrayal of Jesus as some sort of sweet guy next door is a sentimental misreading of the Bible. Jesus didn't attract everyone he met, certainly not the wealthy and powerful. He was a peasant who likely attracted peasants. The Gospels tell us he was radical enough to make even many of the liberals of his day, the Pharisees, uncomfortable.

Uncovering the "real" Jesus is no small task. It might not even be possible. Marcus Borg notes that "except for one or two sentences in a late first-century Roman source written by Jewish historian, Josephus, our only sources for knowing about Jesus are basically the Christian Gospels. So, we don't have a lot of information about him." We know what we know about Jesus through the four Gospel narratives: Matthew, Mark, Luke, and John. But even these narratives do little to give us a comprehensive picture of Jesus. They differ from one another in both major and minor ways, leaving the reader to wonder just what we can really know about Jesus. For those looking for one picture of Jesus, the Gospels can be incredibly frustrating.

GOSPEL TEXT DETECTIVES

Marcus Borg says:

> The quest for the historical Jesus has been the attempt to try to arrange the material in the Gospels into earlier and later layers of material, and I think we know with a reasonable degree of probability that some things in the Gospels are quite late (the product of a developing tradition decades after the death of Jesus) and some things in the Gospels are relatively early. So I think there are generalizations that we can make about the historical Jesus that have a fairly high degree of probability.

John Dominic Crossan likes to say that there's really only one Gospel in the Bible and four "according tos." Crossan believes that the life of Jesus has too much meaning to be limited to only one telling that followers would be tempted to literalize and venerate. The four "according tos" give us four very different glimpses of Jesus. Despite efforts to the contrary, they defy synthesis.

To make sense of the Jesus we find in the Gospels, it's helpful to know a bit about the books themselves. While they may be the first books of the New Testament, the Gospels are far from being the earliest written material in the Christian scriptures. That distinction is held by the authentic letters of Paul, who was writing in the late 50s CE, some twenty years after the crucifixion of Jesus. The earliest source material of the biblical Gospels was probably written twenty or so years after that. And most scholars agree that the Gospels do not appear in the New Testament in the order in which they were written. That's why even the most cursory reading of the four biblical Gospels reveals a number of chronological inconsistencies, not to mention stylistic and content differences.

In addition, the literary genre of "Gospel" itself is anything but ob-jective. These reports are highly subjective, written by individuals speaking to particular communities of believers. Gospels are not intended as historical records or divine dictations. They are a record of the traditions developing around Jesus and the way they might play out in various communities. Some go back to the historical figure of Jesus and others developed out of the experience of early Christian communities.

The similarities and differences between Matthew, Mark, and Luke have given rise to what scholars call the "Synoptic Problem." The synoptic or "common view" of these three texts leads to further questions not only about how similar they are in some places, but how different they are from one another and from John.

The most obvious difference between the first three Gospels and John's Gospel is the order of events represented here in a table from scholar Robert Funk:[2]

The Synoptic Gospels	The Gospel of John
Begins with John the Baptist OR birth and childhood stories	Begins with creation — no birth or childhood stories
Jesus is baptized by John	Baptism of Jesus assumed but not mentioned
Jesus speaks in parables and short aphorisms	Jesus speaks in long, esoteric discourses
Jesus is a sage	Jesus is a philosopher and a mystic
Jesus is an exorcist	Jesus performs no exorcisms
The "Kingdom of God" is the theme of Jesus's teaching	Jesus himself is the theme of his own teaching
Jesus has little to say about himself	Jesus reflects at length on his own mission and person
Jesus takes up the cause of the poor and oppressed	Jesus has little or nothing to say about the poor and oppressed
Jesus's public ministry: 1 year	Jesus's public ministry: 3 years
Temple incident: late in the story	Temple incident: early in the story
Jesus eats a last supper with his disciples	Foot washing instead of the last supper

Along with the chronological differences of the Gospels, there is also a completely different cast of characters in some places, different styles and vocabularies, and different political and theological programs. Even within each Gospel, we find inconsistencies in tone and language and agenda. Those instances jump out as being either out of place or taken from another source.

It's helpful, then, to look at each author to get a better sense of what they're up to and why they make the storytelling choices they do. Author Etienne Charpentier summarizes the characteristics of the gospel writers as follows.[3]

MARK:
The Storyteller. Jesus gives very few speeches in Mark—this is not an intimate narrative. Instead of details, the author emphasizes the mystery of Jesus. This Gospel includes several "don't tell anyone" stories in which Jesus seems to want to keep a low profile. The story also includes multiple geographical impossibilities, making it unlikely that the author had firsthand knowledge of the events in Palestine.

MATTHEW:
The Teacher. Jesus gives five big speeches in Matthew. Considered the most "Jewish" of the Gospels, Matthew portrays Jesus as a second Moses, mirroring the life experiences of the first Moses: exile in Egypt, killing of infants, mountaintop experiences, and so on. Matthew's telling is centered on the concept of the kingdom of heaven.

LUKE:
The Historian. Like Mark, the author of Luke is also poor at geography. Luke's Jesus emphasizes the poor, the outcast (like the shepherds), and the plight of women.

JOHN:
The Greek. Echoing Platonic influences contrasting the ideal and real, John emphasizes "that which is above" and "that which is below." Jesus offers ethereal discourses about water, bread, birth, lambs, light, and himself. The split between Jews and Christians, something that isn't evident in the Synoptics, rises to the point of anti-Semitism in many places in John.

Each of these authors brings his own bias and agenda to his Gospel. While that makes the Gospels unreliable historical documents, it does make them lively, telling contributions to the biblical narrative as a whole. They tell us a great deal about what was important to the early followers of Jesus and what kinds of issues they wrestled with as they formed communities of faith.

THE TWO-SOURCE HYPOTHESIS

For years, careful readers have noted that wherever Matthew and Luke agree, they match Mark nearly word for word. In fact, Matthew reproduces nearly 90 percent of Mark. Luke copies about 50 percent. And they often reproduce Mark in the same order. So it seems clear that Mark was written first and was creatively plagiarized by Matthew and Luke. However, each writer's political and theological agenda influenced the way he told even stories copied from another source. Stories like the baptism of Jesus and the portrayal of Pilate change radically from Mark, to Matthew and Luke, to John.

In the Jesus Seminar's seminal work, *The Five Gospels: What Did Jesus Really Say?*, the two-source hypothesis is graphically depicted to show the streams of influence on Matthew and Luke.[4]

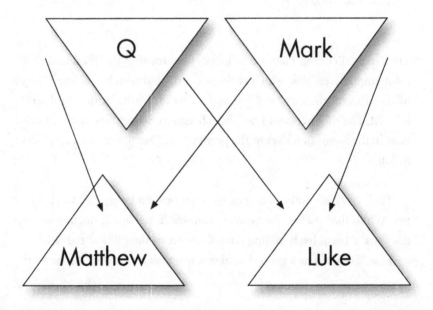

In addition to using Mark as a source, scholars have hypothesized a second source used by Matthew and Luke. Identified as "Q" (from the German word for "source," *quelle*), Matthew and Luke have approximately 200 "sayings" in common that are not taken from Mark. Many were skeptical of this idea, citing no known examples of a "sayings" source. Then, in 1947, the text of the Gospel of Thomas—a Gospel consisting only of sayings—was discovered in Nag Hammadi. That, along with other evidence, confirmed the possibility of Q's existence as a "sayings Gospel" and furthered something called the two-source hypothesis, in which Matthew and Luke drew from both Mark and Q in composing their Gospels.

The Synoptics and John

The differences between the Gospel of John and the Synoptic Gospels have been recognized for centuries. Even Clement of Alexandria (c. 150–211 CE) explained that the author of John was "urged by his friends and inspired by the Spirit" to compose "a spiritual Gospel" (Eusebius, Hist. Eccl. IV.xiv.7) as a complement to the "less spiritual" Synoptics.

In her book, *Beyond Belief,* Elaine Pagels makes an interesting case for John having been written as propaganda opposing the Gospel of Thomas, but there seems to be little evidence to suggest that John was written to either complement or correct the Synoptics. What remains clear is that the topography, order of events, location of events, the teaching style and themes of Jesus—as well as the very self-understanding of Jesus—are radically different in John.

SO WHO WAS JESUS?

Much of what we know about Jesus and his life are not facts of history but images and metaphors. They are not historical but they are no less true.

In *Jesus: A Revolutionary Biography,* John Dominic Crossan gives the example of a hypothetical statue of Abraham Lincoln.[5] Crossan imagines a sculpture of Lincoln standing in front of a large tree stump. On the other side of the stump, kneels an African-American slave, eyes looking up in hope and expectation. The slave's arms are stretched wide so that the chains linking his wrists rest on the top of the stump. Feet planted firmly, lumberjack Lincoln stands poised with an ax above his head ready to come down and shatter the chains of the slave. Crossan suggests that while this is not a depiction of a literally true event, we recognize it as truth just the same. The language of metaphor, parable, and artistic representations often express profound truths better than the raw historical data—a reality that the evangelist authors of the Gospels knew well.

The Synoptics portray Jesus going to those who were hated and despised and declaring God's love for the outcast and the negatively stereotyped. John attests to God having "so loved the world, that he gave his only begotten son" (John 3:16). And while theologians have long debated Jesus's true mission, that of apocalyptic prophet, sage teacher of wisdom, or sacrificial lamb, the variety of images and stories of Jesus seems to point to one reality: an experience of someone who is beyond all description while at the same time being the embodiment of that for which the deepest human yearnings strive.

Amy-Jill Levine says:

> Even though there are discrepancies among the gospels, for the most part if we read through Matthew, Mark, Luke, and John, we can get a good picture of what Jesus was trying to promote. [We get] the personality of Jesus himself, this individual who gathered disciples, who attracted crowds by means of healing and provocative teaching, who was sufficiently testy, sufficiently edgy, that some people wanted to kill him and others wanted to make him king. So although we have differences we also have

similarities. And, I don't think that the differences should outweigh the overall picture we get of an individual who's dedicated toward healing, toward seeking how best to live in conformity to God's will, and toward his own sense that he is instrumental in God's plans.

That charisma led people to call Jesus by many names: Messiah, Christ, King of Kings, Lord of Lords, true God of true God. And yet from the multitude of possibilities, "Son of God" language became one of the dominant metaphors for describing who Jesus was. Throughout the history of Israel all sorts of persons were referred to as "sons of God" in order to speak of their intimacy of relationship with the Divine. But with the birth stories of Jesus, the relational metaphor became a biological claim of divinity. Taking such metaphors literally has had a trickle-down effect, forcing theologians to scramble to come up with concepts like the Trinity—a conceptual stretch that attempts to explain how both the claimed divinity of Christ and monotheism can coexist.

Bishop Yvette Flunder sees Jesus a bit differently:

[I see Jesus] walking around as a horribly oppressed person with a whole lot of clothes on, pressing him—just layers and layers. We've taken 2,000 years to turn Jesus into someone very different than that person who got in the water with John for baptism. There's political stuff, there's economic stuff, there's church stuff. Jesus is even a plank on many political platforms. Jesus is the reason that we go to war, Jesus is the reason we oppress the immigrant, Jesus is even mad at Mickey Mouse or the Teletubbies. But there comes a point when we have to undress Jesus, we have to take all the stuff, all the crap that we've put on Jesus, all of these layers and layers of tradition and all of our different ideas and theologies and get back to the Jesus that stood in the water with John.

WHOSE KINGDOM?

One thing most New Testament scholars agree on—and they don't agree on much—is that Jesus's main aim was the kingdom of God—not some saccharine vision of a future in heaven, but a clear political statement about the here and now. As John Dominic Crossan says:

> Basically, it's awfully simple. It means [asking ourselves] what this world would look like if God sat on Caesar's throne. What would a divine instead of an imperial program look like? What would a divine budget look like? So "kingdom of God" is a way of saying Rome is *not* the kingdom of God. Rome thought (since Caesar was divine and it had a kingdom) that it must be the kingdom of God. What Jesus is really saying, sort of in your face is, "Rome, you are not the kingdom of God. You're not even the *will* of God."

Over and over again, the Gospels ask us to choose our allegiance. Whose kingdom?

The evidence we have about the identity, actions, mission, and vision of Jesus varies widely and wildly depending on the source and theological filter. At best, one can speak of the "lives" of Jesus rather than the life of Jesus. Our awareness of the origins of the Gospels, the traditions that have formed our image of Jesus, and the continuing struggle of faithful people to understand the complexity and radical nature of Jesus's message for the world, are critical in understanding how we might live as followers of Jesus today.

6

A Passion for Christ

Paul the Apostle

Perhaps no single person is more responsible for the existence of Christianity as we know it today than that balding preacher from Tarsus whom we know as Paul.

Idolized by some as the conduit through which God dictated an eternal and unchanging moral code, discredited by others as a misogynist crank, Paul is without question one of the most controversial figures in the history of Christianity. But one thing can't be questioned: his passion for Christ and his apparent willingness to risk life and limb in propagating his interpretation of Christ's message and purpose. Very little, if any, of what most people think of as Christianity has been untouched by the influence of this itinerant tentmaker. That's why any faithful expression of Christianity needs to be based on a thorough examination of the changing understandings and significance of Paul's writings and ideas.

It is abundantly clear from Paul's letters that he was no stranger to controversy. His words continue to be the source of debate today. Yet for all his influence, very little is known about the man responsible for nearly a quarter of what we know as the New Testament. Most of what people think we know about Paul comes from Luke's Acts of the Apostles. However, Acts conflicts in so many ways with the authentic writings of Paul in both chronology and theological content that it's highly suspect as an accurate account of his life.

According to Luke, Paul's birth name was Saul. He was born in Tarsus of Asia Minor (modern-day Turkey), possibly to a Roman family who was committed to his Jewish education and upbringing. Luke notes that the young Saul studied in Jerusalem with Rabbi Gamaliel and persecuted those on "the Way" as heretics before experiencing a profound life-changing encounter with the Christ on the road to Damascus. In a moment, we'll look at the ways these stories conflict with Paul's writings, but even as uncertain as these Lukan story elements are, they nonetheless express the conviction that Paul straddled two very different worlds. He was uniquely situated to translate the universal message of a local Jewish sect into language that the whole world could embrace.

His biography is by no means the most controversial aspect of Paul's life. Reviled and discredited for writings attributed to him, he has the dubious honor of being one of the most admired and hated proponents of Christianity. Women, slaves, Jews, and homosexuals are just some of the groups who can point to Paul's writings as providing fodder for those who seek to defend an unjust and cruel status quo.

At the same time, Paul's work is responsible for many of the structures and doctrines that shore up the institutional church. Letters attributed to Paul have introduced the idea of Jesus as the divine savior from sin and set the foundation for a church that administers sacraments and ordains clergy. Likewise, Paul's writings have been the springboard from which theologians have woven complex theories of blood atonement and recast the faith we now call Christianity into a religion "about" Jesus rather than the religion "of" Jesus.

"Without Paul," says John B. Cobb Jr., "Christianity would have remained a Jewish sect. Now, [Paul] didn't ever intend for it to become anything other than the true Judaism. But there have been other developments in Judaism from time to time and other claims for Messiah that have led to the development of sects, which then after a while are reabsorbed into Judaism. In some way that's better—from the Jewish point of view that may be better. But then the vast majority of us Gentiles would have never heard the gospel or ever been grafted into the roots, the Jewish roots."

To make sense of Paul and his role in casting a vision for the faith, we need to sort out Paul's social, theological, and ecclesiastical legacy. Only then can we establish exactly what can be attributed to him and what cannot.

GENUINE PAUL

The earliest writings in the New Testament are Paul's authentic letters. One indication that the Gospels were written later is that the genuine Paul never quotes from them. Further, Paul seldom quotes Jesus—and when he does, they're not the same sayings we find in the Gospels.

Despite his having written an entire biography of Paul in Acts, Luke seems to be curiously unaware of Paul's life and ministry as reflected in Paul's authentic letters. None of Paul's letters are mentioned in Acts. The language and theology of Paul's speeches as told by Luke are so different in vocabulary and theology from the Paul of the authentic letters that it seems much of Luke's Paul can be chalked up to dramatic license. The authentic Paul emphasizes justification and reconciliation while Luke's "Paul" preaches righteousness and forgiveness. In other words, Luke's Paul preaches in the theological language of Luke, not Paul.

Without Acts, the letters become our primary source of understanding the real Paul. However, many of the books attributed to Paul are either anonymous or pseudonymous. Analysis of the vocabulary, style, and theological focus of the letters attributed to Paul has led scholars to agree on seven letters as having actually been written by Paul, probably in the 50s of the first century. They are: 1 Thessalonians, 1 and 2 Corinthians, Galatians, Philemon, Philippians, and Romans. First Thessalonians is probably the earliest. Romans, the most mature statement of Paul's theological views, is likely the latest.

While the superscription, "The letter of Paul to the..." appears on many other New Testament letters, the use of the superscription can only be traced back to the second century and was most certainly used to lend credibility to an otherwise anonymous work. In Hebrews, Paul is mentioned only in the superscription and nowhere in the body of the letter. In Ephesians, both the superscription and the interior mention Paul, but the content is so wildly different from the authentic letters, scholars agree that it is "pseudo" Paul.

You can still find theologians who will argue about the authenticity of Colossians and 2 Thessalonians, but most agree that Ephesians, Hebrews, 1 and 2 Timothy, and Titus are later creations by authors other than Paul. As John Dominic Crossan notes, "None of this is particularly scandalous. It was quite customary in the ancient world to attribute texts to a dead person who was extremely authoritative. You're saying, as it were, 'If he were only alive today, this is what he would say.'"

The two letters to Timothy and the letter to Titus are good examples of "pseudo-Pauline" literature. Having come to be known as the Pastoral Epistles, many Bibles will still print the heading as "The Letter of Paul to Timothy or Titus." But even the most cursory reading will reveal the profound differences between these Pastorals and the undisputed letters of Paul.

The vocabulary, theology, and style of the Pastorals are closer to that of the second century's early church fathers. The matter-of-fact discussion of church "order" (bishops, elders, deacons, etc.) had not been established when Paul was writing in the first century. In Paul's day, Christians were still a kind of Jewish reform movement, not a "church." The Pastorals reflect some transition time between Paul's loose community structure and the hierarchy of the second-century church.

John Dominic Crossan notes that there is a trajectory from the "radical" Paul to increasingly reactionary Pauls of later generations:

> The Paul of the authentic letters is a sort of a radical Paul who insists on equality. It probably is that the post-Pauline letters are trying to tone down the social radicality of the original Paul. If

you look, for example, at a statement from Paul, Galatians 3:28, where he insists that if you are in Christ—and "in Christ" is important—there is no hierarchy. Once you come into the Christian community, whether you come male or female, slave or free, Greek or Jew, you are equal in Christ. You're all members of the same family. When you start applying that in a world of slavery, in a world of patriarchy, in a world of patronage, you are shaking the foundations of Roman normalcy. So in one sense, this radical Paul who insists on equality in the family of God gets slowly toned down. My point is not that these other epistles are valueless, but you must understand that their purpose is to deradicalize, to sanitize, and in a way to sort of fumigate this dangerous Paul, to make him a little bit more acceptable to Roman normalcy. This is, in fact, in Colossians and Ephesians, in Timothy and Titus, the first move towards accommodation with the Roman Empire. The shadow of Constantine, a few hundred years ahead, is starting to fall over the early church.

SOMEONE ELSE'S MAIL

Although Paul's letters are often read as if they are somehow letters to "us," they are actually glimpses into the everyday circumstances of Paul's efforts to oversee a fledgling movement. Each of the authentic letters reveals a slice of Paul's life that he never intended to be collected and venerated the way they have been. Paul would undoubtedly be apoplectic if he knew that some of his letters, dashed off in impulsive outbursts at disobedient and wavering little faith communities, were now held up as "holy" and as the "word of God." The *Peanuts* comic strip character Linus was wise to express discomfort at reading Paul's letters, saying, "I feel like I'm reading someone else's mail."

All the authentic letters of Paul were "occasional," meaning they were written in response to a particular situation or occasion. In many cases it is clear that someone like "Chloe's people" (1 Cor. 1:11) have tattled or written a letter to Paul to report some kind of problem, compelling Paul to respond. Romans, the only letter written to a church Paul didn't start, was a letter of introduction to a congregation he intended to visit and wanted to butter up before he arrived. That's why Romans stands out as the most comprehensive statement of Paul's theology, independent of parochial crises.

Amy-Jill Levine finds that the occasional nature of these letters tells us something about Paul as well. She says, "One of the things I think that's very helpful about Paul—and he admits it himself—is he's all things to all people. He adapts his message according to the needs of the individual congregations to which he writes, which means he's a good pastor. The same sermon that might work in Church One might not work in Church Two because the congregational needs would be different. Because he's writing ad hoc information targeted to specific congregations, it's extremely difficult to get some sort of systematic program on what Paul actually thought regarding particular practices in churches."

Though they were never intended for universal application, Paul's letters are nonetheless invaluable in guiding and shaping the lives of Christian individuals and communities. For instance, the reason we have written details on how to celebrate the Lord's Supper is because the Corinthians weren't doing it the way Paul wanted them to. Paul sets them straight in 1 Corinthians 11 and casts the model for the practice of communion in the institutionalized church.

THEOLOGICAL SHENANIGANS

Paul's major themes of grace, faith, freedom, and Christ crucified are interwoven through his letters. However, much of Paul's writing remains cryptic, dense, and repetitive. That's not always Paul's doing. In many cases, it's the theological projections from later developments or outright mistranslations that obscure Paul's original meaning. A case in point is Paul's concept of faith.

Translators, often influenced by theological developments in the later church, are also restricted by the limits of language. The English word translated as "faith" is *pistis* in Greek. For Paul, *pistis* was not something to possess. Rather, it was a concept that included a whole way of living. The language of "having faith" would have been foreign to Paul. But there is no English word to translate the breadth of meaning suggested by Paul. Professor J. Paul Sampley has suggested "faithing" as a better translation of *pistis* while others have suggested "faithfulness." John B. Cobb Jr., says, "*pistis* for Paul (and in its general use in his time), included a whole way of living that's better captured in the English word 'faithfulness.' Faithfulness includes trust and assurance, but it also includes the total way of being in the world."

These distinctions are more than esoteric theological shenanigans. They can have profound implications for the way we understand and practice our faith.

For example, in the grammatically confusing context of Romans 3:22, *pistis* can be interpreted in two very different ways. Overall, Paul was interested in the faithfulness (or faithing) of Jesus and his obedience to death. But instead of being translated as the faith *of* Jesus, Romans 3:22 was translated as faith *in* Jesus, essentially suggesting right belief as the priority. There is a significant difference between believing *in* Jesus and faithing the way Jesus did. Such choices in translation can and have contributed to Christianity's emphasis on an aspect of discipleship Paul may never have intended.

HARD TO UNDERSTAND

So also our beloved brother Paul wrote to you according to the wisdom given him, speaking of this as he does in all his letters. There are some things in them hard to understand, which the ignorant and unstable twist to their own destruction, as they do the other scriptures.

—2 Peter 3:15–16

God's law-opposing work in the world. He deserves our responsibility. Some readers are frustrated by Paul the polemicist, who often squares off when cornered and overstates his argument in triplicate twelve times over until his opponent's case is beaten down or neutered. In addition, Paul's efforts to translate Hebrew concepts into a Greco-Roman cosmology can sometimes leave the reader wondering where he's going.

Even the preeminent Pauline bumper sticker, "Christ crucified," a statement meant to be a shocking oxymoron in Paul's day, seems pedestrian and old hat today. Its importance has been commandeered by literal interpreters of scripture, such as Mel Gibson, whose advertisements for *The Passion of the Christ* simply declared, "Dying Was His Reason for Living." We are culturally so far removed from Jesus's and Paul's world that such phrases have lost their edge and become simple litmus tests of right belief. The idea of Christ crucified for today's progressive Christian can be lost in light of gross literal overstatements. But John Dominic Crossan believes, "Jesus died to maintain the integrity of his life. Or, to reverse Mel Gibson's claim, 'Living Was His Reason for Dying.'"[1]

Christ crucified and the resurrection also hold power for the likes of Marcus Borg, who claims them as "the metaphorical embodiment of the path of dying to an old way of being and being born into a new identity."

If there is a constant message in Paul's writings, it's this: Human beings have a capacity for self-destruction that Paul saw as being altered only by the grace of God.

According to J. Paul Sampley, the grace of God for Paul means we are:

No Longer	Now	Not Yet
Weak (helpless)	dying to sin	share glory of God
Enemies	justified	saved (whole)
Sinners	reconciled	perfect (complete)
Ungodly	"in Christ"	

Paul speaks of our solidarity with Jesus, of our having died to sin with Christ (as opposed to Christ having died for our sins). Freed from the "no longer," we are unfinished creatures living in the "now" that the Divine will complete in the "not yet." Those who have died in Christ will be finished as they press on, faithing and participating in the faithfulness of Jesus.

All of this leads to one of the most important aspects of Paul's teaching, namely, that as a by-product of grace, there is hope. In both the courtroom language of justification and the familial language of reconciliation, Paul expresses a belief in a God who is up to something in the world. It's not about people believing in extraordinary things, but about people being in a renewed relationship with the Divine and with their fellow human beings. As we unpack Paul's "Christ in me" and "Christ in us" language, we get a glimpse of the almost mystical sense in which Paul felt God participates in our lives and we participate in God. As such, we are profoundly interconnected as the body of Christ and called to participate in God's program of making the reign of God real in the world.

It's hard to pin down a real center or core truth of Paul's message. But if we're willing to embrace the many different ideas tugging and pulling at one another in creative tension, we begin to sense his passion for Christ and his grace-drenched hope for humanity.

Paul's confidence in the future was based on his perception of what God had done in the past and had promised for the future. Paul lived believing that what God had begun would be completed sometime in the "not yet." In the meantime, the form in which one's faith is best expressed is in a love that cuts across social orders and barriers, a grace that heals all divisions, and a hope that can overcome all the violence, injustice, and grief the world can muster.

Out into the World

Challenges Facing Progressive Christians

Stagnation in thought or enterprise means death for
Christianity as certainly as it does for any other vital
movement. Stagnation, not change, is Christianity's
most deadly enemy, for this is a progressive world.[1]

—Harry Emerson Fosdick

Medieval Europeans believed famines and plagues were sent by God as punishment for sin. Wars were divine earthly retribution. Feudalism, absolute monarchy, and slavery were considered ordained by God. Even the invention of the lightning rod was denounced by clergy "as an impious attempt to defeat the will of God."[2] In the not too distant past those seeking medical help submitted themselves to physicians who slit the skin to bleed patients and let the bad "humours" escape. Even more recently, women were turned away from the polls and African Americans were relegated to the back of the bus.

How the world has changed! Today, we take for granted wireless phones, ease of travel, education for our children, and miracles of medicine. Daily work and life are inconceivable without our computers, cars, comfortable homes, and instant communication. While we still have significant strides to make toward equality for all people, we have made enough progress to be ashamed of the divisions we once held sacred. We've long since left the idea of a flat earth and a three-tiered cosmos behind—and we wouldn't dream of going back a thousand years. And yet many Christians today not only embrace religious ideas that are more than one thousand years old, they believe these ideas are proof of their faith and a litmus test of their relationship with God.

In virtually every field of human endeavor, new discoveries are praised. Not so with religion. In no other area of life is the denial of progress held up as a virtue. Twenty-first-century believers faithfully recite creeds reflecting arcane fourth-century questions, giving little thought to the political and theological terrain that spawned the creeds in the first place.

When the Bible is held up as a final authority trumping all other arguments, it's helpful to remember that the early church didn't have any Bible beyond Hebrew scripture. They were small gatherings of people who sought a deeper understanding of and relationship with the Divine. They came together around the teachings and person of Jesus and developed the foundations of what we know as Christianity out of their own experience and insight.

What most people "know" about the Bible or understand about religion today has been cobbled together out of assumptions, insecurity, and long-held half memories that have little basis in rational thought or historical fact. Yet the resistance some people have to expanding their religious horizons can be fiercely irrational. They don't want anyone to mess with the faith they believe they know so well.

But even the Bible is full of examples of changing perceptions and descriptions of the divine/human relationship. Not only does the character of Jesus change from one Gospel to the next—sometimes profoundly—but the very nature of the Divine changes throughout the course of the biblical story.

hard time accepting in the Acts of the Apostles.

The whole of scripture is awash with change, change, and more change. Yet the fallacy that Christianity is a static belief system offering absolute truths to the faithful remains the overwhelmingly predominant message preached and believed by many in the West today.

FROM LITERAL TO METAPHORICAL

Over the centuries, much of our perception of the Divine has been driven by fear, tribalism, and our own prejudices. The God many of us grew up worshipping simply does not exist. When theologian Paul Tillich popularized the phrase "the Ground of Being" to describe the Divine, he too was wrestling with a reality we all have to face: using clumsy human terms and metaphors to describe the indescribable. While many Christians continue to cling to an image of God as a coercive and wrathful potentate, others are progressing toward a more metaphorical understanding of divinity.

Many people are often surprised to discover that a nonliteral and metaphorical understanding of scripture has been the norm in academic and mainline Protestant clergy circles for more than 100 years. But out of fear or ease of maintaining the status quo, many clergy are apologetic and simply not honest with their people about what they learned in seminary. Mainline Protestant churches have, as a whole, not fared well in the last fifty years membership-wise. Many of those who have left the church altogether are thinking people who can no longer endure the shallow and watered-down theology being preached in an effort to avoid controversy. Indeed, one of the fastest growing segments of American demographics seems to be what John Shelby Spong calls "the church alumni/ae association."

Meanwhile, conservative churches that promote rigid doctrines and unchanging "truths" seem to be growing by leaps and bounds. In a world that so often feels chaotic, it's not surprising that people seek out the comfort of a place where things don't change. Ironically, many of the central, so-called "traditional" doctrines of modern fundamentalist Christians, including the rapture, pre- and postmillennial dispensationalism, and other apocalyptic schemes, are based on the relatively recent *Scofield Reference Bible* of 1909.

It would appear—and scientific studies suggest—that human beings are "wired" for spirituality. No matter how we feel about the church as an institution, and the various ways we express our spiritualities, we long to find others who are wired in similar ways.

Unfortunately, acceptance is often found only when a person submits to the influence of some ultrapersonalized God who can only be accessed through one particular incantation, prayer, or belief system. Many of us let ourselves be led down the primrose path of this or that religious idea, all in the quest for the faith that will prop up our previously held prejudices and justify our own narrow-minded and parochial perspective on the world. At best, we find a group that in the finest of self-help traditions gets us off drugs, drinking, or a penchant for infidelity. Then, as we huddle together in cultural and theological ghettos, too many of us are satisfied with congratulating one another on how right we are while discrediting and damning the beliefs of the rest of the world.

BELIEVING VS. RELATIONSHIP

When missionary John Paton tried to translate the New Testament into the indigenous language of the people of New Hebrides, he ran into a

one's heart to. Believing

tal assent. It suggests something deeper—something that asks for our whole selves. In our friendships and relationships with significant others, we don't believe in the other person (at least not in the same way we talk about believing in God). Instead, we are in dynamic, fluid relationships with other people. We depend on one another, learn to give and take, make an effort to get to know others, and spend time together out of sheer enjoyment.

Believing doesn't mean putting your allegiance in with a set of doctrines or teachings: it means moving from a secondhand religion of following rules to a firsthand religion of relationship, from having heard about Jesus to being in a dynamic and fluid relationship with the Spirit of Christ. The day of Christians living in fear, intimidated by some vague sense of guilt that our Creator is waiting to punish us somehow, is obsolete. We have something other than fear to "lean our whole weight on."

But what is Christianity without "right belief" and the fear of punishment for doing wrong? A criticism often leveled at Jesus and other "liberal" thinkers has been, "You tolerate everything but intolerance!" In fact, progressive Christians cannot tolerate injustice, abuse or exploitation, and are actively committed to eradicating evil in all its forms—including hatred, discrimination and violence. The heart of this religion is compassion, hospitality, and a posture of welcoming the outsider—not because those things are politically correct or trendy, but because such behavior was modeled by Jesus, who always put people before the rules. As Ron Buford says, "He saw what they needed. And no matter what law he had to break, if he had to break a law in order to make that person whole or to make their lives better, he did it." Jesus was about moving beyond belief to relationship.

WHAT WOULD JUSTICE DEMAND?

When the prophet Micah observed that ritual had become an end in itself in Israel, he determined that the people had lost the essence of their faith. Without justice, human beings cannot live together as God intended. Without kindness and mercy, life is unbearable. And unless one walks humbly in the presence of the mystery we call God, we are likely to be humbled in ways we least expect. And so, Micah poses the question that stands at the heart of Jesus's ministry:

> "And what does the LORD require of you
> but to do justice, and to love kindness,
> and to walk humbly with your God?"
> —Micah 6:8

Jesus's life was about living out Micah's call. We don't prove our faith in God by blind and unquestioning obedience to rules. Such obedience, in fact, gets in the way of faith because we so often mistake the rules for God.

Marcus Borg contends that the historical Jesus had the passion of a social prophet, who, like Micah, called people to strive for justice—even if it meant breaking the rules. Jesus was "like a Martin Luther King" says Borg, "with a very strong passion for those who are impoverished by an economic system that operates to the benefit of the elites at the top. He was a God-intoxicated Jewish voice of peasant social protest."

Founder of Soulforce, Mel White, spent most of his early life struggling with the rules imposed on him by religious authorities. But later, he came to see Jesus in a new way, through the eyes of Mahatma Gandhi. White says:

principles to nonviolently free gay, lesbian, bisexual, and transgender people from religion-based oppression. Relentless. Nonviolent. Resistance. That's the heart of the prophetic Jesus. He called us to be relentless, to be nonviolent and to resist injustice and the systems that cause poverty and being outcast and hunger and nakedness.

Perhaps a less saccharine alternative to the popular What Would Jesus Do? campaign would be the Micah-inspired, What Would Justice Demand? It's good to be good—but if we only do so because that's what the rules tell us to do, we're missing the point. Living justly is right because it's what's best for us and for others.

As we try to figure out what it looks like to follow Micah's call in our own lives, it helps to understand the religious life as a journey. Jesus's early followers were called those who were on "the way," suggesting that our spiritual lives are not about following rules or being "saved" so much as they are about life-long journeys of transformation.

VITAL FAITH

In the early twentieth century, Harry Emerson Fosdick was an eloquent spokesperson for progressive Christianity. He preached sermons that even eighty years later would prove scandalous in many of our churches. An apocryphal story is told of Fosdick meeting a young man for a walk in Central Park. "I'm jealous of your faith," said the young man. "I'm afraid to ask questions, because I was raised in a faith that provided all the answers and to ask questions was to show unfaithfulness." Coming upon a reflecting pool, Fosdick mused, "Son, your faith is like this pool: calm, bordered, shallow — you always know what it's going to look like and what the boundaries are. But it's not a "living" faith. It's not going anywhere. Vital faith is like a stream bubbling up from a well deep within the earth. As it makes its way, it twists and turns, sometimes changes course, is deep and slow in some places and fast and turbulent in others, responding to the geographical reality. It's joined by the waters of other streams and together they make their way back to their source."

Stagnation, not change, is Christianity's deadliest enemy. Vital faith has always been dynamic, flowing, and moving. So one of the biggest challenges for thinking Christians today is facing those who conceive of "true" Christianity as something that never changes. While many faith communities have invested untold energy arguing over changing the style of liturgy and music used in worship, what really need to be addressed are many of the basic theological tenets espoused by that liturgy and music. Take, for example, a contemporary worship song in which God is praised for knowing where every bolt of lightning strikes. This might be comforting for those who want to believe God controls the world like a puppet master. It is, perhaps, less comforting for those who have been struck by lightning.

For many religious people, it takes some serious readjustment to change those theological underpinnings and recast Christianity as something fluid. Some are too controlled by fear — of change, of uncertainty, of being called heretical — to make the shift. They keep trying, desperately, to hold on to old conceptions as if their eternal life depended on it. But there are alternatives.

about believing the right stuff or even about being "good." It's about a relationship with the Divine and with one another. It's a relationship that does not leave us unchanged, but transforms us into more and more compassionate beings—as Paul writes, into "the same image [as Christ]" (2 Cor. 3:18). It's not about having all the answers, but about wrestling with and living the great questions of life. When our experience of God is limited to memorizing creeds and parroting beliefs, we fail to experience the depth Christianity has to offer.

This is not a problem for Jews. As Hebrew scripture Professor Harrell Beck points out, "I'm so glad that Judaism has never produced a great systematic theologian. They left that for the Christians! Dogmatic theologians? Perish the thought!"[4] The stories of the Bible express deep theological thought in relational and *not* propositional terms.

Walter Brueggemann explains the profound difference between a faith of rules and a faith of relationship. He says:

In Romans 12 Paul gives that lyrical statement of ethics: "I beseech therefore by the mercies of God to present your body as holy and a living sacrifice to God." And what Paul really lines out is an ethic that is counter to Caesar, counter to Pharaoh. You could imagine a catalog like Romans 12 being a parallel to the Ten Commandments. They are all formulations for counter obedience. First of all, Paul enjoins the church to practice hospitality. We all know that. But imagine hospitality in Pharaoh's world. Second, Paul enjoins gen-

erosity. Imagine generosity in Pharaoh's world. And thirdly, Paul
says you cannot practice vengeance. Now all of us know that those
three summonses of hospitality, generosity, and no vengeance are
as radical as you can get in Pharaoh's world or in Caesar's world.
So my thought is that these are secrets that have been kept silent in
the church so that the church doesn't upset anybody. But there is a
huge hunger in the church because people are asking for an alternative way. The wonderful thing about hospitality and generosity
and no vengeance and Sabbath and no coveting is that it's not liberal and it's not conservative. Everybody can do it. We don't all have
to do it the same way. These are marks of a unified church that no
longer needs to argue about secondary issues. And if we did these
primary marks of the church, there's a fair chance that most of the
secondary issues would evaporate because we wouldn't have extra
energy for them.

Christianity remains an amazingly diverse enterprise as we enter into
the twenty-first century. In contrast to those who preach absolute certainty, there are those who are convinced that there's something more to
Christianity than what they've experienced in the past. They are a group
of seekers who have a hunch about this Jesus. They are not preoccupied
with their own eternal well-being so much as they long to change the
world to reflect Jesus's vision of the reign of God.

These seekers are comfortable with ambiguity and understand that
through difficulties, mistakes, and challenges, it's the journey that's
important. It's what we learn along the way in relationship to the Divine
and to one another that matters most. It takes work as we go down the
road, sharing our experiences, our questions, and our uncertainties with
one another and with God. And grace comes in the midst of the search,
as we journey down the road together. As Bishop Fulton Sheen observed
so many years ago, "The questions of God may ultimately be more satisfying than the answers of men [and women]."[5]

As a corollary to what Spong calls the "killing certainties" of fundamentalist Christianity, it is good to remember the words of the great mystic pastor and poet, Howard Thurman: "Don't ask yourself what the world needs. Ask yourself what makes you come alive, and go do that, because what the world needs is people who have come alive."[6]

The challenge of progressive Christianity in the twenty-first century will be to "come alive," mustering the courage, wisdom, and resources to be a beacon of faithful thoughtfulness for those who have given up on the church, been hurt by slavish adherence to church doctrine, or found themselves unwelcome for reasons they don't understand.

When UN Secretary General Dag Hammarskjöld wrote in his journal, *Markings,* he often expressed the core sentiments held by many exploring progressive Christianity. He wrote, "I don't know Who—or what—put the question, I don't know when it was put. I don't even remember answering. But at some moment I did answer Yes to Someone—or Something—and from that hour I was certain that existence is meaningful and that, therefore, my life, in self-surrender, had a goal."[7]

To "live the questions" is to live into that same sense of ambiguity and certainty, of faith and doubt, that is at the heart of progressive Christianity. Inspired by insights that are at once fresh and ancient, progressive Christians can claim a distinctive voice in the twenty-first century by being in solidarity with the poor, countering the idolatry of wealth, practicing nonviolence, and by seeking justice and inclusivity in a culture dominated by suspicion and fear. In so doing, we may discover that the path of true wisdom is not just asking the questions for which there are no answers, but in living the questions which shape our faith, our lives, and our world.

SECTION TWO

Reconciliation

8

Restoring Relationships

Rootless. Alienated. Estranged. Meaningless. The human condition can be a desperate mix of questions about the basics of "being." In fact, the longing for a sense of connection is at the root of the English word *religion*. The Latin *re-ligio* means to relink, to reconnect. To reconnect, relink, and restore people to relationship with one another and to the Divine is the heart of religion. Our stories, rituals, ceremonies, and traditions grow out of our collective effort to understand just what it takes to be *re-ligio-ed*.

Central to the biblical tradition is the notion that truth doesn't come to us primarily as fact, creed, or scripture. It is best conveyed through story. As our spiritual ancestors endeavored to sort out the process of reconnection, they did so by developing three major themes — what Marcus Borg calls biblical "macro-stories."[1] Borg explains that for the ancient Hebrews enslaved in Egypt, the problem was bondage. Since what was needed was liberation, the tale of the Exodus became one of the most important stories for ancient Israel. For those removed to Babylon after the destruction of Jerusalem, the problem was exile. The solution was maintaining a sense of identity in a foreign land, and if possible, a journey of return. For those grounded in the institution and rituals of the Temple, the problem was sin and guilt. The solution was forgiveness. Individually and collectively, says Borg, these stories serve as the thematic wellspring from which stream the major stories of the biblical tradition.

BONDAGE AND LIBERATION

While liberation from bondage for the Hebrews was a practical matter of getting away from Pharaoh, bondage today is no less real: political, economic, religious, psychological, and spiritual bondage is the stuff of everyday struggle for countless millions.

Marcus Borg suggests:

We hear these as stories of the divine-human relationship in the present as well as in the past. My favorite way of making this point is with the way the story of the Exodus is told in the Jewish celebration of Passover each year to this day. If you've ever been to a Passover Seder, a Passover meal, you will remember that there are spoken words that accompany the meal, like a liturgy almost, but it's a family gathering in a home. At one point in the evening the following words are spoken—this is a close paraphrase, not exact quotation—but it goes like this, "It was not just our fathers and our mothers who were Pharaohs' slaves in Egypt, but we, all of us gathered here tonight were Pharaohs' slaves in Egypt. And it was not just our mothers and our fathers whom God led out of Egypt with a great and mighty hand, but we, all of us gathered here tonight were led out of Egypt by the great and mighty hand of God." Those words are affirming that the Exodus story is true about *us*.

The temptation is to let this story be something that happened long ago about which the facts are worth knowing. But the true power of the story is in what it is saying right now about each of our lives and what it says to the deepest part of our being. Everyday kinds of bondage in our lives take on many forms: grief, anxiety, ego, guilt, regret, addictions, religion, legalism, apathy, destructive relationships, destructive jobs, issues of identity—or just being in a rut.

That's in part why Franciscan priest Richard Rohr says Christianity is not so much a spirituality of addition (where you add this skill and that achievement) as it is a spirituality of subtraction. Especially in the affluent West, peeling away the things that don't matter or that keep us in bondage is the solution to much that ails the human soul.[2]

TOWARD THE PROMISED LAND

Following the American Civil War, newly freed slaves in the South had no place to go. Many returned to plantations to work for room and board—and no pay. Technically, they'd been liberated, but not much had really changed. The same was true for the Israelites. The Torah repeatedly asks, "Where do we go from here?" The whole of Exodus, Leviticus, Numbers, and Deuteronomy is about the subsequent journey of the children of God, a journey of trials and tribulations, learning how to survive, and journeying toward the promised land.

This spiritual journey toward a land of promise has been expressed in countless ways. From personal pilgrimages to holy places to the highly personalized notion of being "born again" to focusing on doing whatever it takes to guarantee a spiritual future in heaven, the promised land is finally none of these. It is best thought of as a way of being where there is peace, understanding, and justice—not just for one, but for the whole community. Jesus called it the reign or kingdom of God.

United Methodist Bishop Minerva Carcaño suggests how the promise of liberation extends into our lives today. She says:

I have experienced liberation. I have been freed from poverty, freed from sexism, freed from racism, freed from all the "isms" that affect my life. And I've been freed from them by God's grace. Prophets of old and prophets of new have said to me, "You are a child of God. You are a sacred being. You are beloved of God." I believe that everyone is a beloved child of God, and I think it's in that message that we are free. I view liberation also in the very concrete ways that we help each other to be free of physical poverty, free of violence, free from all that pushes us down or offends us simply because of who we are. Free from our sin, our tendency to be judgmental of others, our tendency to want more for ourselves than to want to share, our tendency to think that we live in a world of scarcity, and therefore aren't able to share when indeed, we live in a world of great abundance.

Moses may have never made it to the promised land, Martin Luther King Jr. may have never made it to the promised land, but the vision of that promise inspired them to do everything they could to get there.

WITH CANAANITE EYES

As appealing as "promised-land theology" may at first seem, it can also be a quagmire of competing claims. The same biblical texts some interpret as messages of saving hope and promise are seen by others as condoning conquest and genocide. Emilie Townes sees the liberating process itself as "this deep, deep battle I have going on about the whole meaning of the Exodus—because the reality is that the Canaanites didn't do anything. So what do you do? That story becomes much more complex." As a Native American, theologian Robert Allen Warrior challenges us to read the Exodus and Promised Land stories "with Canaanite eyes"—from the perspective of the victims of colonization and conquest. He says, according to the biblical text, the Canaanites "are not to be trusted, nor are they to be allowed to enter into social relationships with the people of Israel. They are wicked, and their religion is to be avoided at all costs. The laws put forth regarding strangers and sojourners may have stopped the people of Yahweh from wanton oppression, but presumably only after the land was safely in the hands of Israel. The covenant of Yahweh depends on this."[3]

Likewise, the early success of the American economy was made possible by the forced labor of millions of African slaves. Civil rights leader

Malcolm X was said to have claimed that his people didn't land on Plymouth Rock, but that Plymouth Rock landed on them. Similar claims can be made against the Afrikaners in South Africa, Spaniards and Portuguese in South America, Belgians in the Congo, and the Dutch in the East Indies.

In adopting the story of the Exodus as their own, African Americans are but one group to have acknowledged the continuing power of the biblical story to inspire people in bondage with the hope of liberation.

> We need not always weep and mourn, let my people go;
> and wear those slavery chains forlorn, let my people go.
> Go down, Moses, way down in Egypt Land,
> Tell old Pharaoh, "Let my people go..."
> —African-American Spiritual

Be it peasant vs. oligarchy in Central America, Palestine vs. Israel, indigenous aborigines vs. the "white fella" in Australia and New Zealand, or countless other conflicts, stories of bondage and liberation continue to play out on a national—and personal—scale.

Emilie Townes likes to talk about liberation as a journey. She says, "For me liberation becomes the process of coming into awareness that there is definitely a better life for people to be had, not just for myself but really for all of us, and that the church should be part of that and where it is not, it is not the church."

EXILE AND RETURN

By the rivers of Babylon—there we sat down and there we
wept when we remembered Zion. On the willows there
we hung up our harps. For there our captors asked us
for songs, and our tormentors asked for mirth, saying,
"Sing us one of the songs of Zion!" How could we
sing the LORD's song in a foreign land?
—Psalm 137: 1–4

Perhaps one of the most important and least acknowledged events contributing to the shaping of Western culture was the Babylonian conquest of Jerusalem in 587/6 BCE. The brightest and best of Jewish leaders were taken into exile in Babylon where they served the courts and needs of the Babylonians for generations. This was not only a political defeat, but also a crisis of faith: Babylon's victory was perceived as a victory for Babylon's patron god, Marduk, over Yahweh of Israel.

Deprived of all the trappings of temple and promised land, the exiles took to writing down their stories of faith in order to prevent assimilation into the Babylonian culture. This "resistance literature" promoted hope in the assurance that Marduk's apparent victory was not the last word and that captivity would come to an end. The traditions and writings of this time period contribute significantly to what we now know as the Torah. After several generations in captivity, a remnant was allowed to return to rebuild their culture and eventually, the temple.

This, however, is not the only biblical story with the theme of exile and return. The authors of Genesis explored exile and return in the story of Eve and Adam's banishment from the Garden. The newly self-conscious humans were not only evicted from Eden, but were cast into a world of anxiety and alienation from one another and the Divine. The journey of return is then played out over the length and breadth of the Bible as human beings seek to reconnect with the idyllic vision of life in Paradise.

SIN AND FORGIVENESS

The theological concept that describes the healing of the once-estranged relationship between God and humanity is called "atonement." Said to be achieved for Christians through the "work" of Jesus (not his life and ministry, but his self-sacrificing death), the idea of atonement has a long and convoluted history.

In the ancient world, it was not unusual for religions to restore relationship to their god or gods with animal sacrifice. Judaism practiced animal sacrifice for countless years. Since the first New Testament writer, Paul, didn't have any Gospels to go on to describe Jesus's life, he went with what he knew, which was "Christ crucified."

Consequently, in 1 Corinthians 15:3–5, Paul wrote, "Christ died for our sins." But there's a problem: in both Greek and English, there are two ways to interpret that phrase. The first, most popular understanding is, "Christ died to save us from our sins." However, an equally acceptable reading of the passage has very different implications: "Christ died *because of* or *on account of* our sins."

Early Christians picked up on the first idea of Jesus's death as sacrifice. The first evangelist, Mark, devoted the first half of his Gospel to Jesus's life, and the whole second half to his suffering and death. By the time the Gospel of John was written, the idea of Jesus as sacrifice had gained so much influence that the storyline was changed: John even changed the day of Jesus's death so it could be said Jesus was slain at the exact moment the Passover lambs would have been slain.

To top it off, The Letter to the Hebrews takes it to the next level, setting Jesus's death against the backdrop of another Jewish holiday, Yom Kippur, or Day of Atonement. In a sad irony, the Jesus of the Gospels, who overturned the tables of the money changers in the temple, protesting not only economic corruption, but the cult of animal sacrifice itself, is simultaneously portrayed in Hebrews as the High Priest that offers the sacrifice *and* as the perfect animal whose blood is spilled in order to satiate God's need for blood.

Culver "Bill" Nelson explains why this is problematic:

I happen to believe that the old notion that God must beat the living daylights out of his own kid in order to be able to forgive us of our sins merely portrays the Divine as an abusive parent, and that's absolutely irrelevant to the thought of modern people, and it should be. What I think really happened historically, is that the story of the purported incident of Jesus turning over the tables of the money changers in the temple occurred right before he was arrested and placed on trial and of course crucified. I think that incident has a much deeper reality than my superficial description of it would suggest. I think Jesus was standing in protest to the nature of the temple itself as an institution that purportedly had to kill innocent beings, birds, animals, and so forth in order for God to be able to forgive us, that God demands this kind of punishment. I think that is an absurdity. I think Jesus was against that sacrificial system. I think he went up against it and the church, within a handful of years, readopted that very system he was against and applied it to him; so that he becomes the Lamb of God.

Clearly, even the early church struggled with the "meaning" of Jesus's death in relation to sin and forgiveness. Over the centuries, many attempts have been made to make sense of the biblical assertions regarding God's bloodthirsty expectations before forgiveness can be meted out. Not the least of these are theories of the atonement fashioned by the twelfth-century theologian, Anselm. Leaving out the notion of grace altogether, Anselm constructed the system that resonates in our churches and psyches to this day: in order to satisfy God's having been insulted by human sin, it is necessary for the perfect God-man, Jesus, to die. This almost purely legal argument eclipsed earlier ideas of Jesus's death symbolizing God's victory over Satan, and has itself experienced nearly a millennia of revision. Two thousand years of fevered speculation on exactly how sinners can receive forgiveness from God is proof of the hunger human beings have for reconciliation with the Divine. The history and development of various theories of atonement will be explored further in Chapter 11, "The Myth of Redemptive Violence."

All this, of course, is a distraction from the very real need of seeking forgiveness from our own fellow human beings. A fixation on sin and the need for divine forgiveness creates an obsession about a "vertical" relationship at the expense of relationships with those around us. Over-spiritualizing sin and forgiveness makes it a higher priority to seek God's forgiveness than the forgiveness of one's neighbor. After all, it is often easier to kneel at the altar over and over again than to knock on a neighbor's door and seek practical resolution to a misunderstanding.

JUST DO IT

We are people in need of forgiveness. But we also need liberation and a sense of belonging. The biblical witness offers us diverse solutions to our diverse problems. Remembering that truth comes as story and that different stories may speak more powerfully to people at different times, we are presented with multiple ways of understanding the quest for reconciliation. To be fixated on one story at the expense of the others diminishes the richness of what the Bible has to offer.

What is important, then, is to begin to live in the stories of reconciliation and make them our own, being present to the immediate and legitimate needs of real people. Together we can continue to move in the direction of reconciliation, restoring relationships with one another and with the Divine.

9

The Prophetic Jesus

*[Jesus] unrolled the scroll and found the place where it
was written, "The Spirit of the Lord is upon me, because
he has anointed me to bring good news to the poor.
He has sent me to proclaim release to the captives and
recovery of sight to the blind, to let the oppressed go free,
to proclaim the year of the Lord's favor." And he rolled
up the scroll, gave it back to the attendant, and sat down.
The eyes of all in the synagogue were fixed on him.
Then he began to say to them, "Today this
scripture has been fulfilled in your hearing."*

—Jesus quoting Isaiah in Luke 4:17b–21

It's no accident that the words most frequently recorded in Hebrew scripture are, "Do not be afraid." Neither is it an accident that the second most frequently recorded passage in Hebrew scripture is the admonition to "care for the orphan, the widow, and the stranger." The prophets tell us that the duty of the people of God is to care about and be the advocates for the poor and powerless. It should be no surprise, then, that according to the Gospels, Jesus's first concern was for those in the community who were most vulnerable and had no voice. This compassion Jesus exhibits is hardly original—the same passion underlies all of the Hebrew scriptures.

Yet speaking out on behalf of people who have no power or advocates has never been popular with respectable society. The prophets and other biblical sources make it clear that care for the downtrodden is the duty of the people of God. But it has always been much easier to make the spiritual life about following specific rules and embracing whatever priorities the community deems as reputable. Confronting the shortcomings of one's culture or society has never been a popular path.

A STRANGER IN THE MIDST OF HIS OWN PEOPLE

For this and many other reasons, Jesus is a stranger in the midst of his own people. According to the Gospels, nearly from the moment he proclaimed the call of Isaiah fulfilled, Jesus has been misunderstood and discredited for his most prophetic statements. As Jesus says in the Gospel of Thomas, "A prophet is not acceptable in his own country, neither does a physician work cures upon those that know him" (Gospel of Thomas, 31).

Today, Jesus has been misused so often by so many, it's no surprise that many of the priorities, practices, and teachings of the Jesus represented in the Gospels are ignored or intentionally contradicted by the institutional church. Jesus has become lost in so many churches that to talk about the radical implications of what's really in the Gospels often triggers howls of "revisionism." Despite the varying witnesses of the Synoptic Gospels, one characteristic is consistent throughout: Jesus raised a prophetic voice that critiqued, questioned, and confronted the status quo.

The bottom line is that in the eyes of the first-century authorities—both religious and political—Jesus was a troublemaker. He was simply too "out there," saying and doing things that were upsetting to the established order. He offered a firsthand relationship with the Divine that bypassed the religion of ritual that was the Sadducees' bread and butter. He ignored the Pharisees' interpretations about what was acceptable to do or not do on the Sabbath. He flew in the face of the Deuteronomic Code of divine earthly retribution and forgave people's sins. And most troubling of all, he not only associated with the wrong kind of people—sinful, impure, disreputable—he even ate with them!

Sister Helen Prejean, who ministers to inmates on death row, reminds us that:

> We live in a culture where the name of God and Jesus is invoked to uphold state killing, to uphold war, to uphold tax cuts where the rich get richer and poor people get poorer. I've come to discover the reason Jesus was a threat to both Rome and the religious hierarchy of the day was because he inaugurated a community that was so radical it threatened everybody. Because, it wasn't just people who could keep the holiness code and do all the hand washing and keep all the laws of cleanliness and holiness. It was people who never washed their hands. It was people who lived what was called sinful lives. And Jesus ate meals with 'em and Jesus inaugurated a community that incorporated even children—they weren't even considered persons. And that's what Jesus did that was so threatening. If he had just been like a dreamy preacher, told everybody to love one another, that wouldn't be threatening to the Romans or anybody. It was that radically new kind of community where wealthy people shared with people who had nothing. No one was in need and everyone was treated with dignity. That's what's so threatening and that's the kind of community we need to have today.

The teachings and the example of Jesus had the effect of undermining and subverting the prevailing religion and politics of both his time and ours. People forget that not only is Hebrew scripture full of the stories of violently rejected prophets, but even Christianity's foremost leaders were so threatening that they were executed by the government. Jesus and Paul directly confronted the political authorities of their day. While the circumstances of Paul's death are unclear, we know that Jesus was killed because his notions of justice and community were so intimidating to the powers that be that they felt it necessary to eliminate him.

BEST IGNORE HIM

If you haven't been made uncomfortable by the teachings of Jesus, you probably haven't understood them. Emilie Townes says, "Jesus was a guy who knew how to get angry, who understood the full meaning of righteous indignation. And when he saw less than what was acceptable, be it sin or whatever you want to call it going on in the Temple, he got upset and acted out about it. For me, that's a model. There are moments when you have to voice the injustice, that you can't mince words about it, that you can't try and be politically correct about it, that you can't be pastoral about it. Sometimes you just have to name a sin a sin and to be willing, then, to take the consequences."

Truth be told, despite efforts across the centuries to tame him, Jesus is still controversial. Beware of all greed, he said, because our true life is not made up of what we own—no matter how much we have. He made radical statements every time he opened his mouth: Blessed are the peacemakers. Those who live by the sword will die by the sword. Do not forget the humanity of even your enemy. Be compassionate with all people just as God is compassionate. If you are not able to forgive, you will not be forgiven. Let the one of you who wants to condemn and to judge be sure you yourself are sinless before you cast the first stone. Do not worship power and status and prestige, and do not aim for those yourself; instead, learn to be a servant.

In a culture where greed and domination are worshipped, talk of the "common good" is suspect, and the media obsesses on the sensationalized exploits of celebrities, the prophetic words of Jesus are countercultural and subversive. Even in the Lord's Prayer, when Jesus teaches his disciples to pray for God's will to be done and for God's kingdom to come on earth, any serious attempt to realize that prayer can only be seen as revolutionary.[1] Author of *Saving Jesus from the Church,* Robin Meyers says, "When Jesus prays, 'Thy Kingdom come, Thy will be done,' what people with wealth and power are saying is, 'No, no, no! MY kingdom stay!' That's what they're praying. They don't want another kingdom to come."[2] The Jesus of the Gospels is a cultural prophet, undermining any culture that worships affluence, appearance, and achievement. For those who wish to protect such things, it's basically safest to just not take Jesus too seriously.

It should be no surprise that Jesus saved his harshest words for the comfortable—those who think they belong in the inner circle with God. He saw them becoming self-righteous and narrow and thinking that the circle of God's family was pretty small. Jesus earned their wrath because he drew the circle wide.

Marcus Borg explains:

The Jesus of history is one who was passionate about the least of these. But I think the church has sometimes, maybe more often than not in its history, used the story of Jesus not to include people and not for the sake of the least of these, but has frequently used the story of Jesus to judge people, to exclude people, even to beat up on people, especially infidels, the non-Christians throughout the middle ages and so forth. But it also continues in our own time. Jesus's passion about the love of God for the least of these gets transformed into, "You've gotta believe the following things about Jesus..." (and those are usually doctrinal things) or, "God's gonna get you in the end, and in the meantime you're not welcome here either."[3]

More often than not, we let the culture around us form us into its mold and then are troubled or even shocked when the Bible contradicts our beliefs or biases about how things should be. But reading the Bible closely—and Jesus's teachings in particular—will be uncomfortable at times. As we listen carefully, we will hear both the prophets and Jesus attempting to move us beyond ourselves and our own concerns. We will find Jesus talking not only about personal change but social change—and these words may cause us to squirm and reexamine our priorities.

MAKING IT REAL

This prophetic Jesus not only challenges our person-to-person relationships but our social and political involvement as well. This is where things become more complicated and more emotional for some people. Catholic Bishop Dom Helder Camara of Brazil experienced this phenomenon firsthand when he began to speak out for social reforms in his country. He said, "When I give food to the poor, they call me a saint. When I ask why there were so many poor, they called me a communist."[4]

Southern Baptist pastor and scholar, Clarence Jordan, lived in Georgia and started an interracial farming community called the Koinonia Farm. It was here that Millard Fuller came for a retreat and formed the idea for Habitat for Humanity. Before Jordan's community gave birth to Habitat, he was a pioneer in the civil rights movement in the 1950s and 1960s. He would often preach as a guest in little Baptist churches, but after congregations heard his message of equality for all people of all colors, he was rarely invited back. On one occasion he gave a sermon that called for our country to stop the practice of segregation. After the sermon, a lady came up to him and said, "My granddaddy was an officer in the Confederate army and he would not believe a word that you just said about race relations." Clarence Jordan smiled sweetly and said, "Well, ma'am, your choice is very clear then. You can follow your granddaddy or you can follow Jesus."[5]

Clarence Jordan was a lot like Jesus. He was willing to let people hear the hard demands of his message and to let them walk away if they found his words too troubling or offensive.

In the Uniting Church of Australia, Rev. Dorothy McRae-McMahon has been an outspoken prophetic voice for justice for many years. From standing up to racist neo-Nazis in the late 1980s to her prolific reworking of the liturgical resources of the church, her voice has been heard loud and clear among those who would otherwise lobby unopposed for the status quo. Although officially retired, her prophetic voice has now taken on a new and vibrant form. Attending the local Uniting Church in Redfern, a Sydney suburb rife with crime and poverty, McRae-McMahon became frustrated at the lack of positive community efforts in the neighborhood.

Along with her pastor, her partner, and a variety of volunteers (including journalism students looking for experience), McRae-McMahon and the South Sydney Uniting Church began publishing a free monthly independent newspaper with the intent of holding government and business leaders accountable, building pride in the community, and reporting positive news. Now with a circulation of over 22,000, *The South Sydney Herald* (www.southsydneyherald.com.au) is a force to be reckoned with in the city. It's not unusual for the Lord Mayor of Sydney or other community leaders to call Rev. McRae-McMahon to complain about how their positions or actions are portrayed in the newspaper — along with the promise to mend their ways. From an otherwise small and eminently ignorable Uniting Church in a voiceless, backwater neighborhood, the voice of the prophetic Jesus is heard.

> *God is in the slums, in the cardboard boxes where*
> *the poor play house. God is in the silence of a*
> *mother who has infected her child with a*
> *virus that will end both their lives. God*
> *is in the cries heard under the rubble*

of war. God is in the debris of wasted
opportunity and lives, and God
is with us—if we are with them.

—Bono, National Prayer Breakfast, 2006

JUSTICE, KINDNESS, AND HUMILITY

Most of us don't really know who Jesus was. His priorities, practices and teachings—even his humanity—have largely been lost to the community of faith that should know him best. Partly out of tradition, partly out of apathy, the prophetic Jesus has too often been ignored. Because, as Amy-Jill Levine says, "Jesus the Jew, Jesus the historical figure, Jesus of Nazareth, was concerned about economics, was concerned about politics, was concerned about justice." To truly embrace the political, economic, and religious implications of his message feels threatening.

The prophetic Jesus was interested in economic reform, politics, and justice for the poor. That concern was so central to the person of Jesus that we truly can't make sense of our discipleship as followers of Jesus if economics, justice, and the needs of the outcast are not part of our discipline and practice.

Although Jesus doesn't ask people to admire him and (in the Synoptic Gospels, at least) never asks people to worship him, Jesus has many millions of admirers and worshippers. Yet those inclined to worship him would do well to note how Jesus always points beyond himself. He invites people to follow him, to imitate him in his commitment to the least and the last, and in his passion to put the mystery of God at the center of one's life.

While uncomfortable at first, the call of the prophetic Jesus is to move people from being admirers to followers—to help people sense that the respectable values of the status quo may not be so important after all. It reminds us—no matter how hard we try to make it about personal piety alone—that the kingdom of God has always been and will always be about politics.

Yvette Flunder encourages us to connect the dots between our theology and our practice, just as Jesus did. She says:

> What I am encouraging people to do and talking to them about is to get out of this either/or-ness. My theology began to evolve to the point where I realized that it is God's will that we be the arms and the hands and the heart of Jesus in the earth, that justice work is very close to the heart of God. I found that when I went to the churches where the Jesus piece, the personal piety piece, was really strong—the Christology, the eternal life, the coming again story—the justice piece was absent. When I went to the justice churches where the need to stand arm-in-arm to end apartheid and the need to stand arm-in-arm for the rights of the farm workers and of the immigrants and to stand arm-in-arm with the many issues that I had, then the sense of the awe and wonder, the Christology was weak. I believe that what we have to do is get these things homogenized. We have got to be able to have relationship with God in Christ, to understand the need for personal piety and meditation and a closeness and relationship, but that needs to be foundational for our justice work.

Micah 6:8 puts it succinctly: "What does the Lord require of you but to do justice, and to love kindness, and to walk humbly with your God?" Jesus followed in this prophetic tradition and put the obligation to fulfill this call squarely on the shoulders of those who call themselves disciples: "Just as you did it to one of the least of these who are members of my family, you did it to me" (Matt. 25:40).

—🪱—

TRUTH TELLER, CHANGE SEEKER, LIFE BRINGER

Galilean truth teller
Propelled by raw, unswerving boldness—
The way of the prophet.
Articulated world reality,
With a "once upon a time" approach.
Jesus held a mirror before the people,
Reflected crises of individual and corporate soul,
Turned their lives inside out and upside down.
Left this question hovering overhead,
Is God the center of your life
Or simply the center of your religion?

In parable and paradox
Rabbi placed pairs on the scales of justice:
Money and God
Religious practices and God
The Sabbath and God
Culture and God
Family and God
Family and work
Asking, challenging "how is it with your soul?"

He called each person Godward.
"Turn toward the Deliverer—
That your vision be refocused
And your lives exude meaning.
With each option, in every opportunity,
Choose, revere, offer Life."

—Cynthia Langston Kirk

10

Evil, Suffering, and
a God of Love

Whatever the status of evil in the world, I know that the
only God in whom I can believe will be a God found
in the midst of evil rather than at a safe distance
from it; suffering the evil rather than inflicting it.[1]

—Robert McAfee Brown

Ever ask, What did I do to deserve this? or I wonder what she did to deserve that? Perhaps you've heard someone claim that, The poor are poor because they're lazy! or AIDS is a punishment from God, or So-and-so is suffering because of [fill in the blank]. The problem is, no matter how often people repeat them, these statements are still false.

The truth is, life is hard. If we look at the way the world really is, we see that bad things happen to good people and good things happen to bad people. That's just the way it is. And that's probably why struggling with the reality of evil and suffering in the world has been one of the foundational questions of existence from time immemorial.

If God is all loving, all good, and all powerful, how can evil exist? For some, the reality of evil is the best argument *against* God's existence.

They want to know, With all the evil in the world, how can you believe in God? Libraries of books have been written on the problem of evil, the source of evil, and why the innocent suffer. Out of all this effort, one thing seems clear: God cannot be all of anything. As grating as this is to our spiritual sensibilities, perhaps it is time for a paradigm shift. Perhaps it's time to recognize something that seems painfully obvious: rather than trying to make sense of an all-loving, all-good, and all-powerful God, maybe understanding the Divine simply as loving, good, and powerful can be enough.

The Greek word for evil, *kakos,* suggests a lack of something, of being not quite whole. Yet at times, evil seems to be anything but lacking. Even the most faithful have cried out in despair, "My God, my God, why have you forsaken me?" In the midst of the pain, struggle, and injustice, it's not always evident how anything good could ever result. But the evidence suggests that sometimes, even the most horrific evil can be redeemed—even in some small way. Suffering can be transformed into endurance, mourning into dancing, and darkness into light. But despite any glimmers of hope, the problem of evil endures. Each new disaster, abused spouse, or ruthless injustice brings with it the painful questions of God's absence in the midst of tragedy and why the innocent suffer.

SUFFERING

In his book *Night,* Nobel laureate Elie Wiesel recounts life in the Auschwitz death camp:

> One day when we came back from work, we saw three gallows rearing up in the assembly place, three black crows. Roll call. SS all around us, machine guns trained: the traditional ceremony. Three victims in chains—and one of them, the little servant, the sad-eyed angel. The SS seemed more preoccupied, more disturbed than usual. To hang a young boy in front of thousands of

spectators was no light matter. The head of the camp read the verdict. All eyes were on the child. He was lividly pale, almost calm, biting his lips. The gallows threw its shadow over him. The three victims mounted together onto the chairs. The three necks were placed at the same moment within the nooses.

"Long live liberty!" cried the two adults. But the child was silent.

"Where is God? Where is He?" someone behind me asked.

At a sign from the head of the camp, the three chairs tipped over.

Total silence throughout the camp. On the horizon, the sun was setting.

"Bare your heads!" yelled the head of the camp. His voice was raucous.

We were weeping. "Cover your heads!"

Then the march past began. The two adults were no longer alive. Their tongues hung swollen, blue-tinged. But the third rope was still moving; being so light, the child was still alive....

For more than half an hour he stayed there, struggling between life and death, dying in slow agony under our eyes. And we had to look him full in the face. He was still alive when I passed in front of him. His tongue was still red, his eyes were not yet glazed. Behind me, I heard the same man asking: "Where is God now?" And I heard a voice within me answer him: "Where is He? Here He is—He is hanging here on these gallows."[2]

Where is God at moments like this? Jeremiah discovered the answer in his own suffering, as he took on the suffering of his people, as he wept and cried out for them. Jesus discovered it in being faithful even to death. Rabbi Abraham Joshua Heschel calls it "divine pathos."[3] Derived from the Greek, *pathos* means suffering. Combined with the prefix *sym* (meaning "with") we have the notion of sympathy—to suffer with. The God of the Jews is understood to have suffered their ordeals with them, giving them strength and hope to endure. Alfred North Whitehead calls God the "fellow sufferer who understands."[4]

The Psalmist sings:

> Where can I go from your spirit?
> Or where can I flee from your presence?
> If I ascend to heaven, you are there;
> if I make my bed in Sheol, you are there. (Ps. 139:7–8)

In the days of the Psalmist, the Jews had no understanding of hell. However, they did speak of a place of the dead called Sheol. Yet the Psalm proclaims that even there one cannot escape God. Such spiritual convictions have bolstered the Jewish people through thousands of years of collective and individual suffering. Despite hatred, oppression, pogroms, and holocaust, they have endured.

While the concepts of pain and suffering are often lumped together, it's helpful to be aware of their distinctiveness: pain is something we can't escape and suffering is what we do about the pain. Suffering is the work we do with the pain. We don't know what the Apostle Paul's "thorn in the flesh" was. But when Paul prays to have this "thorn" removed, the divine response is, "My grace is sufficient for you, for power is made perfect in weakness." Paul then was able to boast in his weaknesses: "I am content," he writes, "with weaknesses, insults, hardships, persecutions, and calamities for the sake of Christ; for whenever I am weak, then I am strong." Individually or collectively, the Divine experiences pain, suffers it, and out of the wreckage helps people rebuild their lives—even though things may never be the same as they once were.

WHERE IS GOD WHEN BAD THINGS HAPPEN?

Rabbi Harold Kushner's son Aaron was born with progeria, a rare and incurable disease that causes rapid aging. When Aaron was three, the doctors explained to the Kushners that Aaron would never grow much beyond three feet in height, would have no hair on his head or body, would look like a little old man while he was still a child, and would die in his early teens. When he was 14, Aaron died of old age.

Aaron's illness and death forced Kushner to reconsider his view of God as an all-powerful force who controls everything with a master plan that humans simply don't understand. The book, *When Bad Things Happen to Good People,* was Kushner's response, emerging with what was hailed as a new understanding of God but what was, in fact, ancient wisdom. Often misquoted as *Why Bad Things Happen to Good People,* the book makes it clear that Kushner doesn't know why any more than the rest of us. Sometimes people make bad decisions. Laws of nature and simple bad luck could also be the culprits. There aren't always reasons why bad things happen.[5]

As Jesus and the disciples pass by the Pool of Siloam, they come upon a blind man. The disciples ask the standard question of conventional wisdom, "Who sinned, that this man was born blind?" Jesus answers that it was no one's fault. His blindness has nothing to do with his sins or his parents' sins. The parents were no more responsible for their son's blindness than the Kushners were for Aaron's condition. Bad things happen—often without explanation.

In Luke 13, two calamities had just occurred that were the talk of Jerusalem. The Roman governor Pilate had slaughtered a group of Galileans, and a tower near the same Pool of Siloam had collapsed, killing eighteen people. One was an atrocity, an act of political violence. The other was a tragedy, a whim of fate. Were those killed at the hands of Pilate worse sinners than all other Galileans? Were those who perished in the tower catastrophe worse sinners than all the others who lived in Jerusalem? Jesus essentially says, "Look, they were in the wrong place at the wrong time." Bad things happen—often without explanation.

In December 1982, the twenty-one-year-old son of William Sloan Coffin, then pastor of Riverside Church in New York City, drove off a bridge into Boston harbor and drowned. Trying to comfort him, a woman said to Coffin, "I just don't understand God's will." Angry, Coffin shouted back at her, "I'll say you don't understand God's will, lady. Do you think it was the will of God that Alex never fixed that lousy windshield wiper, that Alex was probably driving too fast in such a storm, that Alex had probably had too much to drink? Do you think it is God's will there are no street lights along that stretch of road, no guard rail separating the road and Boston Harbor?"

Coffin later commented, "For some reason I can't get it through people's heads that God doesn't run around the world pulling trigger fingers, clenching knives, turning steering wheels. God is dead set against all kinds of unnatural deaths. This is not to say there are no unnatural deaths. There are. But the one thing that should never be said about any violent death like Alex's death is that it is the will of God. My own consolation lies in knowing that it was not the will of God that Alex died—but that when the waves closed in over the sinking car, God's heart was the first of all hearts to break."[6]

As the waves receded from 2004's South Asian tsunami, leaving hundreds of thousands of dead, religious leaders of all faiths struggled to speak to the "why" of such incomprehensible disaster. American television evangelists voiced repugnant and arrogant opinions from, "God was punishing those Muslims and Hindus for the way they treat Christians in their countries" to "God was using the tsunami to warn the rest of us to mend our ways or else." Likewise, 2005's Hurricane Katrina inspired Billy Graham's son, Franklin, to claim that God targeted New Orleans because of its being a "wicked city" full of sexual perversion and satanic worship.

These shockingly offensive attempts to offer superficial answers in light of catastrophes of such magnitude make it clear that if we are going to make any sense of a post-tsunami, post-Katrina, post-any-natural-disaster God, then God needs to be understood quite differently.

Rev. Glynn Cardy of New Zealand said that to suggest that God intentionally held back, "allowing the [tsunami] in order to teach us a moral lesson, makes God a monster."[7] He's not the only one to suggest that it's time to change metaphors. In the aftermath of the tsunami, the idea that God is "in control" is so troublesome as to be utterly useless. But to think of the Divine as that power called love, the one who "suffers with" and comforts the afflicted regardless of the outcome, has spiritual integrity born of real-life experience.

In another Kushner book, *The Lord is My Shepherd: Healing Wisdom of the Twenty-Third Psalm,* the rabbi notes that in times of trouble, "God does not explain; God comforts."[8] Through grace, suffering makes compassion possible, and what is more central to the life of faith than striving to be more compassionate?

Since the terrorist attacks in New York on September 11, 2001, Americans have joined the rest of the world in trying to deal with the pain of confronting random evil on a massive scale. Within days of the attacks, some church leaders and websites were celebrating the story of Stanley Praimnath, the man who was allegedly saved because his Bible was sitting on the desk under which he sought shelter. The message was, See? God will protect you! However, his story may have been manipulated by naïve (or unscrupulous?) religious people. Praimnath himself says, "So here I am, running, screaming, like everybody else. And here I am, got delivered, and I'm angry. Angry because all of these good people who were there, the firefighters, the cops, the EMS workers, all of these good people who were left in this building...that couldn't come down from the 81st or 82nd floor because of all of this debris. They perished. So I'm angry."[9]

Where is God amidst suffering and death—especially the death of the virtuous? In Psalm 23, the psalmist suggests that God is our strength and our comfort, even in death. Kushner writes, "When my time comes, I will feel less alone because I know that God is not only grieving for me but is with me at that moment."[10]

There are those who continue to blame people with AIDS for their own predicament—It's their own fault. They shouldn't have messed around or they shouldn't have shared a needle. Before actor Anthony Perkins died of AIDS-related complications, he said, "I believe AIDS was sent to teach people how to love and understand and have compassion for each other."[11] "I know their sufferings," God declares in Exodus 3:7. In our affliction, God is afflicted.

So where is God? There, as an adolescent child dies of old age. There, brokenhearted, as a child of yours drowns. There, as the victims of terrorism perish in violent deaths. There, as hundreds of thousands are overwhelmed by the waves of a tsunami. There, as the messenger dies on a cross.

There's a lot of pain and suffering in the world—and the Divine is there. Our call as compassionate people of faith is to work toward overcoming evil and injustice in whatever forms they manifest themselves and to stand as witnesses to the presence of God. As we do all we can to facilitate healing and reconciliation, offering comfort in a hurting world, we become the embodiment of an answer to the question, Where is God when bad things happen?

SATAN GETS A BUM RAP

Martin Luther mocked him, Milton immortalized him in *Paradise Lost*, and Dana Carvey's "Church Lady" taunted him on *Saturday Night Live*. To Paul, he was "the god of this world," who, along with his helpers, figures in the New Testament nearly twice as often as the Holy Spirit. He is the Devil, Beelzebub, Mephistopheles, Satan—the most familiar figure in Christian lore next to Jesus (and despite efforts at using inclusive language for God, the effort to refer to the embodiment of evil as anything other than male has been sorely lacking).

Although Christianity has made Satan the proper name for the archenemy of God and the personification of evil, the character only appears in all of Hebrew scripture a few times in just four books. In fact, the Hebrew word *satan* is not a proper noun at all. Whenever it appears, it does so preceded by the definite article *ha*. The phrase *ha satan* (like the earth creature *ha adam* in Genesis 2) can be more faithfully translated into English as "the adversary" and can be used to refer to anyone playing an opposing role. When Jesus calls Peter Satan, he's not suggesting that Peter is possessed by Satan or influenced by Satan, but calling Peter what he is—his adversary.

In what is probably the oldest book in the Bible, Job characterizes *ha satan* as a legitimate member of God's council. But after the opening two chapters, *ha satan* is never mentioned again. The snake in the garden is often referred to as Satan, but such references are just theological spin. The snake is simply a clever creature that generations of theologians have associated with the devil. Likewise, nowhere in the Bible is Satan cast down into the fiery pit for rising up against God. The "Lucifer" or "day star" that is cast down (i.e., put out of power) in Isaiah is the ruler of Babylon, Nebuchadnezzar. The angels that disobey are not sent to hell but to Sheol, a place understood in Hebrew as simply nothingness. Satan's supposed dominion over a place called hell is not biblical, but Greek mythology and medieval fantasy woven together by Dante, Milton, and others.

Nevertheless, the Greco-medieval vision of Hell remains a dominant element in the worldview of many Western Christians today. The threat of being punished for eternity by an all-loving but sadistic God seems to be so prevalent that the average church-goer might be forgiven for assuming that fear of a literal Hell is actually the heart of the so-called good news. The not-so-biblical version of Hell has become such a pillar of the evangelical enterprise that those who understand the gospel as simply glorified fire insurance or a Get Out of Hell Free card are left asking, If there's no Hell, then why be a Christian?

Acknowledging this awkward fixation, Rob Bell published his disavowal of Hell in 2011's *Love Wins*, unleashing a tidal wave of theological apoplexy in evangelical circles. Ironically, for calling into question ideas that are only tenuously supported by the biblical text, Bell was condemned as a heretic.

Some Christians, hell-bent on fostering arcane notions of the underworld and its minions, continue to point to the Bible as "proof" of their claims. However, the textual evidence called definitive by some has proven to be later additions to the tradition. For instance, the idea of demons and Satan entering into human beings to incite evil deeds was developed by New Testament authors. They even cast the radical monotheist Jesus as a dualist, operating as though there was a secondary "evil" god working in opposition to the "good" God. Luke's Jesus is said to have claimed seeing Satan descend like a lightning bolt (Luke 10:18). But when read in context, it is clear that Jesus is simply referring metaphorically to the work the disciples are doing casting out demons. This "satanification" of the New Testament reached its zenith with the book of Revelation. In order to achieve a memorable finale to his story, the author of the Apocalypse merged his dualistic vision of the Christian myth with ancient dragon and beast myths, pitting the forces of evil against a Rambo-like Christ figure, forever compromising what many have come to believe to be the nonviolent teachings of the historic Jesus.

So Satan and Hell remain as two of the most misunderstood concepts in our tradition. The Enlightenment made it possible to begin explaining evil in ways that didn't include a mythological being and a literal Hell—but the imagery and concepts are so primal and powerful, that the idea of battling a literal Satan and fear of eternal punishment are still among the primary factors motivating Christians today.

Evil is. But there isn't a unique being shaping and defining it. Satan is simply the embodiment of the not good over the good. The Devil, Satan, or demons are not objects, things, or persons. They are conditions of hatred, spirits of injustice, attitudes of jealousy, structures of destruction. Little demons with pitchforks and pointed tails running around don't explain evil. The power of the demonic is the power of us—the power to reject God and to thwart the emergence of life, love, and what is possible. In the words of Alexander Solzhenitsyn, "If only there were evil people somewhere insidiously committing evil deeds and it were necessary only to separate them from the rest of us and destroy them. But the dividing line between good and evil cuts through the heart of every human being...."[12]

The Lord's Prayer specifically asks God to "deliver us from evil," but what that deliverance looks like depends on us. We need more than individualistic deliverance from pious notions of holiness. We need an awareness of our complicity with the complex systems of the world and the evil and suffering they cause. In the midst of the pain and suffering in the world, Christians remember the pain inflicted on a man of compassion, truth, and integrity. In his suffering we see our call as people of faith to resist evil and injustice in whatever forms they manifest themselves. Wherever and whenever we can, our call is to do all we can to help alleviate suffering and pain and to not stand idly by. We are, as Paul reminds us, to "not be overcome by evil but overcome evil with good" (Rom. 12:21). And there, in the midst of real life, we may not find the "why," but instead see "what to do next" while juggling evil and suffering with a God of love.

—⁂—

THEOLOGY OF EVIL AND SUFFERING

Haiku Trilogy

Lines in the sand
Deaths in the Sonoran Desert
Divine lament

Child sentenced to death
Dying slowly in Auschwitz
God on the gallows

Rage upon anger
Exploded at Virginia Tech
Come Holy Comfort

—Cynthia Langston Kirk

The Myth of Redemptive Violence

We are going to deal theologically with the problem of
violence forever because it is intrinsic to our inheritance.
The question for God and for all of us who follow this
God is whether we can resist that stuff that is
intrinsically present in our existence.

—Walter Brueggemann

Tennyson wrote that despite any love we may profess of God, despite our claims to revere love as Creation's final law, we, and nature along with us, are "red in tooth and claw."[1] After countless generations of ruthless competition for survival, it's our nature as human beings to carry within us the primal urge to act out in violent ways. We are a violent species—and as a practical matter, violence more often than not "works." If a turn to violence can get the desired result, why bother with any namby-pamby alternative?

According to Culver "Bill" Nelson, myths are not true or false. The question one must ask of a myth is, is it alive or dead? In 1966, John Lennon was vilified for claiming that the Beatles were more popular than Jesus. While he was probably right, he could have also said that the myth of redemptive violence is more popular than Jesus. From even the most cursory evaluation, it's clear that the myth of redemptive violence is not only alive and well, but has completely eclipsed Jesus's teachings, example, and the basic principles of Christianity. In fact, the myth of redemptive violence managed to infiltrate the writings and teachings of Christianity from such an early date, that many people are unable to separate one from the other.

In his seminal article on the subject, "The Myth of Redemptive Violence," Walter Wink describes how violence essentially functions as a god, enjoying faithful obedience from its followers and seeming to come through when all else fails. First captured in writing around 1250 BCE, the myth of redemptive violence is at the heart of the Babylonian Creation epic called the *Enuma Elish*. The epic tells how the very order of the universe is established through "god on god" violence with the defeated female deity being dismembered and her corpse strewn about to create various elements of the cosmos.

"The simplicity of this story commended it widely, and its basic mythic structure spread as far as Syria, Phoenicia, Egypt, Greece, Rome, Germany, Ireland, India, and China," writes Wink. "Typically, a male war god residing in the sky fights a decisive battle with a female divine being, usually depicted as a monster or dragon, residing in the sea or abyss (the feminine element). Having vanquished the original enemy by war and murder, the victor fashions a cosmos from the monster's corpse. Cosmic order requires the violent suppression of the feminine, and is mirrored in the social order by the subjection of women to men and people to ruler."[2]

The biblical witness tells of Yahweh creating human beings from the dust of the earth and animating them with the very breath of God. But the competing narrative of violence comes from an extreme act of violence in the Babylonian creation story. In order to create servants for the gods, the god Marduk executes a fellow god to use his blood to create human beings. Marduk then establishes a divine hierarchy in which a strict adherence to order is upheld through violence and the threat of violence. Obedience is the supreme virtue and is enforced in the daily ordering of human relationships: women subdued by men, slaves subdued by masters, peasants under kings, people under rulers, laity under the priests (pardon that visual image).

Essentially, the myth of redemptive violence is what Wink calls, "the original religion of the status quo."[3] It not only exists to legitimate power and privilege, it perpetuates the value of ideas like peace through war, security through strength, and the notion that fear can only be overcome through domination.

THE ART OF WAR

Compared to war, all other forms of human endeavor shrink to insignificance. God help me, I do love it so![4]

—General George S. Patton, Jr.

The virtue and superiority of violence are certainly not concepts that died off with the Babylonians. It's gobbled up by young and old alike in our cartoons, comics, video games, and movies. We absorb violence through sports, foreign policy, nationalism, militarism, and, judging by the popularity of Lao Tzu's *Art of War* among business people, in our corporatism as well. Violence is entertaining, exhilarating, and as Chris Hedges has argued so poignantly, it gives many of us meaning.[5]

Sadly, it seems that violence has one of its biggest advocates among the followers of the Prince of Peace. They not only use Christianity to perpetuate the myth of redemptive violence for their own benefit, but it's almost as though many televangelists and the Religious Right wouldn't know what to do if they didn't have violence as a means of defending their views and inspiring the loyalty of their followers. Some even do so with barely concealed glee that God would use violent means to express displeasure with the behaviors with which they disagree.

After the attacks on 9/11, Jerry Falwell was quick to assign blame to his laundry list of opponents in the culture war. Responding to a question from Pat Robertson, Falwell pointed to a violently vindictive deity who was responding to Americans who:

> ...threw God out successfully with the help of the federal court system, throwing God out of the public square, out of the schools. The abortionists have got to bear some burden for this because God will not be mocked. And when we destroy 40 million little innocent babies, we make God mad. I really believe that the pagans, and the abortionists, and the feminists, and the gays and the lesbians who are actively trying to make that an alternative lifestyle, the ACLU, People For the American Way—all of them who have tried to secularize America—I point the finger in their face and say "you helped this happen."[6]

Pat Robertson was also quick to define 9/11 as an act of divine earthly retribution with, "Well, I totally concur." Justifying what he believed were God's actions by blaming his political opponents for having forced God to do what had to be done, Robertson said, "The problem is we have adopted that agenda at the highest levels of our government."[7]

In fact, promoting solidarity with a violent, tribal deity has become something of a specialty for Pat Robertson. From threatening Disneyworld with killer hurricanes for promoting "Gay Days" to openly praying for God to take out Federal judges, Robertson has seduced supporters eager to believe that God would use violence to further God's agenda. How much easier it is for us to use violence to solve our disagreements when God models such behavior for us on so grand a scale!

And it's not just the celebrity pastors. Advocating violence seems to trickle down into the core message of churches large and small. Steve Anderson, pastor at Tempe, Arizona's Faithful Word Baptist Church, came to national prominence after preaching that someone should "abort" Barack Obama, a call that triggered an inquiry from the Secret Service. Anderson's whole-hearted advocacy of violent means is based on his conviction that "God is a God of wrath and vengeance." Anderson reserves a particularly strident condemnation for gays and lesbians, preaching that God commands that they all "should be taken out and killed. The same God who instituted the death penalty for murderers is the same God who instituted the death penalty for rapists and for homosexuals, sodomites and queers!"[8]

The commitment to a bloodthirsty and vindictive God runs deep in American religion. Over the last few years, nationally known pastors like Bishop Carlton Pearson and Rob Bell have been condemned by Evangelical and Pentecostal leaders for suggesting that they could no longer believe in a God of love who tortured people for eternity in a literal hell. Such changes of heart are a positive development, but the status quo of pop Christianity, integrating faith and violence on almost every level, can be an overwhelming cultural force.

The myth of redemptive violence has so infiltrated our culture that even our language is overwhelmed with a continual drumbeat of violence. From seemingly innocuous phrases like, "Shoot me an e-mail" to the "war on poverty" to "He's da bomb" and even the "Fight for Peace" are simply "to die for" in our culture.

We spank children to teach them not to hit one another. We sanction the killing of killers as a deterrent against killing. We advocate the arming of citizens to promote personal safety. Is it any wonder that people are being deluded into complying with a system that allies them with violence not compassion, with death not life? We are a wholly compromised culture that can't even imagine the existence of any alternatives. In short, Wink says the myth of redemptive violence "is the simplest, laziest, most exciting, uncomplicated, irrational, and primitive depiction of evil the world has ever known."[9]

But our complicity is not our fault. Really.

ORIGINAL SIN

Father, bless me for I have sinned, I did an original
sin...I poked a badger with a spoon.[10]

—Eddie Izzard

We're only human. Flawed, full of selfishness, omissions, laziness, half truths, rebelliousness, and willfulness. Many Christians might explain the shortcomings of being human with a vague reference to something called "original sin" (along with it having something to do with sex). But beyond that, original sin just lurks around as one more of those Christian ideas lots of people recognize but can't explain. Those people are often surprised to find that original sin is nowhere in the Bible (explaining in part why the idea of original sin never developed in Jewish theology).

Matthew Fox points out that Elie Weisel goes so far as to say that original sin is alien to Jewish thinking. "That's a much stronger statement than saying it's not just in the Bible," says Fox. "It introduces an attitude of self-doubt and lack of reverence for self and one's beauty that is thoroughly the opposite of Jewish consciousness."

According to Fox, Jesus himself never heard of original sin. The term wasn't even used until the fourth century, so "it certainly is strange to run a church, a gathering, an *ekklesia*—supposedly on behalf of Jesus—when one of its main dogmatic tenets, original sin, never occurred to Jesus. Western Christians are so attached to original sin—but what they're attached to is St. Augustine. The fact is that most Westerners believe more in Augustine (and his preoccupation with sex), than they do in Jesus."

Part of Augustine's reason for going into the priesthood in the first place was to seek absolution for his early uninhibited sex life. It's not surprising that he would connect sex as the primal transmission of sin from one generation to the next. He suggested that since Adam sinned, all of his descendants are inheritors of this "stain" of sin.

To make his point, Augustine looked to Romans 5. There, Paul sets up an argument that Adam's sin necessitated Jesus's sacrifice in order to appease God. "Adam did it, Jesus undid it" is one of the foundations of the theory of blood atonement. Our inherent sinfulness was so great that our profoundly offended God could only be appeased by the violent spilling of blood. Although our blood being spilled was deserved, Jesus's blood would suffice.

Here the crucifixion falls right into the hands of anyone wanting to prove the efficacy of redemptive violence. Although "Christ crucified" was Paul's primary message, it is clear from his multiple attempts to explain its meaning that even he wasn't exactly sure how it all worked. Whether describing it as expiation, ransom, or redemption, Paul's efforts have left a lot of room for multiple theories to emerge.

> *Satisfaction Theory:* Derived from ancient Jewish ritual practices (including the Day of Atonement) where animals were sacrificed to satisfy God's need for blood. Jesus becomes the ultimate sacrifice to appease a God who is so offended by human sin, that only the spilling of his own son's blood will bring satisfaction. Incidentally, Canaanite religions were not the only ones to sacrifice their children to appease Baal and other gods. There are a number of biblical examples of Judean kings and leaders who also ritually sacrificed their children, much to Yahweh's displeasure.

> *Substitution Theory:* In this theory, the death of Jesus is not a sacrifice, but a pay-off to God. Human beings are so sinful that each of us deserves a horrible lingering and bloody death. However, Jesus loves us so much that he was willing to step in and be our substitute. God would just as soon kill us for our sins, but the slaughter of the innocent satiates the Divine's blood lust.

> *Ransom Theory:* If through sin, humanity is now stuck in and operating on the Devil's "turf," then God had to pay off Satan in order to win our freedom. How? By paying with Jesus's death.

Victory Theory: This is seen not as a payment to the devil (which is the equivalent of giving in to terrorists), but a defeat-in-principle of the power of evil. Through Jesus's "obedience unto death," he showed he could take anything that the Devil could dish out.

Moral Theory: Embraces the idea that the real point of Jesus's obedience and death was to provide an example for humanity to follow—to stay faithful to one's convictions even in the face of injustice, brutality, and ignorance. The universe is structured to deal with consequences. Consequences are not punishment, they're just consequences. Jesus had to deal with the consequences of his actions and so do we.

These theories offer vastly different "cosmic" dynamics. The first two are directed toward God by appeasing or compensating God for humanity's trespasses. The second two are aimed at Satan and mark the end of "demonic control" through two diametrically opposed methods—did God pay off or punch out the Devil? The last "moral" theory suggests a change of disposition, not of God or Satan, but of humanity itself.

The satisfaction theory has tended to be the most popular. It is reflected in Campus Crusade's "Four Spiritual Laws," the Roman Catholics' sacrifice of the Lamb of God on the altar, and in the hymns of American Protestantism ("There is a fountain filled with blood," "Are you washed in the blood of the Lamb?" and "What can wash away my sins? Nothing but the blood of Jesus").

Though Jesus was still executed, the theory that is least dependent on justifying the violence done to him is the Moral Theory. Not surprisingly, it has also been the least popular among orthodox theologians. Instead of glorifying the redemptive power of violence, it suggests that the virtue in the story comes from Jesus's obedience, even as he suffers the violence inherent in all things human. Those who are convinced of humanity's original sin find this theory unsatisfactory, for if humanity only needed an example to follow, we must not have been so sinful after all.

John B. Cobb Jr. notes, "Paul speaks of blood (he does use the word), but it is simply a way of referring to death. It has no reference to blood being peculiarly salvific. The atonement doctrine, which puts an emphasis on Jesus's blood as being the sacrifice, is really a mistranslation of Romans Chapter 3 where it simply means that Jesus's faithfulness to death is the saving factor. So it's too bad, but for a thousand years since Anselm, we've been fixated on the atonement doctrine."

John Dominic Crossan also bemoans the influence of Anselm on the last thousand years of Christianity:

> Anselm lives around the year 1000. He lives in a feudal society. In a feudal society the Lord cannot say, "I forgive you." Can't do it. That would derogate his standing, his status and his honor. It would be like a federal judge coming in one morning saying, "This a beautiful day, you're all free." Can't do it. So Anselm was thinking that God is like a feudal lord or a federal judge. God can't forgive. Just can't do it. Somebody has to pay. So he comes up with substitutionary atonement as his attempt to make sense of what happens. Otherwise, he doesn't know why on earth Jesus died. And the reason he doesn't know is because he's a bad historian. It's as simple as that. He doesn't know the history. If he knew the history he would know that Jesus is God incarnate and the normalcy of civilization will not tolerate people who stand for justice. The point [is not simply] getting rid of substitutionary atonement because it's very bad theology. I think, quite frankly, it's a crime against divinity.

The existence of all these mostly violent theories of atonement and their lack of any uniform understanding of what happened on the cross is due to the biblical witness being unclear. Paul, the Gospels, and Hebrews all suggest different ways of grappling with a mystery. Since the theories of atonement have never been made uniform in scripture (let alone Christian theology), and lurk in a mishmash of imagery in each of our own religious upbringings, it's no wonder that we have ideological pandemonium in the streets.

ORIGINAL BLESSING

The opponents of the idea of the vague and inherited guilt of original sin have been numerous and clever in their critiques, from Franz Kafka's *The Trial* to Matthew Fox's *Original Blessing*. John Shelby Spong puts the question in everyday language when he asks, "What would be the influence on a child's life if the parents, seeking to improve their parenting skills, purchased a book that instructed them everyday to inform the child that they are a horrible person? 'You are incapable of doing anything about your destiny.' 'You are not even good enough to pick up the crumbs under the family table.' Would that create a healthy adult? Yet this is the message the church has given people for centuries. Why portray God practicing parenting skills that would be so clearly unhealthy for our own children?"

History is rife with the evidence of human beings' capacity for evil. Be it the holocaust, Islamic terrorists, or Christian militias praising the carnage of the Oklahoma City bombing, anyone's faith in human goodness and the idea of progress can be shaken. But to spend energy concentrating on how sinful and hopeless human beings are is to fail to appreciate the incredible good that human beings are capable of—wonders of science and symphonies, art and generosity, the gentle touch, the healing word. Evil is not hard to find in human life, but neither is it the ultimate and defining characteristic of humanity. Perhaps it's like a roadside accident that attracts the morbid attention of passersby, but we spend an inordinate amount of time dwelling upon and struggling with the mystery of evil when the real mystery is where *goodness* comes from. It should come as no surprise that irrational urges toward violence and evil are part of our primal being. But the true wonder is in human beings showing signs of transcending those patterns with mercy, compassion, and forgiveness.

In *Original Blessing,* Matthew Fox recovers an ancient, biblically rooted tradition in Christian spirituality in which the Creator takes great delight in creation—including humanity. Likewise, John Shelby Spong suggests that in a post-Darwinian age, it doesn't make sense for us to continue wallowing in the notion of our having once been innocent garden dwellers, now exiled. Far from being "fallen" creatures trying to return to a mythical Eden, human beings are "emerging" as a species from more primal and baser instincts to become more responsible and mature beings. Granted, our emergence has included a knack for ever-increasing efficiency in killing one another, but alternatives have also emerged.

SATYAGRAHA

*Truth is God; Non-violence is Love in Action; and
Peace, the result of enduring conflict resolution,
is the Fruit of Satyagraha.*[11]

—Mahatma Gandhi

Gandhi believed that at the root of every conflict there is untruth, and that the only permanent solution was truth. In an effort to systematize his belief, Gandhi conceived the practice of Satyagraha. Combining *Satya* (truth) with *Agraha* (firmness), Gandhi advocated the "unwavering search for the truth." He was convinced that the only way of getting to truth is through love, and that the only practical definition of love is when the security and well-being of the other person becomes as important as your own.

It followed that the unwavering search for the truth would be characterized by nonviolence. Following its success in the Indian subcontinent, the principles of Satyagraha were adapted and successfully utilized in effecting change in the United States by civil rights leaders like Martin Luther King Jr. And while this ideal of nonviolence is overshadowed by the dominance of the myth of redemptive violence, the practice of "relentless nonviolent resistance" continues to be used today by groups like Soulforce (www.soulforce.org). Carrying on Gandhi's teachings, Soulforce reminds its adherents that the nonviolence movement seeks justice and reconciliation, not victory—and that refraining from violence is not only a discipline of the fist, but of the tongue and heart, as well.

SAVING WORK?

All who take the sword will perish by the sword.

—Jesus, Matthew 26:52

Our culture has been and will continue to be awash in depictions of and the practice of violence as the ultimate solution to human conflicts. But the witness of Jesus's life, teachings, and death model a different paradigm. Jesus inaugurated a new order based on partnership, equality, compassion, and nonviolence. His teaching carries us beyond pacifism, beyond just war theory, beyond domination and its spiral of violence to the remarkable possibilities of nonviolence and understanding.

As John Shelby Spong says:

Jesus did not die for your sins, let that be said a thousand times. Jesus did not come from God to rescue fallen, sinful, inadequate, incompetent people like you and me. That is an image of a God who comes to us from outside to rescue this terrible and fallen creation. That is an idea from which we need to escape. Jesus has to become, not the Divine Invader, but the human face of what God looks like in human form. That is because, when you look at Jesus he lives fully. Nothing diminished his life. He never diminished anybody else's life. People betrayed him and he responded by loving them. People denied him and he responded by loving them. People forsook him and he responded by loving them. People tormented him and he responded by loving them. People killed him and he responded by loving them. How else could he communicate to people like you and me that there is nothing we can ever do, there is nothing we can ever be that will place us outside the boundaries of the love of God. It is not that we are some worthless inadequate person that God has to come in and rescue, it is that God's love is so abundant and so overwhelming that this love calls us to live, and to love, and to be all that we can be so that God can live in us and through us. That is a very different way to think about God.

For twenty-first-century Christians, the promise of God's saving work in Jesus is less about suffering and satisfaction on a cosmic level than it is about living a life of integrity. To say "Jesus died for our sins" is not substitutionary or ransom based, but biblical shorthand for Jesus having died as a result of our collective sin; that is, from the normal operating procedure of unjust, oppressive, insecure, and violent human beings. Yet despite who and what we are, the mystery of grace is modeled in Jesus's obedience unto death, an obedience that remained forgiving and gracious even in the face of misrepresentation, humiliation, and extreme violence. Being faithful to convictions like justice, nonviolence, and the needs of the poor and the downtrodden are ways not only to take atonement out of the musty halls of speculative theology, but to actively counter the myth of redemptive violence in the world.

12

Practicing Resurrection

If Christ has not been raised, then our proclamation
has been in vain and your faith has been in vain.

—1 Corinthians 15:14

Even as Jesus's virgin birth and healing miracles are embraced as meta-phor, the resurrection remains for many the one core, nonnegotiable, and historical fact at the heart of Christianity. Yet the only way one can maintain an unquestioning and literal interpretation of the events surrounding that first Easter is by steadfastly avoiding the reading of the Bible.

Paul, author of our earliest New Testament writings, tells us noth-ing of the third day's events jumbled together later by the Gospel writ-ers. Instead, he opts for trying to explain the "idea" of resurrection to the Corinthians with a tortured discourse on its importance. Evidently having been asked how a body is raised, Paul blurts out in response with "Fool!" before explaining that "It is sown a physical body, it is raised a spiritual body" (1 Cor. 15:36, 44). Nowhere does Paul speak of Jesus's body having been resuscitated or of his postresurrection interaction with the disciples. It took another twenty to fifty years before those stories would become a part of the Gospel narratives. However, Paul does proclaim that, regard-

less of the details, the events of Easter reversed the outcome of humanity's actions and character. He attributes knowledge of this to Jesus having
appeared in visions to select witnesses—including himself.

Since Paul died before any of the Gospels were written, he never had
a chance to read the various accounts. If he had, he would have undoubtedly written a letter of protest over their many inconsistencies.

The risen Christ doesn't even show up in Mark, the earliest Gospel. Mark's abrupt and unexpected ending verges on the anticlimactic:
the women find the tomb empty, are instructed by a young man to tell
the disciples to go to Galilee to meet Jesus, but instead scatter in fear and
tell no one anything. That's it. The end. No angels, no soldiers, and no
Jesus appearances. Such a cliffhanger was simply too much for later writers, so over the years a variety of new endings were written to "flesh out"
Mark's unsatisfactory finish. Several of these now appear in most Bibles
as footnotes or as the "shorter" and "longer" endings of Mark. We're left
with the account written closest to the action being woefully short on
any of the details we've come to associate with Easter.

As Matthew and Luke wrote their Gospels some fifteen or twenty
years later, they each had a copy of Mark in front of them. We know this
because they copy much of Mark almost verbatim. What is interesting
is what they choose to change about the stories. Their adaptations seem
to reflect other information they might have had or serve as a means of
driving their own theological agenda.

Even a casual reading of Matthew and Luke reveal a number of edi-
torial liberties: Mark's young man is transformed into a supernatural
angel in Matthew—and *two* angels in Luke! Matthew has the women
embracing the resuscitated body of Jesus at the tomb and appearing to
the disciples out of the sky on a Galilean mountaintop. Luke places the
action in Jerusalem and not in Galilee. Although Luke's Jesus can appear
and disappear seemingly out of thin air, he also does his best to prove
he is not a ghost by eating, teaching, and having the disciples investigate
his wounds. Matthew doesn't feel a need to explain how the risen Jesus,
at some point, is no longer with the disciples. But Luke, still centered in

Jerusalem (and in a dramatic preparation for his sequel, *Acts*), introduces the story of the Ascension. But here, Luke even contradicts himself. In his Gospel account, he places the Ascension on Easter while in
Acts, the Ascension is forty days *after* Easter.

The moving resurrection account in John enhances the physical
nature of Jesus's body even further with Mary mistaking him for a simple gardener and Jesus having to insist that she not "cling" to him. Jesus
ascends at this point only to appear to the disciples later that night in the
Upper Room. A week later he appears to the disciples again, this time to
upbraid "doubting" Thomas (and any readers of like mind) for their lack
of faith. In a much later Galilean appearance, the disciples have returned
to their nets. Jesus materializes to direct them in a great catch of fish and
ends by empowering Peter to be on about feeding his lambs. John ends
by assuring readers that "there are also many other things that Jesus did;
if every one of them were written down, I suppose that the world itself
could not contain the books that would be written" (John 21:25).

The above seems especially true when considering the resurrection
accounts. If we try to make them fit together, we find that the "many
things" Jesus did and the events that transpired were mutually exclusive
of one another. As we become familiar with the texts themselves, it's clear
that stories developed over time and that none of the accounts can be
claimed as definitive — or historical.

Although painfully obvious, the inconsistencies of the Gospel accounts
have proven oddly insignificant to generations of believers. Through will-
ful ignorance or just plain not paying attention, the stories of this supposedly ultimate and defining moment of the faith have been synthesized
into supporting various notions of resurrection as a physically resuscitated
body. Looking back through the lenses of time and tradition, it's clear to
see how even Paul is now almost impossible to read without the influence
of the later Gospels distorting and redefining his original meaning.

Yet *something* happened in the days following the crucifixion that
transformed the disciples from uncertain followers to heralds of the

Jesus message, evidently willing to die for their convictions. John Shelby Spong says:

> There is no question in my mind that had there not been some transforming experience that happened to the disciples after the death of Jesus that convinced them that he had conquered the boundary of human death there would be no Christianity. But what people don't understand is that the idea that this experience meant the resuscitation of a deceased body that could walk physically out of a tomb on the third day after crucifixion is a very late developing tradition. You will not find it in Paul; you will not find it in Mark. Most people are surprised to know that in the first Gospel, Mark, written in the early seventies, the risen Christ never appears to anybody! It's only in the later Gospels that he not only appears, but offers his flesh to be inspected and eats and walks and talks and interprets scripture. It is a very late development in the tradition. There is a powerful Easter experience that starts the whole Christian faith, transforms the disciples, changes them from cowards who had forsaken him and fled and brought them back into being heroic followers of this Jesus, and that changed the way they understood God. So whatever that Easter experience was they could never again think of God without seeing Jesus as part of that definition. They could never again see Jesus without feeling that God was part of the divine definition. Something incredibly powerful happened, but it had nothing to do with the resuscitation of the body.

Whatever the events were surrounding that first Easter, early followers of this Galilean peasant were propelled into a new way of living and relating to one another. They were compelled to reevaluate their Jewish heritage in ways that accounted for their experience of Jesus, both in his temporal life and as a spiritual presence in the present.

With only the Gospel accounts as our guide, we, too, are left to reevaluate our heritage in ways that account for the clearly nonhistorical resurrection stories and our experiences of a spiritual presence we call the Christ.

SEEING EASTER THROUGH

You can't go on seeing through things forever. The whole
point of seeing through something is to see something
through it. It is good that a window is transparent
but the point is that we should see the
street or the garden beyond.[1]

—C. S. Lewis

On a side street in Jerusalem, a garden tomb is maintained as an example of first-century tombs and as a destination for pilgrims. It is hewn out of rock with a track for a disk-shaped stone to be rolled over the door. A rolling stone was important, because burial in those days was not what we practice today. At most, the body was in the tomb for a year or so as nature reduced it to bones. The bones were then removed and placed in an ossuary, or bone box. Much has been made in recent years of the discovery of such bone boxes allegedly tied to Jesus's brother, James, and other family members. But ossuaries and stones aside, what do we do with the image of an empty tomb? With five different biblical interpretations of resurrection, we *still* don't know what really happened.

With all the discrepancies and differences in the text, there is ample evidence for those of similar temperament to look at Easter and easily see through it all. For many of these folks, it's okay to see the stories as simply stories.

But the vast majority of believers are conditioned to embrace only the most simplistic and superficial view of Easter. The whole story is an inconvenience getting in the way of the triumphal and happy ending.

For those whose faith is dependent on a literal, physical resuscitation of Jesus's body, any suggestion to the contrary is tantamount to heresy.

But wherever one finds oneself, seeing through it all or seeing only what is convenient, the question remains: Can we see it through? Regardless of how transparent the stories are as stories, regardless of any fixation on just the happy part of the story, what meanings do we see beyond the literal? What inspiration do we take with us into our life and relationships?

Jesus's teachings are rarely about religion. They're not about the next life either. They're more about everyday life and relationships. They seem to suggest that God intends us to take one world at a time, and make something of it. A "see-it-through" Easter faith is one that grapples with daily life, which brings Jesus back to life by caring about what happens to others. Not just to a spouse, a child, an aged parent, or a colleague, but to someone whom we don't know—better yet, to someone outside our "tribe"—someone we've been taught to not like at all.

PRACTICING RESURRECTION

Practice resurrection. Part of who
you are is who you will be.[2]

—Wendell Berry

While there are those who limit resurrection to a miraculous event that happened to Jesus long ago and that will in some distant future be the fate of true believers, such literal interpretations have ceased to have meaning for many rational, faithful, and even mystically oriented Christians today. The followers of Osiris, Attis, Mithra, and the many other resurrected gods have recognized and celebrated resurrection in various ways over the centuries. Today, the metaphor of resurrection stands for many Christians as a symbol of the call to new life, as an appeal to practice resurrection here and now.

The reality of the human condition leaves many "entombed" by their attitudes, circumstances, or life choices. Metaphorical "rocks" are everywhere: the rock of disappointment, of insecurity, of poverty, or of guilt. We're often sealed in by the rocks of arrogance, confusion, addiction, or indifference. Our eyes adjust to the darkness of the tombs we choose. Almost anything that stands between a person and the transforming presence of the Divine can be seen as a stone in need of being rolled away.

Perhaps one of the largest stones in need of being rolled away is the popular Christian notion of what life after death means for the individual believer. The idea that worthy believers will somehow be resuscitated in another life is the conventional wisdom expressed at most every funeral in Western culture. Grieving loved ones, those preparing to die for a cause, or those who are forced to endure hardships in this life are assured that there is a better life somewhere beyond this mortal coil.

One is hard-pressed to find any but the slimmest support in the New Testament for our popular notions of life after death. Indeed, most examples counter such common thinking. For instance, Matthew sets up a story where Jesus is confronted by the Saducees, a Jewish sect that did not hold to a belief in a general resurrection. Matthew casts them proposing a hypothetical resurrection question to try to trip Jesus up: "If a woman is married multiple times in succession because each of her husbands dies, whose wife will she be in heaven?" In dismissing their question, Matthew's Jesus makes it clear that any of our earthly categories of being or personal identity cease to have meaning beyond this life: "For in the resurrection they neither marry nor are given in marriage, but are like angels in heaven" (Matt. 22:30).

Regardless of how little biblical evidence there is for popular ideas of life after death, many people take comfort in the simplistic notion that they will somehow be with their loved ones in the next life. This idea has become so fixated in the minds of many faithful that it could often be perceived as the primary reason people claim an allegiance to Christianity. As such, it becomes a major obstacle in understanding any deeper meaning of resurrection—and to living one's life in the present.

Whatever perspective one has on life after death, the eternal is not something off in some vague, unknowable, distant future. Whatever the eternal might be, it begins here as part of who we are today. The message of resurrection is new life *now*.

DON'T BE AFRAID TO LIVE

The message of the resurrection is not simply, "Don't be afraid to die." Surely it is that. And all of us when we lose someone we love, or on our own day of dying will need the comfort of the resurrection. But I believe the message of Easter is not simply "Don't be afraid to die," but "Don't be afraid to live—to live for those things worth dying for." [3]

—DeWane Zimmerman

Winnie Varghese warns us that bringing new life to the world is threatening to the powers that be—that new life doesn't come without a cost. She says:

Resurrection is the central teaching of the Christian church. When we try to live authentically, to do what Jesus has called us to do, when we do this work of inclusion and of welcome, we get death threats. There is death all around us. If death is the end then we are sort of defeated by this world. The teaching of resurrection is that we are not defeated by the powers of this world. The Christian teaching is that there will always be hope for the fullness of God's justice in every time. We will fight for it because we have a story of resurrection. We are not defeated by death. Our God is not defeated by death. But it doesn't mean we don't die.

As motivation to live every moment to its fullest, Socrates exhorted his followers to practice dying as the highest form of wisdom. Such immediacy can radically change one's world and teaches the importance of reevaluating priorities. In his book, *A Year to Live*, counselor Steven Levine put his experience with hospice patients to the test. His daily encounters with those who had been given a terminal diagnosis revealed to him people with transformed lives. Their perspective on life changed, their priorities were reordered, and many of the circumstances and choices that had crippled them before their diagnosis evaporated into new life. Levine set a date for his own death and lived as if he would die on that day. His book is the record of his radical experiment to get a glimpse of that transformation for himself. In so doing, he gave himself permission to address his unfinished business and enter into a new and vibrant relationship with life. He gained a new appreciation for the need to live each moment mindfully, as if it were all that was left.

Life is precious. It's to be shared with generosity. The Gospels are clear about this. What should also be clear is that resurrection isn't just limited to the experience of Jesus or to however we understand a life after death, but in passing from death to life here and now. The message of resurrection and of Easter hope is that we can live fully in this life, giving of ourselves, and risking for love's sake.

For Sister Helen Prejean, "that's the heart of the Christian life." She says:

[In the words of] St. Paul, "Dying and behold we live." And it's not just in the act of our death it's the way we pour out our life. You know, the *giving,* the expenditure of our life for the community, in *love,* is a form of dying. And when we can be driven by love, when we can be motivated by love to give our lives on behalf of others and not count the cost, that, too, is a form, is it not, of resurrected life. That we are alive even as we give our life and we die. And when we recognize that in the saints, in people who do it, they always say, "Well, *love.* It's not labor, it's not a sacrifice, it's love" because they're caught up! There's a transformative love where you can give your life and you give it in love.

Help someone who's hurting. Open the eyes of love for someone who is blind. Free a captive. Heal a wound. Feed someone who is hungry. Give the gift of yourself—for the gift of who we are was given to us in order to be given away.

Martin Buber tells the story of an aging pious man, Rabbi Susya, who became fearful as death drew near. His friends chided him, "What! Are you afraid that you'll be reproached that you weren't Moses?" "No," the rabbi replied. "That I was not Susya."[4]

The secret to practicing resurrection is in giving away who we are and what we have—completely and wholly—to something greater than ourselves. It's in escaping from the circumstances and choices that entomb us and entering into new life here and now. In life and in death, Jesus modeled this generosity and transformation for followers then and now. As we embrace resurrection as a credible and meaningful principle for living, we, like Jesus, may become more than anyone around us—or even we ourselves—could have imagined.

13

Debunking the Rapture

The Rapture is a racket. Whether prescribing a violent script for Israel or survivalism in the United States, this theology distorts God's vision for the world. In place of healing, the Rapture proclaims escape. In place of Jesus's blessing of peacemakers, the Rapture voyeuristically glorifies violence and war. In place of Revelation's vision of the Lamb's vulnerable self-giving love, the Rapture celebrates the lion-like wrath of the Lamb. This theology is not biblical. We are not Raptured off the earth, nor is God. No, God has come to live in the world through Jesus. God created the world, God loves the world, and God will never leave the world behind! [1]

—Barbara Rossing

Over the last 150 years, countless millions have been caught up in various forms of Rapture theology. Scripture, torn from its context, is manipulated as a weapon of fear and intimidation. An offended God is portrayed as being out for vengeance—and people are encouraged to embrace a self-centered satisfaction in being personally "saved" at the expense of the suffering and death of family, friends, and neighbors.

Barbara Rossing writes, "The Rapture vision invites a selfish noncon-
cern for the world. It turns salvation into a personal 401(k) plan that
saves only yourself."[2] Meanwhile, a ravaging warrior Jesus is preparing
to return to violently punish those who aren't the right kind of believers.
Best get right or be "left behind."

While Tex Sample was riding in the car with another man, the talk
turned to the Bible:

> He was telling me about that passage in Thessalonians where it says
> that when Christ comes again we will rise up in the air to meet him.
> He interpreted that passage very literally and began to tell me what
> would happen if the second coming should occur while we were
> riding together. He told me that he would be leaving the car very
> fast. He seemed convinced that I would not be leaving the car at all.
> So he told me that I would need to be prepared to grab the wheel
> as he left so that I would not crash. I remember thinking as he was
> describing these things that if he left that car that fast he was far
> more likely to be *ruptured* than raptured.

While this belief system seems too abhorrent to be the obsession of
anything but a few fringe thinkers, *Time* magazine discovered that fully
59 percent of respondents to their poll said they believe the events of Revelation are going to come true.[3] In fact, despite a record of having never
been right on anything, the sensational prognostications of Rapture pro-
moters have, in our day, fueled what can only be called its own end times
industry. After spending more than $100 million on billboards warn-
ing of the end of the world in 2011,[4] radio personality Harold Camping
garnered worldwide ridicule for his "Great News!" prediction. Sadly, his
retirement from the business of predicting Judgment Day only leaves a
niche for the next charlatan to rise up and hornswoggle the vulnerable.

The pastors, teachers, and authors who have visited this indignation
on so many trusting people are either conniving snake-oil salesmen who
should be ashamed of themselves or poor souls who actually believe this

foolishness and are to be pitied. Regardless of their motives, they have struck fear into the hearts of innumerable innocents with elaborate constructs of immanent cosmic destruction. Their shameless schemes have ruined lives and raked in millions worth of profit, while the original purpose of apocalyptic literature and the true context and meaning of the book of Revelation have been buried behind unbiblical Nostradamus-esque prophecies.

THE COMING OF DARBY'S SECOND SECOND COMING

Little did nineteenth-century evangelist John Nelson Darby know that when he conceived of what was to become "premillenarian dispensationalism," his musings would one day capture the imagination of millions and become the foundational cosmology for millions more. According to the scriptures Darby cobbled together, the Bible sketches out a cosmic calendar of events leading to the end of time. Before the end comes, Jesus returns to spirit away all true believers into heaven in an event dubbed the "Rapture." Never mind that the word never occurs in scripture—according to adherents, the event is clearly described in the text. After seven years, when those who have remained behind suffer great "tribulations," Jesus returns a second time (the *second* second coming) to exterminate the evil forces gathered at Armageddon. After the battle, there will be one thousand years of peace and prosperity.

To anyone outside the Rapture cult, the sheer fabrication of the idea is painfully obvious—and because its sources are disparate and unrelated texts, everyone in the clique claims and argues over a different story. Be it Dispensationalism, Postmillennialism, Historic Premillennialism, Dispensational Premillennialism, or some variation on one of the above, the texts cited by Dispensationalists are taken completely out of context and have absolutely nothing to do with one another, let alone the make-believe Rapture. Unconsciously drawing on the dualism of Zoroastrianism and the Manichaeism declared a heresy by the early church,

Rapture proponents believe that the world is evil and that the righteous must escape before a vengeful God destroys it. The message of Revelation has been warped to sensationalize the death and destruction of masses of people, to prop up fundamentalist Christians' own prejudices, and sanctify the status quo.

Many of the core doctrines of modern fundamentalist Christians, including the Rapture, have their primary source in the relatively recent *Scofield Reference Bible* of 1909. This reference Bible includes section headings and margin notes that support Darby's theology and the investigations of earnest prophesy sleuths. The Moody Bible Institute is just one of the schools and other institutions that have raised generations of Rapture-anticipating Christians who promote their message through local churches, conferences, publications, radio, and TV.

One of the best sellers of the genre has been Hal Lindsey's *Late Great Planet Earth*, published in the 1970s. Continually updated to recast the current political landscape as the definite proof of the Rapture's immanence, it has paled in significance with the popular success of Tim LaHaye and Jerry Jenkins's *Left Behind* novels. First published in the late 1990s, they are now cross promoted through a variety of media, including movies, DVDs, and video games.

It would be one thing if this were just bad theology embraced by harmless kooks. But in fact, it has become so influential that it is affecting public policy and international relations. Rossing contends that a side benefit of the *Left Behind* novels is its having established a power platform for the Religious Right. In the course of the story, readers are not so subliminally influenced "on a whole range of conservative political issues including anti-abortion, anti-homosexuality, anti-environmentalism, militarism, and Middle East policy, as well as opposition to the United Nations."[5] The faithful are relieved of any need to be concerned for the environment or any other aspect of the world; for in the course of their personal salvation, the earth and all the evils therein will be destroyed.

But sociologist and Baptist preacher Tony Campolo has argued to the contrary, saying:

What the Bible makes clear is that we are to stay here in this world struggling against the powers of darkness. No wonder America spits on the UN—and they put down what government can do. I think that we need to challenge the government to do the work of the kingdom of God, to do what is right in the eyes of the Lord. That whole sense of the rapture, which may occur at any moment, is used as a device to oppose engagement with the principalities, the powers, the political and economic structures of our age.[6]

DOOMSDAY IS COMING . . . OR IS IT?

When Revelation was written, it was not unique. The genre of apocalyptic literature was popular with both Jews and Christians. Apocalypse simply means "unveiling." Since the idea of gradual change wasn't a common concept in the ancient world, this literary form was originally intended to reveal a hopeful vision for people. Progress was seen as a series of ages, one after the other, that changed rapidly. In Hebrew thought, there are three "ages": (1) Original paradise, (2) the cursed world, and (3) the Messianic kingdom. An "apocalypse" was therefore the Hebrew way of expressing hope for the victory of God and the triumph of righteousness.

As Christians entered the story, they took over that phrasing of expectancy and aimed it squarely at the oppressive rule of Rome. While the New Testament is aglow with "Christ is coming!" the notion of the second coming was, for the early Christian, a very specific way of expressing hope in overcoming their suffering under the heel of empire. It was essentially resistance literature hiding the promise of triumph in fantastical images and language. The "end," as announced in Revelation, is not the end of the world, but the end of the Roman Empire. (Take heed, present-day imperial powers!)

Unfortunately, the historical and political implications are lost on present day Rapture proponents. "Christ is coming!" seems to be the central message of the gospel for many Christians. They either sit still and do nothing and expect the world to grow increasingly chaotic until Christ comes—or worse, they intentionally do what they can to achieve what they think will promote or hasten the end:

- A group of über-Christian Texas ranchers have been doing their part to "bring it on" by helping fundamentalist Israeli Jews to breed a pure red heifer, a genetically rare beast that must be sacrificed to fulfill an apocalyptic prophecy found in the book of Numbers.
- At www.raptureready.com, you can track how many weeks you have left to get your affairs in order. The "Rapture Index" tracks all the latest news in relation to biblical prophecy. Among its leading indicators of Apocalypse are oil supply and price, famine, drought, plagues, wild weather, floods, and climate.
- After 9/11, there's been yet another wave of Apocalypticism in American culture: Christ is coming—literally, externally, on the clouds of heaven—to make things right and set up his literal kingdom here.
- John Hagee, pastor of the 17,000-member Cornerstone Church in San Antonio, Texas, has said, "Mark it down, take it to heart, and comfort one another with these words. Doomsday is coming for the earth, for the nations, and for individuals, but those who have trusted in Jesus will not be present on earth to witness the dire time of tribulation."[7]

"NO SIGN WILL BE GIVEN"

It's a scenario that always seems to pop up when frightening circumstances arise and people's only hope seems to lie in divine intervention. But even in Greek tragedies, such plot twists were mocked as cheap.

Called *deus ex machina* (god out of a machine), it is used only when the plot and circumstances of the play become impossibly complicated and irresolvable. Then, at the last minute, an actor playing a god is lowered by a crane into the midst of the action to rescue the righteous and save the day. Questionable plot and slapdash exegesis notwithstanding, the Rapture starts at the end with a Christian deus ex machina and leaves befuddled Bible readers to work out the circumstances that trigger the crane's descent.

Despite the Gospel of Matthew's warning that only "An evil and adulterous generation seeks for a sign, but no sign will be given to it except the sign of Jonah" (Matt. 16:4), whole denominations of people are totally absorbed with the minutiae of biblical prophecy and second-guessing the unfolding of history. The sign of Jonah, as Culver "Bill" Nelson says, "...is not about a dumb fish!" Ironically, the "sign of Jonah" is a reminder of God's unpredictable grace. Jonah experienced firsthand how God short-circuits any legalistic understanding of rules or events that force the Divine to behave in a prescribed manner or show favoritism to one particular tribe or another.

Author Robert Jewett writes, "To let the gospel work on us is to overcome the prejudices and fears that close the mind. It is to allow common sense and prudent judgment to prevail. To live by this sign is to learn to laugh as the author of Jonah did at the silly, chauvinistic behavior of himself and his people, so certain that God preferred them over the Ninevites."[8] As Jesus reminded his followers in the Sermon on the Mount, God makes the "sun rise on the evil and on the good, and sends rain on the righteous and on the unrighteous" (Matt. 5:45). In other words, God doesn't play favorites.

And yet, a tremendous amount of intellectual energy is spent combing the scriptures for passages that support the shallow tenets of fundamentalist biblical prophecy. Devotees have convinced themselves that the Hebrew prophets, the writers of Christian scripture, and Jesus himself were in on secret knowledge that is waiting just for the uncovering—if only they can tease out the clues.

But no matter how it's spun through a very narrow reading of scripture, the apocalyptic vision set forth by evangelists is of a god restoring
justice through divine retribution—what John Dominic Crossan calls
"divine ethnic cleansing." This ideology, espoused so dramatically by the
Left Behind series, has essentially hijacked Jesus's message, taken advantage of a culture of fear, and rationalized voyeuristic primal urges that
enjoy wrath and war.

Crossan invites us to consider the implications of the Rapture theology rampant in our culture:

> Is the second coming of Jesus violent? In which case it negates the
> first coming—and it was all some kind of a joke or a preamble
> or a mistake. Yeah, maybe Jesus just got it wrong, just couldn't
> get the message that "We have a violent God." And it's clear in the
> Book of the Apocalypse [that] even though the ending is mag-
> nificent, it is the other side of serious slaughter. That's also in the
> *Left Behind* series. I would ask you to consider it also in the *Nar-*
> *nia* series. I do not want you to think that the sensibility of those
> two series is the same. It is not. But, if you have seen *The Lion, The*
> *Witch, and The Wardrobe,* you have the Lion and the Witch. You
> have the Lamb and the Whore. It's gendered, first of all. And in
> that story, no matter what they say, it is an allegory of Christianity
> in which Jesus comes, Jesus is executed, Jesus rises from the dead,
> and Jesus, having risen from the dead, destroys the powers of evil
> in a violent army attack. It is consistent with the New Testament
> if you take the Book of the Apocalypse or the Book of Revela-
> tion as the final act. Do we expect a violent return of Christ? And
> is that our great Christian treason? That we betrayed the God
> who is revealed to us in Jesus as nonviolent resister and we want
> him to come back and for God's sake get it right this time? We
> want a God who'll kick butt. Is the return of Christ violent? If
> it is maybe then Job's wife has the proper response, "Curse God
> and die."

JESUS IS COMING. LOOK BUSY.

*Revelation calls us to "come out" of the beast's realm of
violence and injustice so that we can participate in the
beloved city of God. That call... is the key to
Revelation's ethical imperative. The book
wants us to follow the Lamb in a
life-changing exodus.*[9]

—Barbara Rossing

Some believe Jesus was an apocalyptic preacher. Indeed, there are passages in the Gospels that paint such a portrait. But if Jesus was an apocalyptic preacher, he was wrong, since the end of the world didn't come in his lifetime (nor has it since). But the question isn't whether or not Jesus was wrong. Nor is it whether he preached divine retribution—on occasion the Gospel writers certainly put such words on his lips. The real question is: Was Jesus's message of "the kingdom of God" an inclusive realm marked by justice and divine love or not?

There are many strands in the fabric of scripture, and apocalypticism is certainly one of them. But it's not the only one. Simply put, the apocalyptic image of Jesus returning in power on a majestic white horse with sword in hand to slaughter the evil masses absolutely contradicts the Jesus who taught us to love our enemies, the humble Jesus who rode into Jerusalem on a donkey and would later tell his disciples that "Those who live by the sword will die by the sword." How could one who practiced nonviolence and compassion denounce his core values and embrace brute force, violence and vengeance? It is simply inconceivable that the God revealed to us in Jesus Christ would resort to retribution. It is more than inconceivable; it is unbelievable.

In *The Rapture Exposed*, Rossing asserts that Revelation's true message is a "vision of hope for God's healing of the world."[10] A divine plan to dramatically and violently enter into history and remake the world is a lie. The literal "second coming" will never happen—and yet we are called to participate in the coming of the kingdom here and now. Slow it may be, but the will and principles of a just and gracious God are being worked out in human life and institutions—in us! *We* are the second coming, called to manifest a message of hope to a world in fear.

John Dominic Crossan says:

> No Jew would think about ending the world because the world is God's creation and according to Genesis 1 is all good. God would never end the world. And of course they don't think *they* could do it, like we know *we* can do it. What they want God to do is end evil and injustice and violence on this earth. So eschatology is the hope that *God* will overcome someday, as it were. Now, if you talk about apocalyptic eschatology that would be somebody who says, "Well, I have a revelation from God that it's going to be soon. Maybe next week, maybe in our lifetime, God is finally going to clean up the world." It's like a great spring cleaning of the world. So what Jesus is saying and what Paul is saying is the great spring cleaning is not just imminent, it has already started. That's the novelty, the creativity, of Christian faith. They're not saying it's coming soon. They're saying it has already begun. And they are saying it's going to be over soon—they were wrong on that second one by 2,000 years and counting. But the first one is the heart of Christian faith. Do you believe it has begun? And what are you doing to get with the program?

Insofar as one perceives the mystery of the Divine as the benevolent ground of all being and that this mystery has been revealed in Jesus, then there is nothing to fear from the ravings of apocalyptic preachers and authors. Our call continues to be one of offering an alternative to the fear and violence embraced by so much of the Church. The message of Revelation is but one facet of our overall responsibility of bearing hope and reconciliation to a troubled world—doing our part to bring healing to the nations, one person at a time.

14

Honoring Creation

Our religion... is written in the hearts of our people.
Every part of this country is sacred... every hillside,
every valley, every plain and grove...." [1]

—Chief Seattle

In no small part due to nineteenth-century Native American leader Chief Seattle, traditional Native American spirituality is often associated with honoring the sacredness of all creation. For Chief Seattle, the Divine reverberates from every corner of creation, a perspective he shares with the Judeo-Christian heritage:

> The heavens are telling the glory of God;
> and the firmament proclaims his handiwork.
> Day to day pours forth speech,
> and night to night declares knowledge.
> There is no speech, nor are there words;
> their voice is not heard;
> Yet their voice goes out through all the earth,
> and their words to the end of the world.
> —Psalm 19:1–4

When reading Genesis 1, it is helpful to note that the Hebrew word translated as "created" is not in static past tense. It can also be interpreted as "In the beginning, when God *began to create* the heavens and the earth…," suggesting that God initiated a creative process that continues even to this moment. The God of Genesis is a creating God. As we are made in God's image, we are made not only to bring order out of chaos but also to be creators. We are not shameful fallen creatures, redeemed only by some cosmic and violent act beyond our control. We are emerging beings, blessed to be a blessing, and bearing special responsibility toward the creation in which we live and move and have our being.

PRAYING WITH OPEN EYES

Never lose an opportunity of seeing anything that is beautiful for beauty is God's handwriting—a wayside sacrament. Welcome it in every fair face, in every fair sky, in every fair flower, and thank God for it as a cup of blessing.

—Ralph Waldo Emerson

Although many Christians feel duty-bound to talk about morality and sin, these are not the only themes in scripture. "I don't think morality is the basic theme of the Bible," writes author Katherine Paterson. "I think its theme is closer to…beauty. By itself, morality is not beautiful enough."[2] When God saw everything that God had made and declared it good, it wasn't a moral judgment, but an aesthetic one. Creation was beautiful, delightful, and even awe-ful. Emily Dickinson remarked that the only commandment she ever obeyed was, "Consider the lilies."[3] More than a simple stop-and-smell-the-roses sentiment, it's a call to cultivate a deeper sense of awareness and awe—an appreciation of the beauty and mystery that transcend the mundane.

Author Barrie Shepherd was stirred to awe while observing porpoises lunge through the surf:

And so I caught the deep and dreadful brushing-by of mystery,
Exulted, silent, in the moving, living presence of an alien world
That swept along our shores, just as it does, and is,
    In each and every moment, whether we watch or pray or wake
        or sleep.[4]

Perhaps praying with one's eyes open is more a part of the spiritual life than many have considered. St. Ignatius of Loyola, founder of the Jesuit order, encouraged an attitude of finding God in all things and all things in God. Not to be confused with the "God *is* everything" of pantheism, theologians have dubbed the subtle yet very different understanding of "God *in* everything" as pan*en*theism. Although most recently popularized in the "Creation Spirituality" writings of Matthew Fox and the evolutionary thinking of Michael Dowd and Jan Phillips, this sacramental embrace of creation has its roots in the earliest expressions of Christianity, the practices of mystics, the philosophy of Teilhard de Chardin, and the first "Process" thinkers, Alfred North Whitehead and Charles Hartshorne. Embracing a consciousness of the Divine in everything and everything being enveloped by the Divine counters the dualistic idea of God being somewhere "out there" with a profound and immediate awareness of the divine presence here and now.

The writer John Steinbeck captures what this awareness feels like. He writes:

And it is a strange thing that most of the feeling we call religious, most of the mystical outcrying which is one of the most prized and used and desired reactions of our species, is really the understanding and the attempt to say that man is related to the whole thing, related inextricably to all reality, known and unknowable. This is a simple thing to say, but the profound feeling of it made a Jesus, a St. Augustine, a St. Francis, a Roger Bacon, a Charles Darwin, and an Einstein. Each of them in his own tempo and with his own voice discovered and reaffirmed with astonishment the knowledge that all things are one thing and that one thing is all things—plankton, a shimmering phosphorescence on the sea and the spinning planets and an expanding universe, all bound together by the elastic string of time. It is advisable to look from the tide pool to the stars and then back to the tide pool again.[5]

Consider the lilies of the field and the porpoises of the seas—the tide pool and the stars. Being awestruck implies a sudden experience of mystery, an awareness of beauty and power that transcends the mundane. That awareness and awe of seeing God in all things and all things in God is an integral part of the spiritual life—and pleads for a response.

JUST GET IT OVER WITH

Your attention please. Thank you for choosing earth as your planetary vehicle. We hope you enjoy the many wonderful features of this planet as you hurtle through the cosmos. Please note however, that in the event of continued inaction in the face of global warming, your seat cushion can be used as a flotation device.[6]

—Blue Man Group

Unfortunately, the hoped-for response from some Christians has not been gratitude or responsibility, but exploitation. Long before the rise of the Religious Right in America, colonial and imperialist Christian attitudes were driven by the conviction that God has granted human beings "dominion over . . . every living thing that moves upon earth" (Gen. 1:28). Today, some rapture-oriented Christians believe that once things get bad enough, Jesus's followers will be taken out of the world to a better place.

They believe that the divine plan is for God to dramatically and violently enter into history and remake the world. From this perspective, environmentalists are obstructionists, and Christians who defend the environment out of a sense of obligation to be good stewards are seen to be working counter to God's will.

During a panel discussion in the Montana State Legislature focusing on the Endangered Species Act, former state Representative Casey Emerson (R-Bozeman) wondered aloud whether "so-called environmentalists" had read the Bible passage stating that people must subdue the Earth. He added, "There are some species that ought to be killed off to subdue the Earth."[7]

A story circulated for years regarding President Reagan's secretary of the interior, James Watt. He allegedly testified before Congress that: God gave us these things to use. After the last tree is felled, Christ will come back. Although now accepted as apocryphal (and not representative of a current change of heart among many evangelicals), people were quick to believe the story as true. Watt's alleged sentiments were not far from the prevalent attitude of many who believed that, in light of the imminent return of Jesus, protecting natural resources was unimportant. Always reliable for a steady stream of outrageous comments, Ann Coulter declared, "God gave us the earth. We have dominion over the plants, the animals, the trees. God said, 'Earth is yours. Take it. Rape it. It's yours.'"[8]

While such extreme attitudes toward the resources of creation have not often been openly promoted, they can be seen as a symptom of the anthropocentric arrogance that sees humanity as the sole purpose for creation. Our dominion has been interpreted as permission to exhaust creation's resources for our own purposes, with creation serving as a mere backdrop for the human/divine drama.

Whether we mean to participate in this view of dominion, Megan McKenna points out that we humans are advancing the destruction of creation in measurable ways. She says:

By the year 2045 half of everything that has been created will be gone. We are cataloguing things that exist and we are losing at least 10,000 of them a year. What will it be like if your children or your grandchildren never saw a whale? Or a pod of dolphins? Or they don't eat fish anymore by the year 2040? Farm-raised fish will kill you! Most of [the environmental destruction that's] happened on the earth has happened in the last fifty years, when Christian nations have been the apex of society, using religious texts to validate what they do. Never once are we asking, "Are we insulting the God of Creation by the way we live and what we do — and using the God of Creation to destroy it?" That's spitting in the face of God.

Little time is given to the thought that with or without us, the cosmos will continue on its way. Creation is an ongoing process and, even though humanity would like to think itself the pinnacle of creation, the mystery of the Divine continues to create and be celebrated by creation itself.

WWJE?

Whatever my own practice may be, I have no doubt that
it is part of the destiny of the human race, in its gradual
improvement, to leave off eating animals, as surely as
the savage tribes have left off eating each other when
they came in contact with the more civilized.[9]

—Henry David Thoreau

For many, human dominion extends to controlling the ultimate fate of countless other animal species, not only the exotic and wild, but the utilitarian and domestic. The last century has seen meat production and consumption grow exponentially in Western countries. At the same time, studies have shown that a vegetarian diet is, in fact, healthier for human beings. Meat-free diets lower the rate of cancer, heart disease, diabetes, and other serious health problems. And the consequences go far beyond impact on an individual's health: industrial-scale meat production compromises water, soil, and the atmosphere. The United Nations' Food and Agriculture Organization's 2006 report, *Livestock's Long Shadow,* states that the production of meat generates "more greenhouse gas emissions than all forms of transportation combined."[10] In a concurrent study, researchers at the University of Chicago determined that moving from a meat-based diet to a vegan diet saves more energy than swapping an SUV for a hybrid vehicle.

Far from being some far-fetched, made-up, bleeding-heart notion, vegetarianism clearly had its fans among the storytellers who handed down the ancient stories of Hebrew scripture. A close read of Genesis reveals a storyline that assumes vegetarianism as the biblical ideal for not only human beings but the animals, as well. From the idyllic world of Eden through the end of the flood—and then picked up again as Revelation's vision for the New Jerusalem—all animals and humans are vegetarian. Even Isaiah foresees a return to a vegetarian world where the lion, lamb, and little child can all peacefully coexist.

While literalists dream up scenarios as to why the lions didn't eat up the lambs on the ark (perhaps, they posit, God put them all into a trancelike hibernation for the journey, and so on),[11] the solution is an obvious plot element right there in the text. According to the second creation story in Genesis 2, God gives all plants to humans and animals to eat—but does not give them permission to eat one another. Genesis claims that humanity—along with every other creature—was created to be vegetarian. It's only after the author of Genesis has all the animals safely off the ark that God changes the rules. In Genesis 9, God permits Noah to become the first carnivore and says, "Every moving thing that lives shall be food for you; and just as I gave you the green plants, I give you everything" (Gen. 9:3). So while the ideal of vegetarianism in the

Bible seems to have simply been good storytelling back in the day, it's not without its powerful implications for today. For the twenty-first-century, theologian John Sniegocki advocates vegetarianism as "a powerful way of modeling God's love through nonviolence, compassion for animals, care for the earth, care for our bodies, and responsible use of the earth's resources."[12]

Part of honoring creation will involve unlearning the notion of dominion as license to do whatever we want with creation. A dominion patterned on care and responsibility will help address the unsustainable use of land, water, and energy that our culture has fallen into. As we wrestle with the depletion of resources that threaten the future of humanity, even the food we choose to eat can become a part of our spiritual discipline.

ALWAYS BE GOOD TO YOUR MOTHER

*We just don't know how to be good to each other or decent
to each other — and we don't treat the rest of creation
beyond humanity all that hot most of the time.*

—Emilie Townes

Robert Musil is the Professor of Global Environmental Politics at American University. He points out that if Jesus was serious when he said, "Just as you did it to one of the least of these who are members of my family, you did it to me" (Matt. 25:40), then we should take seriously that more than 5 million poor children die each year from diseases related to the environment. Asthma, dysentery, cholera, and malaria are all exacerbated by pollution, poverty, war, and the disruption of our global climate. In many instances, rising temperatures lead to the spread of disease-carrying mosquitoes. Drinking water fouled by floods or hurricanes can bear bacteria that in the belly of a poor, malnourished baby means not merely diarrhea, but death. He says, "The biblical texts we need for this journey are not only those about the goodness of God's creation, the lilies of the field, the coming of rain in the desert. The essential texts describe Jesus's ministry, his call to heal, to bring hope to suffering humanity, to do justice, to bring peace to those—especially the most vulnerable—who are in danger."[13]

According to Musil, the environment is not simply some lovely, green thing outside of us, apart from us. It is in us as well. Every molecule passes through us, through the ecosystems that we are part of and that sustain us. Modern medicine has confirmed the biblical claim that we are equal in the eyes of God, regardless of borders. From studies by Philippe Grandjean, we know that a single molecule of mercury or PCBs released into the environment can make its way—through evaporation, rain, and the food chain—from a broken electric generator in Texas all the way to the Arctic. There, a pregnant Inuit is eating what appears to be a perfectly healthy fish. The mercury enters her bloodstream, crosses her placenta, and harms the learning and development of her unborn child. Musil says, "If we are to halt this threat to creation, we need to include coal miners, children with asthma, people who live near or work in the factories that make most of us comfortable while spewing pollution and promoting cancer. We must care and act on the injustices of poverty and war. As Christians, we care about all creation..."[14]

Many Christians are finally beginning to understand the interconnectedness of all creation from a religious perspective—the sense of oneness with God, with each other, and with Creation. Matthew Fox even suggests Mother Earth as a metaphor for the crucified and resurrected Jesus; innocent of any crime, she has blessed us for billions of years and is now being killed by pollution. Even so, she rises daily to redeem us, holding out hope for a radical change in the human heart and spirit. Fox says:

> To be compassionate as God is compassionate is to both rejoice in
> the delight and beauty and joys of the world, of creation, but also
> to defend them. To defend creation. And to defend what's beauti-

ful. You know, Thomas Aquinas in the thirteenth century has an amazing teaching about the word "salvation." And he says it not once but several times. He says the first and foremost meaning of salvation is to preserve things in the good. That's an amazing definition of salvation. He's not saying to escape hell or to earn brownie points for life after death. The first and foremost definition of salvation, he says, is to preserve things in the good. I cannot imagine a more apt definition of salvation for our times of ecological peril and disaster than that definition from a premodern theologian, Thomas Aquinas. We are here to preserve things in the good, and that is blessing. Blessing is the theological word for goodness.

SECTION THREE

Transformation

15

A Kingdom Without Walls

I didn't know so many people were Jewish![1]

—Isaac Schnitzer

It was the Schnitzers' second Hanukkah in Billings, Montana, and five-year-old Isaac wanted the menorah to be in his bedroom window. But as Isaac and his sister, Rachel, prepared for bed, a brick hurled from the street sent shards of glass flying through the room.

The day after the incident, an FBI agent advised the family to get bulletproof glass in their windows and to take down the menorahs. Instead, they decided to put the menorah back in the window and call the local newspaper.

The next morning, a member of the local Congregational church read the story and phoned her pastor. Echoing the World War II legend from Denmark where Nazi occupiers were thwarted by King Christian and thousands of other non-Jews who donned yellow Star of David armbands in solidarity with their Jewish neighbors, a plan was hatched.

Within days, the word was out and paper menorahs were distributed for display in windows throughout town. The Target store had some plastic menorahs but soon sold out. An antique store in Billings reported a Christian woman buying a very expensive, antique menorah to place in her window. The marquee at the Catholic High School read, Happy Hanukkah to our Jewish friends.

Soon, hundreds of homes in Billings had menorahs in their windows. Some were shot out by bullets, some shattered by bricks. Hate calls were made to Christian families. Margaret MacDonald, whose idea it was to put up the paper menorahs, said she thought it would be a simple thing for people to do. But when she went to put the menorah in her own window, she hesitated: "With two young children, I had to think hard about it myself. We put our menorah in a living room window, and made sure nobody sat in front of it." The community would not be intimidated. Each night of Hanukkah, more and more menorahs were placed in windows. The local paper printed a brightly colored full-page menorah, urging its 56,000 subscribers to place them in their windows.

On the last night of Hanukkah, hundreds of homes had menorahs in them. As the Schnitzers drove around town that night, Isaac saw all of the houses with menorahs in their windows and exclaimed, "I didn't know so many people were Jewish!"[2]

EMBRACING THE STRANGER

Nancy Ammerman says that "One of the messages that Christianity has to offer is the message of both a radical equality and a radical grace. The notion that we are neither a Jew nor Greek, male nor female, slave nor free. That somehow it's possible, not so much to do away with those differences, but nevertheless to find a way to be together around those differences."

There's a story about author Nikos Kazantzakis that points to our common humanity. The story goes that as he walked along a dusty path in his native Crete, an elderly woman passed by, carrying a basket of figs. She paused, picked out two figs, and presented them to the author. "Do you know me, old lady?" Kazantzakis asked. She glanced at him in amazement, "No, my boy. Do I have to know you to give you something? You are a human being, aren't you? So am I. Isn't that enough?"

Over and over, Hebrew scripture lists three groups of people as worthy of special kindness, extra thoughtfulness, and intentional consideration: strangers, widows, and orphans (see Lev. 19:10; Deut. 10:18; 14:29). The legal mandates in the Old Testament are unique among the other known judicial systems in the Ancient Near East in their consistent and outspoken advocacy of the weakest, least protected, and disadvantaged members of the society.

"Strangers" are listed with "widows and orphans" because strangers were alone—they lacked any kinship connection that would otherwise protect and support them. Jesus ate with the outcast and the stranger, and preached that "Just as you did it to one of the least of these who are members of my family, you did it to me" (Matt. 25:40). Paul defines the mark of the true Christian as one who extends hospitality to strangers (Rom. 12:13).

Ephesians 2:11–22 takes it even further. They used to be "aliens," strangers, they had "no hope." But "in Christ Jesus" these strangers become part of a common humanity with believers. The dividing walls have been "broken down." Essentially, the anonymous author of Ephesians says, "Don't exclude people because they aren't the way you want them to be. Don't let your pre-conceived notions be the guiding principle of how you relate to others. Remember, not too long ago, *you* were the strangers. Some wanted *you* to be circumcised to be part of the fellowship. Remember that?"

William Booth, the founder of the Salvation Army, spent many years reaching out to the poor and needy on the streets of London. An apocryphal story from the day captures the essence of his work. Every Christmas, London churches sent out representatives to the streets to invite the poor to Christmas celebrations. Huge crowds would gather to take advantage of this annual outpouring of generosity. The Anglicans began by announcing, "All of you who are Anglicans, come with us." The Roman Catholics followed: "All who are Catholic, come with us." Then the

Methodists, the Lutherans, and all the other denominations announced, "Whoever is one of us, come with us." Finally, when all of the church representatives had made their invitations and left, a large crowd of people remained milling about. At that point, William Booth would step out of the crowd and shout out to the people, "All of you who belong to no one, come with me!"

LET LOVE BE DANGEROUS

"You shall love the Lord your God with all your heart, and with all your soul, and with all your mind." This is the greatest and first commandment. And a second is like it: "You shall love your neighbor as yourself." On these two commandments hang all the law and the prophets.

—Matthew 22:37–40

God asked Jonah to go to Nineveh. Instead of facing his prejudice against the Assyrians, Jonah ran away. After a deep sea detour of some repute, he finally made it to the Assyrian capital. Much to his self-righteous chagrin, they embraced God's love and forgiveness with such fervor and humility that even the cattle were wearing sackcloth and ashes. Compared with earlier biblical sources that suggested that God was some sort of exclusive tribal deity, the book of Jonah stands in direct opposition. Instead of sounding the alarm to circle the wagons against "the other," the story of Jonah trumpets the conviction that God's grace is extended to all people, even the ones for whom we might hold human hatred and prejudice.

John Shelby Spong believes that the story of Jonah is about human prejudice. He says:

It's about a prophet who is called by God to speak to people for whom the prophet does not care. He refuses to speak and goes in the opposite direction. But God keeps pushing him back to Ninevah. To me, that story is designed to demonstrate that the love of God does not have boundaries. Nations have boundaries and tribes have boundaries and prejudices have boundaries and fears have boundaries. But the love of God has no boundary! And any time you impose a human boundary on the love of God, you have done something evil, cruel, destructive, and ungodlike. If God can love even the Ninevites, there must be something bigger going on here. It goes beyond just tolerating people. It goes on to acceptance and affirmation of people—not despite their differences, but because of their differences.

Spong believes that such efforts are at "the very heart of the Christian gospel," saying that the wars in his life have primarily been "against prejudice expressed toward black people, prejudice expressed towards woman, prejudice expressed toward gay and lesbian people, prejudice expressed toward Jews and other religious groups. If the love of God is bounded by my tribe or my race or my gender or my sexual orientation or my religion, then the love of God becomes one more human idol."

For many years, the Center for Progressive Christianity has promoted eight points by which progressive Christianity is defined. Directly confronting the prejudices we harbor as human beings, the points include a list suggesting those who are called to be in a community without boundaries:[3]

- Believers and agnostics
- Conventional Christians and questioning skeptics
- Homosexuals and heterosexuals
- Females and males
- The despairing and the hopeful
- Those of all races and cultures
- Those of all classes and abilities
- Those of all ages

These people don't have to be like one another or become like one another—but they are still together in fellowship. Embracing such diversity serves as an antidote to those who would claim to be the sole arbiters of a holiness based in conformity of both belief and behavior. To paraphrase C. S. Lewis: Can you think of a type of person who might make you uncomfortable if they sat next to you? May that person come into your life soon! That's where true discipleship is tested.

Jesus repeatedly shattered the rules of ritual purity and cultural expectations of separation from "the other." The stories of Jesus healing people in Matthew 9 are a perfect example of Jesus's willingness to break down the walls separating people: the paralyzed man, the blind and mute man—all people whom the "righteous" would have labeled as sinners and thus deserving of their fate. Jesus also showed compassion to:

- A tax collector who was cheating the people: He was considered a traitor, hated by fellow Jews for helping the occupying forces of Rome bleed the country dry and line his own pockets.
- The woman with the hemorrhage: Ritual cleanliness laws conspired to exclude women from religious life. Some women would *never* be ritually "clean." By even touching the woman with the flow of blood (or being touched by her), Jesus was made unclean—but his response was one of love.
- The synagogue leader: A respected leader with a sick daughter who came to see this radical rabbi only after he had exhausted every other avenue to save his daughter. Despite his daughter having died, Jesus was gracious and went with him, healing her.

We're called to love our neighbor as we do our own self. That love is more that just a superficial, Hi, how are you? It involves cost, risk, and vulnerability to provide a safe place for people who are lonely, rejected by society, or beat up by others or the circumstances of life. Observing Mother Teresa's work with India's "untouchables," poet Sydney Carter was moved to reflect: "Let love be dangerous."[4]

In 2002, a group of Phoenix clergy calling themselves "No Longer Silent: Clergy for Justice" (www.nolongersilent.org) issued the *Phoenix Declaration* calling "for an end to all religious and civil discrimination against any person based on sexual orientation." As stated in the Declaration, the clergy were inspired by "the courage of all people who have refused to let the voice of intolerance and violence speak for Christianity. The determination of these people, especially GLBT (gay, lesbian, bisexual, transgender) persons, to meet hatred with love and to answer violence with compassion is an inspiration to us all, and prophetic witness of God's activity in our world."[5]

Mel White's story of coming to terms with being on the wrong side of one of those walls is a compelling testimony to just how determined people are in denying the existence of "the other." He says:

> I grew up in a wonderful evangelical Christian home, and I thank God for it. We went to church every time the doors were open. And I'm still glad—let's get that square. I'm still an evangelical. I believe in Jesus as my Lord and Savior, I believe that God is Creator of all things, and that the Holy Spirit is alive and well and working today. And I'm gay as can be. I've been in a partnership with a gay man for thirty years. I'm an old, extinguished gay. But I have to say that along the way it wasn't easy to accept myself because of the people around me who took the Bible literally and condemned me and forced me to go through all kinds of therapies to try to get over being gay, to exorcise the demon of homosexuality. I went through exorcism, electric shock, all kinds of aversive therapies like eating terrible tasting things when I saw a gay man, or a man who was impressive to me. I went through all that and finally slit my wrists. And my wife of twenty years said, "You know, you're gay. You've tried. I like gay men, I just didn't want you to be one. But you are one, Mel. So I give you your freedom." And we've been close friends ever since. If you're a gay person, a lesbian person, bisexual, transgender person, accept who you are. Accept it as a gift from God.

Finally I could accept it. It took a lot of scar tissue to get to the place where I could love a man and not be embarrassed. Everything in me was same sex attraction, from the very beginning. But [for] all those years I thought I was sick and that I was sinful; that I was sick and should be cured; that I was sinful and should be forgiven; all those wasted prayers; all those wasted therapies. God made me gay. God loved me as a gay man and continues to love and work through me. I wish I could say to young gay, lesbian, bisexual, transgender people across the country and around the world, "Love yourself 'cause God sure does. She made you just like you are and wants you desperately to accept that as a gift. Instead of trying to give it back, accept it."

HOSPITALITY OR HOSTILITY?

Hospitality has long been a core value in the Jewish tradition. One story of Abraham's hospitality even has him running to greet the strangers at his camp (Gen. 18:2). In ancient days, the practice protected people from the dangers of traveling alone. There were no safe and cheap shelters for travelers. Along the way people could be brutalized, robbed, wounded, or lost. As once practiced, it was expected that food offered to a stranger had to be as abundant as possible, even if it meant, as it often did, that the family had to do without in the coming days.

Jesus radicalized any romantic notion of hospitality into the care and love for those with no social standing, those of limited resources and questionable credibility. In the judgment parable in Matthew 25, the king says to those being given the kingdom: "I was naked and you gave me clothing, I was thirsty and you gave me something to drink, I was a stranger and you welcomed me." Essentially, followers of Jesus are challenged to overcome fear of the stranger and give attention to the lonely, the excluded, the unfamiliar.

The word *hospitality* is translated from the Greek *philonexia*. Its root is the same word from which we get the word *xenophobia*. Our treatment of the "alien" or "foreigner" reveals our core values of hospitality or hostility toward those who are different. Seeing the face of Christ in the stranger at our door is often a challenge. But the spirit of hospitality found in the Bible recognizes the child of God in everyone and obliges us to treat one another accordingly.

John Shelby Spong explains:

What you also meet in the Jesus story is that he calls us to a humanity beyond our prejudices. Oh, we all have prejudices. Some hide them better than others but we all have prejudices. Jesus lived in a world where people hated Samaritans. Samaritans were unclean. Samaritans were a half-breed mixed race. Samaritans were heretical thinkers. They didn't practice the true faith of the Jews. The Jews hated the Samaritans, looked down upon the Samaritans, but they never really realized that if you look down upon someone else that what you're really trying to do is to build yourself up. And then you ask yourself, Why do I feel so inadequate that I have to build myself up by tearing somebody else down? That's what prejudice is. Prejudices develop so that you and I can hide our insecurities even from ourselves. We think, it's okay to hate these people because they're quite hateable. So it's not prejudice, it's just objective. That's the way we deal with it. But if you are fully human you have no need to look down on other people. Prejudice kills the humanity of the prejudiced person. We certainly kill the victim. But what we really need to understand is that you cannot be human and look down upon another single solitary human being. For prejudice kills the humanity of the perpetrator of that prejudice.

Ancient literature and fairy tales are full of stories in which gods and other supernatural beings disguise themselves as mortals, sometimes as the lowest of the low, and roam throughout the world to see how people will treat them. As the Epistle to the Hebrews says, "Do not neglect to show hospitality to strangers, for by doing that some have entertained angels without knowing it" (13:2).

Jim Wallis tells of how the Sojourners Community opens a food line to the hungry and homeless of Washington who live within sight of the White House. Before the volunteers open the doors, they gather around the food, hold hands, and are led in prayer by Mary Glover, the best pray-er of the community and someone who herself stood in that food line a few years earlier. Echoing Jesus's admonition, "Inasmuch as you have done it to one of the least of these, you have done it to me," she prays: "Lord, we know you'll be coming through this line today. So help us to treat you well."[6]

Springboarding off the *Phoenix Declaration* and drawing on input from members of No Longer Silent, Scottsdale Congregational UCC, and other colleagues, Eric Elnes crafted what was to become the *Phoenix Affirmations,* a set of twelve principles set forth to articulate the values of an emerging twenty-first-century faith. The fifth of these affirmations points to the priority of "Engaging people authentically, as Jesus did, treating all as creatures made in God's very image, regardless of race, gender, sexual orientation, age, physical or mental ability, nationality, or economic class."[7]

Acknowledging that the church has not always lived up to its call to walk with Jesus on this particular path, Elnes notes that a growing number of Jesus followers "feel called to move beyond their immediate comfort zone to recognize that the guest list for God's party is a lot larger than previously imagined."[8]

The significance of a shared meal in Jesus's day has been somewhat lost to our twenty-first-century way of thinking. Many of the people with whom Jesus dealt never had a full stomach. Naturally, "heaven" for them was imagined as a banquet. One of the clearest ways Jesus showed his openness and acceptance of all types of people was in sharing meals with them. Ironically, the shared meal of communion is today one of the principle tools used to exclude people from Christian fellowship. In direct contradiction to Jesus's own practice, many denominations enforce elaborate rules clarifying who can receive communion and who cannot.

John Wesley, the founder of the Methodist movement, began his career as an Anglican priest and a rigid legalist. But over the years his understanding of communion was only one of his views that changed significantly. Deeming communion a "means of grace," Wesley left a legacy in which the United Methodist church now practices open communion in which anyone can participate. As a witness to the free gift of grace and the open table fellowship practiced by Jesus, no one is turned away from the table, not even the unbaptized.

NO EARTHLY GOOD

Jesus loves everybody—get over it.[9]

—Jerry Barlow

Story after story of Jesus portrays him as hanging out and eating with the wrong people at the wrong time, touching people he shouldn't touch, and going against the expectations of the proper and pious religious folks.

One of the most striking examples involved a woman and a dinner party. The woman in Luke 7:36–50 was considered immoral by many in the religious community. Yet here she shows up at a party where she isn't welcome, hasn't been included, clearly isn't wanted, and is, in fact, condemned for attending.

She begins to wet Jesus's feet with her tears and shocks Middle Eastern sensibilities by letting down her hair to dry his feet. As she anoints Jesus's feet with ointment, the pious host, Simon, declares, "No self-respecting or true prophet would allow this sinner-woman to touch him."

Jesus asks Simon, "Do you see this woman?" Far from being an ophthalmological question, Jesus is asking, "How long are you, a decent,

God-fearing man, going to be blinded by your rigidity?" More interested in the notoriety of having the famous rabbi at dinner than anything else, Simon had neglected the basic courtesies of washing the feet of one's guests—an act of hospitality extended here by the outcast and not the host himself.

Simon's condition was what might be called hard-heartedness. Marcus Borg writes, "Throughout the Bible, the heart is a metaphor for a deep level of the self"[10]—below even thinking and feeling. Closed hearts are described in the Bible as hard hearts, shut hearts, and stony hearts. With this malady come blindness, lack of understanding, darkened minds, lack of gratitude, insensitivity to wonder and awe, and a lack of compassion.

Jesus's annoyance at Simon reveals a lack of patience for such hard-heartedness. Jesus's people *were* the outcasts, *were* the strangers, *were* the whores and the beggars and the forgotten. The people Jesus spent his time with were the very people kept far away from the Temple by the rigid rules of the ruling religious class.

One doesn't have to look hard to see the twenty-first-century version of these same rigid rules of exclusion at work in our churches today. We have built theological walls of every conceivable type—language, actions, beliefs, liturgy, music, requirements, expectations, education, rigidity, race, class, sex, orientation, gender identity, etc.—all meant to keep out the people we think are somehow less deserving of inclusion than we are—all to promote the worship of the idols of conformity and status quo. Without giving a second thought to what it says to the outsider, some of us cling to these walls for the reassuring comfort that what we know and are familiar with will not change. For others, these walls are the final proof that what Christianity has to offer is primarily hypocrisy and selfishness. And yet there is something deep inside us that, if given a chance, revels in experiencing moments of unity and reconciliation.

Professor Stephen Patterson suggests that it's in those very moments that we get a glimpse of Jesus's original vision, an alternative to the voices of those that would mistake homogeneity for holiness:

There's a lot to be said for homogeneity. There's a lot to be said for a beautiful lawn all green, no blotches, waving in the wind—a rich wheat field, all the same, all together. But there are other visions. Jesus has another vision for the empire of God. He has another vision for our communities of faith. He has another vision for our church. Let me say just this: that sometimes being the Church, being the Body of Christ, means being in a place you're not supposed to be, doing things that you're not supposed to do, being a weed in the midst of a garden that does not want a weed. And sometimes it means attracting unwanted guests. The unclean and the unwanted, the uncherished of the world, [whom] God longs for us to draw to ourselves and shelter.

As a student at Boston University School of Theology, Tex Sample studied preaching with Allen Knight Chalmers. Deeply involved in the civil rights movement, Chalmers had helped free the Scottsboro Boys in the 1930s and while at Boston University was the president of the NAACP Legal Defense Fund, involving him in civil rights struggles and action all over the United States. Sample recalls:

Chalmers would be with us in class through the week, and then often on the weekend was gone to some troubled place to see what could be done. During those years, he had a black student in class that he was unusually close to and they loved each other very much. The black student was out of Alabama and wanted to go home one Christmas for the holidays. His wife was pregnant, well along in the pregnancy, but she checked with her doctor and the doctor indicated that it would be all right for her to go home if they would take it easy on the trip down and not rush coming back, but just take an easy, easy trip.

The trip home was fine. They had a wonderful time visiting with family and friends and when they came back, they were somewhere in North Alabama and she was having very sharp contractions; at least that's what she thought. They then began to rush to find a hospital. The first hospital they went to told them that they did not serve colored people and so they were then frantically searching trying to find a hospital that would take them. By the time they found a hospital, they had lost the baby and the mother very nearly died.

When that student got back to Boston University, he was a cauldron of fury and he would have absolutely nothing to do with Chalmers, though they had been warm friends. When Chalmers would meet him in a hallway, the young man would turn on his heel and walk away. Chalmers had made phone calls, had tried to see him, all to no avail. One day while Chalmers was in his office, he looked down the hallway and could see the young man coming up the hallway toward his office. Chalmers simply stepped back into his office and waited for the young man to get immediately in front of his door. When he did, Chalmers, a big man, reached out and grabbed him and yanked him into his office and just hurled him across the room to the other wall. Then Chalmers shouted at him, "Listen, you have *got* to talk about this. You've *got* to talk and you are going to talk *now*. You are not leaving this office unless you go right over me!" He said the young man responded at first with something that sounded like a growl and then it became a shout. He said, "God damn you. God DAMN you! If it weren't for you, I could hate *every* white man on the face of this earth!"

Sample wonders, "Where can the people who are marginalized in the world, the people who are poor, the people who are outcast, find those that they can trust? Is it you? Is it me? Can it be the church?"

The gospel makes an appeal to us to tear down the walls, to reach out to those who are strangers, those who are far off, those against whom we harbor prejudice—even our enemies. The gospel engenders a radical hospitality that requires boundaries be crossed, barriers be dismantled, and walls be torn down.

—∿—

KIN_DOM WITHOUT WALLS

Imagine a place
Where mercy resides,
Love forms each heart,
Compassion lived out with grit and determination.
A place where lavish signs
Mark each path barrier free.

Imagine a place
Where skin tones are celebrated
Like the hues of tulips in springtime.
Where languages inspire
With symphonies of diversity.
Where Respect schools us
In custom and history
And every conversation
Begins with a bow of reverence.

Imagine a place where each person wears glasses,
Clarity of vision for all.
Recognizing each one, everything
Made in the image of God.

Imagine a place
Where carrots and pasta
Doctor's skills and medications
Are not chained behind barbed wire—
Food, shelter, health care available for all.

Imagine a place where
Every key of oppression
Was melted down to form public art

Huge fish, doves, lions and lambs
On which children could play.

Imagine a place where
People no longer kept watch
Through the front window
To determine whether the welcome mat
Would remain on the porch.

Such is the work
The journey
The destination
In the kin_dom of God.

—Cynthia Langston Kirk

16

Social Justice
Realizing God's Vision

*Justice is not a fancy word which we can slip in and out
of prayers harmlessly. God's justice affects the fabric
of this world and the integrity of its people.*

—John Bell

Speaking an authoritative word from Yahweh, the prophets of Hebrew scripture stood in judgment over the political and religious leaders of the people. Today, the popular notion of a prophet has been gutted of any suggestion of spiritual or moral insight in favor of the image of a prognosticator of sensational and superficial coming events.

But the call to pursue social justice has deep roots in the biblical tradition and has been at the heart of efforts to address social, environmental, and moral injustices around the world. Theodore Parker, the great Unitarian preacher and activist, believed that the significance of religion in the first place was in its active "meddling" in public issues and "everything that affects the welfare of [humanity]."[1] In a society which is often unjust, inequitable, and whose very structures are responsible for generating untold suffering and poverty, we are right to wonder, "Is there any word from the Lord?" (Jer. 37:17).

THE PROPHETS OF HEBREW SCRIPTURE

Everybody cryin' mercy,
when they don't know the meanin' of the word.
Everybody cryin' justice,
so long as it's business first.[2]

—Mose Allison

Some 750 years before the birth of Jesus, things seemed to be going fairly well in the Northern Kingdom of Israel. Yet God called a shepherd and dresser of sycamore trees named Amos to preach harsh words to a comfortable people. Amos denounced Israel and its neighbors for their reliance on military might, for grave injustice in social dealings, for their abhorrent immorality, and their shallow, meaningless piety. Needless to say, he was unpopular with religious and political leaders—and anyone else whose status, wealth, and security relied on maintaining the status quo.

Sadly, today's popular understanding of prophecy has essentially been gutted of its distinguished biblical heritage in favor of divination of the future, clairvoyance, and a scandalous misuse of the Bible to predict the apocalypse. Wallowing in angst-ridden conjectures of divine retribution and blame, these somber predictors of doom string together unrelated biblical texts in order to stuff their coffers by scaring the masses.

Far from foretelling some inescapable future, the prophets of Hebrew scripture stood in judgment over the political and religious leaders of the people and proclaimed a conditional future: what happens next is directly contingent upon how the religious, ethical, and political corruption of the day is dealt with.

While different in style, tone, and context, each of the Hebrew prophets had the same concern about justice and community, about being the people of God, together. They were not solitary figures, isolated from the experiences of the real world, but members of the community living in the midst of life and all its struggles. Be it the three major prophets—Isaiah, Jeremiah, and Ezekiel—or the twelve shorter works known as the "minor" prophets (the term refers to their length, not their importance)—Hosea, Obadiah, Nahum, Haggai, Joel, Jonah, Habakkuk, Zechariah, Amos, Micah, Zephaniah, and Malachi—their dominant concern was the relationship of a people to their God.

With the exception of Jonah, who's remembered more for his actions than his words, these books are comprised mostly of what the prophets said as spokespersons for God. And unlike the message of today's "prophets," what they said had less to do with foretelling the future than telling what God's will is for the people of God.

It's important to remember that the judgment they predict isn't an unavoidable divine punishment but an effort to call people back into a relationship with God. No matter how dire the circumstances, their words were tempered with the simple expectation that is at the heart of biblical faith: hope for the future.

A DIFFERENT GOD

In his historical novel *The Source,* James Michener tells the story of a Canaanite village in prebiblical days. The time was 2,200 years before Christ, and the Canaanites in that village worshiped numerous gods of the earth. It was a fertility religion, and among the many gods was the goddess Astarte. In every home there were voluptuous clay figurines of Astarte and her male companions. These people, sad to say, practiced human sacrifice to the god Malek, in the belief that if they sacrificed the lives of their firstborn sons, the gods would be so pleased that they would make the people more fertile. Temple prostitutes were provided by the priests to the men of the village as part of their fertility rites.

Timna, the protagonist in Michener's story, could not accept the sacrifice of her firstborn son, nor could she accept the behavior of her husband with a particularly young and erotic temple prostitute. Michener writes, "Timna, still grieving for her son, watched the performance dispassionately and muttered, 'What folly! The fertility is in the soil. It is in me.' And while others celebrated she walked slowly homeward, seeing life in new and painful clarity; with different gods her husband Urbaal would have been a different man, and she went into his godroom, looked with abhorrence at the four Astartes, and methodically smashed [them] along with their phallic companions."[3]

With a different god, he would have been a different man.

According to John Dominic Crossan, one of the most pressing questions for twenty-first-century Christians is, "What is the character of your God?" The character of the God in whom we place our allegiance shapes our character as people of faith. The prophets remind us of God's character. Although Crossan is quick to point out that we can't generalize the message of the prophets as, for example, nonviolence (the first two prophets, Elijah and Elisha, were extremely violent), a recurrent, pronounced theme on the prophets' lips is divine justice. The God of the Bible is a just God. Although God's justice is often misunderstood as a retributive justice, it instead is a justice about *distribution*, says Crossan. In other words, God is concerned about fairness and equality, not vengeance and retribution. A violent god begets a violent people. A god who seeks fairness and equality begets a people who seek fairness and equality.

TAKE THIS HEART

I don't know what your destiny will be, but one
thing I do know: the only ones among you
who will be really happy are those who
have sought and found out how to serve.

—Albert Schweitzer

Professor of Old Testament Harrell Beck, says:

For many years of my life I detested the text of Isaiah 53:10: "It has pleased the Lord to bruise the servant." So I decided to go to the Jerusalem Bible to see if the Catholics could help me out. They read it, "It has pleased the Lord to *crush* the servant!" But then I've lived long enough to discover that the only people who have really made any difference in my life are the people who God has taken and sand-papered the cockles of their hearts until they could not walk by a hungry child, a crying woman, or a hardened man without responding. It has pleased the Lord to bruise the servant. And I thank God for what is, in many ways, the ultimate maturity of the spiritual life. It's no accident that the 53rd Chapter of Isaiah and the song of the suffering servant is more quoted in the New Testament than any other single chapter of the Old—and is half the text of Handel's Messiah. Can you hear me? Submission—that submission which understands that the gospel is bad news before it can really be good news.[4]

Jesus calls would-be followers to "Repent, and believe in the good news!" (Mark 1:15). This repentance leaves behind destructive, violent, unjust beliefs and practices in favor of becoming collaborators with God in seeking justice. Benedictine Sister Dawn Annette Mills suggests that the word *repent* carries with it the call "to crumble."[5] In modern-day vernacular, she suggests repentance is something like the roto-tilling of the heart. Time and again the Bible speaks of hardened hearts as a metaphor for ignorance or acceptance of suffering and injustice. Repentance leads to the softening of one's heart. Likewise, hardened soil also needs water for softening. Mills suggests tears as an effective strategy for softening hearts. Concern for justice can then take root.

The last song on U2's 2004 album, *How to Dismantle an Atomic Bomb*, is really a psalm—a sung prayer entitled "Yahweh." The song closes with the line, "Take this heart and make it break." A hardened heart is of no use to God. God desires our hearts to crumble and break on account of injustice—thus prompting us to rise up impassioned in God's name to do something about it.

Mills points out that the Latin behind the word *compunction* means "punctured; a punctured heart."[6] The role of the prophets is to pierce our hearts and make them break on account of injustice.

Rabbi Abraham Joshua Heschel once wrote:

A student of philosophy who turns from the discourses of the great metaphysicians to the orations of the prophets may feel as if he were going from the realm of the sublime to an area of trivialities. Instead of dealing with the timeless issues of being and becoming, of matter and form, of definitions and demonstrations, he is thrown into orations about widows and orphans, about the corruption of judges and affairs of the market place. Instead of showing us a way through the elegant mansions of the mind, the prophets take us to the slums.... Their breathless impatience with injustice may strike us as hysteria.... But if such deep sensitivity to evil is to be called hysterical, what name should be given to the abysmal indifference to evil which the prophet bewails?[7]

Echoing Rabbi Heschel, Culver "Bill" Nelson says, "The prophets set before humans the awesome dimension of justice and righteousness and fairness and human caring—and lots of people prefer to live in their logic-tight compartments in a little cubicle away from the world where they are comfortable, rather than where they are caring."

Psalm 51 declares "a broken and contrite heart, O God, you will not despise" (Ps. 51:17). When nursing a bruise or a hurt, all it takes is for someone to brush up against it and you twinge from the sharp pain. Such sensitivity is a prime characteristic of a person of faith. Hearts are softened by tears shed in the face of injustice. Hearts are broken from confronting an "abysmal indifference" to suffering and evil. What breaks your heart? What brings tears to your eyes? Poverty? Abuse? Disease? Inadequate housing? Capital punishment? War? Illiteracy? Greed? Perhaps God is inviting you to do something about it. "Repent, and believe in the good news."

DOING JUSTICE, LOVING KINDNESS, AND WALKING HUMBLY WITH GOD

As a people of faith we must live our lives not
always comforted by the holy but haunted
by God's call to live a prophetic life.

—Emilie Townes

The author of James asks, "What good is it, my brothers and sisters, if you say you have faith but do not have works? Can faith save you? If a brother or sister is naked and lacks daily food, and one of you says to them, 'Go in peace; keep warm and eat your fill,' and yet you do not supply their bodily needs, what is the good of that? So faith by itself, if it has no works, is dead" (James 2:14–17).

Being a disciple is not only a matter of receiving, but doing. Upon closer investigation, it seems that what passes for Christianity today is really two different religions. One encourages people to ask, What can God do for me? (Save me, give me victory, make me prosperous and successful) while the other asks, What can I do for God? (What gifts have I been given to serve the less fortunate and change the world for the better?) When someone asks you, Are you saved? what he means is, Have you had a personal experience of God's grace in your life so that you can accept Jesus as your personal Savior? What he doesn't ask is, Have you been in relationship with the poor in this world? Have you fed the hungry? Are you seeking justice for the oppressed?

John Dominic Crossan makes a clear distinction between the two types of justice in the Bible: personal/individual justice and systemic or structural justice. He says, "Personal/individual justice is: I don't cheat you, I don't defraud you. It's personal and individual between two people. But there is also another type of justice, systemic and structural justice." Jesus and the prophets of Hebrew scripture were all too familiar with the ferocious resistance their particular systems fielded in defense of the status quo. Both had to deal with a reality of human civilization that is as familiar to us today as it was to them: that the wealthy and powerful in any given society manipulate the system to serve their own self-interest.

As those with influence work to bend the arc of the universe towards privilege, the system is structured to favor the affluent, to the detriment of the less advantaged. As such, Crossan warns that systemic injustice is usually far more subtle than any personal slight: "It's the line item in a budget that guarantees that half a million kids will be hurt six months from now and, sort of, *nobody* did it. It just sort of…happened."

Serving as an accomplice to the quiet manipulations of structural injustice, the church often misdirects people's attention away from larger issues to stress a highly personalized piety. Marcus Borg observes: "Here is how it works: whenever Christianity becomes concerned primarily with the virtue of individuals, it tacitly legitimates whatever social system is in place." Borg goes on to say that:

> Systemic justice is concerned with the way the structures of society work. And this is critically important: the litmus test for whether or not a given system is just or not is you look at the results. Systemic justice is a results-oriented justice. If you have a system that produces a pretty large and radically impoverished class, then no matter how fair the rules are enforced and no matter how democratically those rules are made, it's not a just society. If you have a society in which 1 percent of the population own 43 percent of the wealth, it's pretty clear that 1 percent has structured that society so it kind of worked out that way—and they have a tremendous amount of power to sustain it. That's the figure in the United States, by the way. The wealthiest 1 percent of us

own 43 percent of the wealth in this country. What I want to do is to get the bottom 99 percent of us angry as hell about the way the elites are structuring this society in their own narrow self-interests to the detriment of all the rest of us.

As disorganized as many perceived the Occupy movement that rose up in the later part of 2011 to be, one thing is certain: the movement was a vehicle for diverse groups and individuals to come together and declare with one voice, The system is broken! Once the task of lone prophets, questioning the justice of the system has been democratized. From Zuccotti Park to Tahrir Square, be it in the blogosphere or on Facebook, in tweets or on the street, the information and organizational tools are available to virtually anyone moved to speak out for justice.

For many, though, the thought of seeking social justice is an intimidating proposition. Perhaps revealing your opinion in an op-ed letter, confronting a bully, standing on a picket line, or braving the elements with your local Occupy group all seem out of character somehow. Yet God's vision for the world can only be realized as each one of us sets ourselves to practicing even the smallest task toward the goal.

Emilie Townes offers this perspective:

> The prophetic life is one in which you live your faithfulness out of a steadiness, and that is often hard for us to do. We do really good with these rushes of faithfulness [but] the mortal life is the life of the mundane. It is doing the right thing day after day after day and moment after moment. It is not these big movements. It is not these big statements of great profound eloquence. It really is doing it every day. I cannot say it often enough: treating people fairly, decently—respecting them for who they are—knowing that none of us is perfect.

In 1966, thirty long years before the fall of apartheid, South African students heard Robert Kennedy proclaim:

Some believe there is nothing one man or one woman can do against the enormous array of the world's ills. Yet many of the world's great movements of thought and action have flowed from the work of a single person.... It is from numberless diverse acts of courage and belief that human history is shaped. Each time a person stands up for an ideal, or acts to improve the lot of others, or strikes out against injustice, he or she sends forth a tiny ripple of hope. And crossing each other from a million different centers of energy and daring, those ripples build a current that can sweep down the mightiest walls of oppression and resistance.[8]

The prophets appealed to the people of God to wake up to the injustices being perpetrated right in their midst. Each person standing up, striking out against injustice—even in the midst of the mundane—sends out a ripple of hope.

At its core, biblical faith has a sense of expectation called hope. The prophets clung to the conviction that judgment proclaimed out of hope for a renewed relationship with the Divine would yield a better, more just, and peaceful future. Far from being hateful or unpatriotic, today's prophets engage in social criticism out of that same hope, a conviction that "doing justice" is essential to expressing both a vital faith and building a world at peace.

17

Incarnation
Divinely Human

The day will come when the mystical generation of Jesus
by the Supreme Being as his father, in the womb of
a virgin, will be classed with the fable of the
generation of Minerva in the brain of Jupiter.[1]

—Thomas Jefferson

We really don't know the what, where, or how of Jesus's birth. Maybe April? That's when Luke's shepherds would likely have been out on the hillsides. Certainly not on December 25th—that's the birthday of Mithra, patron god of the Roman Legions whose birthday was co-opted by Christians some 400 years later. Luke says the family lived in Nazareth and traveled to Bethlehem where there was no room at the inn, but shepherds and angels were in attendance. Matthew tells us the family already lived in a house in Bethlehem. And Herod, the wise men, and a wandering star played the big parts.

Our earliest witnesses to Jesus's life, Paul and Mark, are evidently unaware of anything miraculous about his birth—in fact, Paul says just the opposite. As Paul introduced himself and his message to the Romans, he described Jesus as having been "descended from David according to the flesh" (Rom. 1:3). He mentions no virgin birth or any of the elements most people have come to associate with the Christmas story. To Paul's mind, Jesus was only declared to be the "Son of God" by having been resurrected from the dead (Rom. 1:4), a decidedly adoptionist—and according to later church councils, heretical—interpretation of the data.

The Gospel of Mark skips all of Jesus's evidently unremarkable early life and jumps straight to the beginning of his ministry—while John goes the other direction and places Jesus at the beginning of time, participating in the very act of Creation.

SO WHAT WILL IT BE?

We haven't even begun to consider the multitude of other Gospels that didn't make the cut into the canon of scripture. Some were left out for theological reasons, some for political reasons, but most were dropped when the church was trying to develop an identity and, in modern terms, spin the story of Jesus in the third and fourth centuries. A dip into the Infancy Gospel of James will net the reader strange and wonderful details of Jesus's birth, most of which, while not the "official" story, have nonetheless taken root in our psyches through their representation in historic art, oral tradition—and Christmas cards! It's in the Infancy Gospel of James that you find a clear statement that Joseph is an "old man"—much older than the "girl," Mary (Chapter 9), that Mary rides a donkey to Bethlehem (Chapter 17), and that the manger was in a cave (Chapter 18). In Chapters 19 and 20, Salome doubts the testimony of the midwife claiming that a virgin has given birth, declaring, "As the Lord my God liveth, unless I thrust in my finger, and search the parts, I will not believe that a virgin has brought forth." Upon further investigation, Salome satisfies herself that Mary still bears the physical characteristics of a virgin, despite having just given birth. Salome then cries out in woe over the iniquity of her unbelief, doing her part to set in motion the doctrine of Mary's perpetual virginity.

JUST ANOTHER VIRGIN BIRTH

*The two men who contributed most to the church's thought
of the divine meaning of the Christ were Paul and John,
who never even distantly allude to the virgin birth.*[2]

—Harry Emerson Fosdick

From Roman emperors to the Buddha to the Greek Adonis to the Mesoamerican Quetzalcoatl, virgin and extraordinary births are commonplace in cultures around the world. Be it Zoroaster of Persia or Krishna of India, Mithra, Prometheus, Indra, or Horus born to the virgin Isis, Jesus is in not so rare company when it comes to his conception and birth.

Mythologist Joseph Campbell notes, "[Virgin birth stories are] recounted everywhere; and with such striking uniformity of the main contours, that the early Christian missionaries were forced to think that the devil himself must be throwing up mockeries of their teaching wherever they set their hand."[3]

John Dominic Crossan offers some examples, including the testimony of the historian Suetonius, who relates the birth of Caesar Augustus as a divine act:

His mother actually fell asleep in the Temple of Apollo, Apollo impregnated her and that makes him a divine son of god apart even from Julius Caesar who was his adopted father and also divine. Back home in bed, by the way, Octavius imagines the sun arising from his wife's womb. So this is a classical way of saying Caesar is destined by God to run the world. The birth of

Alexander, sort of the model for Augustus, was actually a virgin birth—the marriage had not been consummated when he was born. So in this world if you wanted to say this is the person that should be running the world, whose program establishes global peace, global justice (all that good stuff) you will start with a virgin birth and/or a divine birth, at least.

Toward the end of the first century, the regions in which the Gospels were developing were undergoing culturally disruptive and often violent change. The year 70 saw the Roman Legion obliterating Jerusalem and its Temple and scattering Jewish refugees throughout the Mediterranean. As the teachings of Jesus spread throughout the empire and as his credibility came into direct competition with other religious figures, stories developed about his birth that sounded strangely similar to the births of the pagan deities that dominated the known world. By the 90s, various versions of Jesus's miraculous birth were widespread and Matthew and Luke incorporated two of these versions into their Gospels.

This wasn't an intentional effort to deceive their audience. Culver "Bill" Nelson explains:

The virgin birth story was an honest mistake. Most liberal theologians believe that the author of the Gospel of Matthew (or someone who supplied the writer with source material) scanned an unknown ancient Greek translation of the Hebrew scriptures. He found what he believed to be a reference to Jesus's birth in Isaiah 7:14. This has since become a famous passage often recited at Christmas time. He simply copied it into Matthew (1:23) as a method of showing that prophecies in the Hebrew Testament were fulfilled in Jesus's life. As it happens, the Greek translators had made a mistake. When they were translating the Hebrew writings into the Greek Septuagint and similar translations, they converted the Hebrew word *almah* as the Greek equivalent of our English word for virgin. Almah appears nine other times in the

Hebrew scriptures. In each case it means "young woman." When the scriptures referred to a virgin (and they do over fifty times) they always used the Hebrew word *betulah*. So Isaiah appears to have referred to a young woman becoming pregnant, a rather ordinary event.

Whether it is from the study of comparative religions or a thoughtful understanding of the Judeo-Christian texts themselves, Jesus's virgin birth takes its place among the almost countless extraordinary births meant to engender divinity and importance to political and religious figures across time. While unquestioning belief in the historical fact of the virgin birth remains a litmus test for many "true" Christians, this literal interpretation of the notion of incarnation limits the presence of the Spirit to one time, one place, and one unique person.

This claim to Jesus's unique and holy nature has been the focal point of debate and rancor for nearly 2,000 years.

MAKING SENSE OF ESSENCE

Foreshadowing elements of Jesus's birth and life, *The Wisdom of Solomon* was but one document circulating in the years prior to Jesus's appearance that likely contributed to his later legend. It reads:

> I also am mortal, like everyone else, a descendant of the first-formed child of earth; and in the womb of a mother I was molded into flesh, within the period of ten months, compacted with blood, from the seed of a man and the pleasure of marriage. And when I was born, I began to breathe the common air, and fell upon the kindred earth; my first sound was a cry, as is true of all. I was nursed with care in swaddling cloths. For no king has had a different beginning of existence; there is for all one entrance into life, and one way out. Therefore I prayed, and understanding was

given me; I called on God, and the spirit of wisdom came to me. (Wisd. of Sol. 7:1–7)

But the story of an unassuming human who called on God and to whom the spirit of wisdom came was not always an impressive sell in the shadow of the Pantheon and mystery religions of the day. Yet it was enough for many followers in the early centuries of Christianity. Although eventually declared a heretic by later councils, the third-century Bishop of Samosata was not alone in his belief that Jesus was the "Son of God" simply on account of his holy life and good deeds.

Was Jesus simply a man whose remarkable life could only be spoken of in terms of divinity? Was he God incarnate, only pretending to be a human being? Was he something in between? Did he somehow possess the same or similar "essence" of the Divine? These and other questions of Christology, or the nature of Christ, became the central debate among Christians in the fourth century. The infighting became so acrimonious, with gangs of hoodlums fighting on behalf of one bishop or the other in the streets of Alexandria, that Constantine saw it as a threat to his unification of the East and West into the new Roman Empire.

After several failed diplomatic attempts to negotiate an agreement between the bishops, the emperor called the first ecumenical council to order in Nicea to try to reach consensus on issues of Christology. Meeting in 325, the approximately 300 bishops set to arguing over the essence of divinity—while Constantine called it "a fight over trifling and foolish verbal differences."[4] At issue was what has come to be called the Arian Controversy. The Arians from the East believed that Jesus was not born divine but made divine in life. Their leader, Arius, was eventually voted down, exiled by Constantine, and his writings burned.

Although the Council of Nicea produced what we now call the "Nicene Creed," it was not adopted as the official position of the church for more than 100 years. Subsequent councils continued to argue over the definition of incarnation itself, with arguments raging over Jesus's "nature," whether he was "begotten or made," or whether Jesus was of the same or similar "essence" as God.

Bernard Brandon Scott is nearly apoplectic over how the creeds hijacked the direction of the early church and distorted what it meant to be a Jesus follower. He offers an appeal:

> Notice what's missing from the creed, you don't have to *do* any-
> thing. It's all about belief. If you look at early Christianity, prior
> to Constantine, it's about praxis; it's about what you have to *do*.
> But after Constantine it's about what you have to believe. As a
> result you can force people to have an ideological program that's
> identical but you don't have to do a darned thing. We have lived
> with this ever since and it's a disaster.

Contributing to the problem is the subtle way the creeds spiritualize Jesus's life at the expense of his example and teachings. Robin Meyers bemoans the fact that in the creeds, you have the "world's greatest life reduced to a comma." Meyers says:

> Look at the Apostle's Creed and the Nicene Creed: "Born of the
> Virgin Mary, *comma,* suffered under Pontius Pilate...". There
> is the entire life of Jesus, all of his teachings, the parables, his
> interaction with the poor, his way of telling bent over people to
> stand up straight—metaphorically speaking and literally speak-
> ing—all reduced to a comma. The most amazing thing I ever
> heard was put this way to me by a person in The Jesus Semi-
> nar, who said, "In the Sermon on the Mount there is not a word
> in that sermon about what to believe, only words about what to
> do. Fast forward 300 years to the Nicene Creed and the essence
> of what is supposed to define a Christian has not a word in it
> about what to do, only about what to believe." So something's
> gone clearly wrong.

Likewise, Diana Butler Bass, author of *Christianity for the Rest of Us*, points to the need to reevaluate our historic emphasis on the creeds: "I think the shift from having faith *in* Jesus to having beliefs *about* Jesus was a negative thing for the church. And to have a person's orthodoxy, a person's right relationship with God tested on the nature of what we believe about something is deeply troubling to me. It's troubling to me as a Christian; it's troubling to me as a postmodern person; and I just don't think it works anymore."

Yet today, countless Christians blithely recite the creeds without any sense of their original intent, the manner in which they came into being, or any thought that their original meaning could have ceased to have any relevance to contemporary life. Many Christians simply assume that it is and always has been a fact that "Jesus is God"—without thinking about any of the theological implications of such an idea for a so-called monotheistic religion.

As a monotheistic Jew himself, it doesn't make any sense that the historic Jesus would have even considered such a claim. It's not surprising, though, taking into account the propagandistic nature of the New Testament writings, that Godlike status was soon attributed to Jesus. Theologians looking for ways to make sense of the "person" of Jesus and compete with the reputations of other "God-men" in antiquity cobbled together ideas like the Trinity, something never overtly mentioned in the biblical text.

The humble mortal we call Jesus would likely be horrified at his deification by generations of well-meaning followers. It is simply inconceivable that the sage teacher and rabbi who pointed beyond himself to the kingdom of God would have elevated himself to the second member of the Trinity, let alone "God from God, light from light, true God from true God." Yet for many Christians, this is the perplexing nature of incarnation—despite options for more practical interpretations.

John Dominic Crossan says, "When I say 'the incarnation,' here's what I mean: That as a Christian, if I want to give you my best explanation of what God looks like in sandals, I'm going to say 'Jesus.'"

Evidently, the earliest disciples experienced the Spirit of Life in Jesus in a way that made his presence so transformational for people that the only way they felt they could describe their experience was by attributing it to the Divine. The challenge for today's Jesus followers is to get back on the other side of all the divisive claims *about* Jesus and his claimed status and embrace his life and teachings as the focus of a life of faith here and now.

Grounded in the prophetic tradition of Judaism, the historical Jesus was your standard-issue human being, but one who had a unique and powerful way of expressing compassion, righteous indignation, and visions for a just world, all wrapped up with the integrity to die for those convictions. Make him into God and all those virtues go into the "so what?" category. Big deal. It's just God playacting.

On the other hand, if Jesus really was truly human (and not some Docetic illusion) then it makes his having completely rebooted his followers' concept of the Divine even more remarkable. Brian McLaren says:

> Jesus's contemporaries didn't just think he was a godly man. There were a lot of godly people. They didn't simply take their pre-existing idea of God and claim that Jesus resembles that idea of God. What happened in their encounter with Jesus was much more radical than that. They found themselves deconstructing their original idea of God in light of their experience of Jesus. So that they gradually moved into a new concept of God, one re-imagined in the image of Jesus—God with us, not distant from us; God who suffers with and for us, not one who inflicts suffering upon us; a nonviolent God who forgives us as we torture him, not a God who threatens to torture us unless we submit.

As far as the synoptic Gospels seem to indicate, Jesus went out of his way to try to live in a manner that short-circuited an "us versus them" mentality, gathering together people who were excluded by purity laws and extending to them what appeared to the authorities as undeserved grace. Yet it seems that even in the first generation of his followers, Jesus was elevated to Divine status, laying the groundwork for an imperial us versus them belief-based movement. The early church then wielded the creeds as dogmatic, belief-oriented proof of one's allegiances claiming, in no uncertain terms, "You're either with us or against us—and we're with *God!*"

But for many today, the creeds have become divisive and counter-productive. Demanding that incarnation be interpreted in a strict technical manner only furthers the councils' failed attempts at arriving at an objective explanation of who Jesus was. Furthermore, in an increasingly pluralistic and secular world, such exclusive claims foster conflict among those who continue to play the my-god-is-bigger-than-your-god game. Perhaps it is in the "comma" that seekers can find a glimpse of Jesus's true essence: the witness of his life, his teachings, and his dynamic (and very human) relationship with the mystery that is the Divine.

INCARNATION FOR THE REST OF US

Where love and caring are, there is God.

—Taizé chant

The seventeenth-century English poet John Donne tells the story of one man's search for God. When told that God lived at the top of a mountain at the end of the earth, he makes the journey there and begins to climb. At the same time, God thinks, "What can I do to show my people I love them?" So God decides to travel down from the mountain and live among the people as one of them. As God goes down the opposite side of the mountain from the man climbing up, they miss one another. At the summit, the man discovers an empty mountaintop. Heartbroken, he concludes that God must not exist.

Despite speculation to the contrary, God doesn't live on mountain-tops, at the ends of the earth, or even in "some heaven, light years away."

From the mystics of old to today's evolutionary theologians, the collective wisdom suggests a profoundly intimate and interconnected Divinity. The true "essence" of incarnation is God's indwelling in all of creation, from the smallest yet-to-be-identified particle to the furthest reaches of the cosmos.

Limiting the Divine to one place or one time or one culture-bound expression creates barriers to deeper understandings of the mystery of life. Indoctrination into one way of thinking makes it difficult to change our ideas of God and Jesus and how they relate to one another. John Shelby Spong suggests that, even in the midst of change, there is hope. He says:

> The virgin birth story is no longer taken literally. In the life of Jesus, however, we still believe that there was a literal experience of a living God. Maybe that forces us to rethink God and if we can stop thinking of God as a great big parent figure up in the sky — a supernatural being who is external to life — we can begin to think of God as the life power itself, the power of love itself, the "Ground of Being" as Paul Tillich described it, which is always emerging in you and me and which emerged in Jesus of Nazareth in some remarkable kind of way that opens new doorways into the Holy for us.

Christians who want to take Jesus seriously need to take his humanity seriously, for Jesus has revealed what it means to be fully human. By living into the fullness of his humanity, Jesus demonstrated a way of being that could only be described by his early followers as divine. As Athanasius suggested even in the fourth century, "He became what we are that he might make us what he is."

Robin Meyers says:

> Incarnation means, to me, that the Spirit of God was pleased to dwell fully in Jesus of Nazareth. He was a reflection of God. He

was not metaphysically made up of one substance with God. But when people looked at him, and listened to him, and received his ministry they felt the presence of God in some powerful and definitive way. That's the Incarnation, [and it's] very important for us to hang on to. It's one of the things that makes Christianity unique. There's really no other world religion that is so fully grounded in a person, in a human being.

Throughout most of Christianity's history, God has been understood as an external deity manipulating and coercing our lives from on high. So it was necessary to try to connect the divinity "out there" with our lowly lives "down here." The Gospel writers tried to explain it with virgin births and resurrections. Councils tried to define it with formulas and creeds. What traditional Christianity has been left with is a legacy of two millennia trying to describe and explain a Divinity that is incarnational. Christian believers have had to settle for some version of a belief that, "in some incomprehensible way," the mystery of God was perceived to be incarnate in Jesus.

But for process theologians like John B. Cobb Jr., incarnation need not be an exercise in theological and cosmological gymnastics. Cobb points out that the Divine is (and always has been) intimately involved in "every moment of human experience:"

> In human beings, God is the source of novelty, of purpose, of meaning, of openness to others, of freedom, of responsibility, and of much else besides. Far from diminishing our humanity, God is the giver of that humanity. The more fully God is present, the more fully we are human.[5]

God is "in process" with humanity, constantly changing and evolving with us. So despite the fact that each of us is a clumsy mix of good and bad—assumptions, prejudices, actions, and intentions—God is sometimes able to have God's way with us. If there is any truth to the Christmas affirmation, "God is with us," then the Divine can't be anything but involved in our affairs, getting dirty with us, and sometimes, because the Spirit is incarnate in us, effecting beauty in and through us.

While firmly in the "Random Acts of Kindness" category, Sylvia Slaton's story is nonetheless a story of incarnation. After feeding expired parking meters in downtown Cincinnati so the parked cars would not be ticketed, the sixty-three-year-old grandmother of ten was convicted of obstructing official business and fined $500. A lifelong Sunday school teacher in her Presbyterian church, she stood up to the city, became a local folk hero, and inspired a generation of guerilla parking-meter feeders. Years later, having resolved their differences, the city honored Sylvia with a memorial parking meter.

Be it the sublime or the ridiculous, for better or for worse, what we *do* is the measure of the incarnation in the world. Approaching life incarnationally can have consequences. One needs to be prepared for situations that take risk, that can be messy, that include speaking out or standing up for people; that might even mean making a personal sacrifice for someone else's sake.

The incarnation is finally not just about Jesus alone but about us. How will we respond to the call to make the love of God real in the world? Wherever we find ourselves, the mystery of life dwells within us, not limited to a time or place, but manifest in every aspect of our lives.

18

Prayer

Intimacy with the Divine

When St. Paul said that we are to pray without ceasing,
he surely did not mean we ought to say prayers without
ceasing. When people envision the kingdom of heaven
as a place where people are praying all the time,
I'd just as soon not go if that is the reality
that you have to deal with.

—John Shelby Spong

Rabbi Harold Kushner thinks he knows God's favorite book of the Bible. It's the Psalms. In the rest of the Bible, God is said to speak to us—"through seers, sages, and prophets, through the history of the Israelite people. But in the Psalms, we speak to God. We tell God of our love, our needs, our gratitude."[1] But more than that it shows enough confidence in the relationship to shake our fist in anger. The Psalms show the nature of covenant relationships to be conversation, familiarity and the confidence to express anger, lament, and dissatisfaction with the way things are. What we think of as prayer—along with other concepts of intimacy with the Divine — are testimony to humanity's striving toward relating to that unknowable yet inescapable sense of "the More."

THE PROBLEM
WITH PRAYER

Prayer is in dire need of a makeover. Tired clichés and rote childhood memories are the extent of many people's prayer repertoire. Prayers that have been taught to children in good faith can verge on the downright creepy when considering their potential for theological and psychological distress:

"Now I lay me down to sleep, I pray the Lord my soul to keep.

If I should die before I wake, I pray the Lord my soul to take."

Many people approach prayer in a way that makes God into a cosmic vending machine: insert prayer into slot, make your selection, and if you're good, voila! The outcome you had in mind. The proof texts quoted regarding prayer would seem to support such an understanding:

"Whatever you ask for in prayer with faith, you will receive" (Matt. 21:22).

"Ask, and it will be given you" (Luke 11:9).

In Matthew 7, Jesus seems to say that whatever we ask will be given to us. In Luke 18, Jesus tells a parable about persistence in prayer: pray, pray, pray and God will eventually give in. Matthew 18:19 has Jesus saying, "If two of you agree on earth about anything you ask, it will be done for you by my Father in heaven."

The problem lies in taking all of these verses out of context. Far from being willy-nilly guarantees of whatever you want, they are instead about making the reign of God real on earth through acts of healing, reconciliation, and justice. When the disciples ask Jesus how to pray, they are taught the "Lord's Prayer," a prayer to sustain and guide them in doing whatever work is necessary in bringing about the kingdom.

PRAYER ABUSE

Truth be told, most people are "foxhole pray-ers," crying out in the midst of disaster: "Lord, if only you'd get me out of _____, I promise to do _____!" And if we're not making deals with God, we're treating the Divine like some sort of Santa Claus for adults: "I want, I want, I want…" Oftentimes, prayer is confused with magic—passionately stringing together the proper words into incantations in hope of conjuring up the power to realize our desires.

The type of prayers where we ask for things on behalf of others is called "intercessory" prayer. Prayers for one's self—heal my cancer, end my loneliness, solve my problems—are called "petitionary" prayers. Although they're the type of prayers people pray all the time, they're dangerous. As many people still perceive the Divine to be in the reward and punishment business, when the prayers aren't answered, people beat themselves up with guilt because they're obviously not good enough or faithful enough for God to answer in the affirmative.

Such an attitude is easy to understand when one reads a passage like James 5:16: "The prayer of the righteous is powerful and effective." If my prayer is not effective, I must not be righteous enough. Taken to its logical outcome, this type of prayer assumes the existence of a malleable deity obliged to change the direction of the whole world just to please the desires of a supposedly righteous person or two.

In the movie *Bruce Almighty*, Jim Carrey's character, Bruce, is imbued with the power of God. After several miserable attempts to respond to every individual prayer being lifted up to God, he finally succumbs and answers, "Yes," to everything. In the pandemonium that ensues, it becomes clear that a good deal of what people pray for is not healthy, reasonable, or legal.

As 1985's Hurricane Gloria bore down on the east coast of the United States, televangelist Pat Robertson prayed for God to change the storm's course to avoid hitting his Virginia headquarters. When the hurricane did indeed veer to the north, Robertson claimed that the phenomenon was proof of God's love for and approval of his ministry. Too bad for the folks on Long Island whose homes were destroyed and lives devastated.

In Q&A sessions following his lectures, John Shelby Spong is inevitably asked about his practice of prayer. Growing out of a deeply personal experience, he's quick to point out how our understanding of prayer reflects our view of the Divine—often with unintended consequences:

> My wife had a diagnosis of cancer in December of 1981 with the expectation of maybe two years to live at most and a lot of prayer groups were formed across New Jersey, well beyond the boundaries of the Episcopal Church—and I appreciated that because that was a love gift. These people were saying we care about you; we care about your wife. We want somehow to do something for you, to be with you in this crisis. You accept that gift graciously. My wife lived six and a half years from diagnosis to death, not two years, and as she passed the two-year boundary, the prayer groups began to take credit for her longevity as if their prayers were actually curing her or pushing back the disease. It was almost as if it were a battle between God and Satan and they were on God's side. Satan was being pushed back because these God-fearing people were praying. Again, without meaning to be pejorative and with deep appreciation for the love that was expressed in that, I could not help but wonder if God really would operate that way. If God would allow my wife to live six and a half years instead of two years because lots of people prayed for her because I was a well-known public figure in New Jersey. I thought, suppose a garbage collector in downtown Newark, which is America's poorest per capita city, had a wife who had cancer. I just cannot imagine God saying, "Well, I am getting a lot of prayers about the bishop's wife so let's give her an extra four years. Nobody, however, is praying for this garbage collector's wife, so I will let her die quickly." I cannot imagine that. And if I could imagine that, I would become an atheist. If that is the way God operates, I want no part of that manipulative deity.

Yet faithful people continue to lift up the scripture passages that seem to suggest, "Just pray enough and God will provide." Personal experience and common sense tell us that such claims are simply not so. In the American Civil War, both world wars, and countless other conflicts, opposing forces prayed to the same God for victory. Meanwhile, it's not hard to understand how a concentration camp survivor could ask, How can I still pray to God after the holocaust?

Imagine the victims of a horrible plane crash arriving at the pearly gates only to be informed by God, "Sorry, I would have loved to intervene but there weren't enough of you praying for it." Or the alternative: God reaching down to catch the plane and, defying all physical laws of the universe, lightly sets the plane down upon the earth — "Whew, good thing you all prayed!" Neither scenario makes sense.

On the other hand, there's a whole new branch of neuroscience devoted to uncovering the connections between one's mind and body. Called "psychoneuroimmunology," it explores the effect that one's emotional and spiritual well-being have on the immune system. Double-blind studies have indicated that people who pray and are prayed for recover more quickly than those not prayed for — a continued testimony to what we have yet to learn about our deep interrelatedness as a part of creation.

So pray for healing — not because you will always get well, but so that you can connect with the still mysterious and natural power of healing. Pray for safe travel — not because God will necessarily catch your plane, but so that you can be prepared for whatever happens. Pray for the end to a drought, for a job, for a "fill in the blank" — not because prayer is going to control the weather, a future employer, or anything else, but so you can avoid the temptation to despair of God's goodness in time of difficulty.

Isn't that defeatist? Darkly existentialist? No, it's acknowledging the reality that life is what it is. "There is a time for every matter under heaven" (Eccles. 3:1) gives a rhythm to being human. Personal experience confirms that the rain falls on both the good and the bad. And for many, prayer helps in raising an awareness of the Divine who shares in both the joys and sorrows of life.

Spong believes:

> There is something that we do not yet understand about how love connects us, how life is bound together, how we are far more interdependent than we think. God is the very relationship that binds us together and somehow when we open ourselves to that, it can be an effective way of loosing God's power in the world. I believe God's power, which is love and life, is always beneficial, always enhancing, and even therapeutic.

TOW-TRUCK THEOLOGY

Episcopal priest Robert Farrar Capon was once asked about the efficacy of prayer. He responded that many people simply have the wrong idea about prayer. God is not in the business of prioritizing who will be protected or saved based on whoever is more worthy than someone else.[2] Imagine the situation: you get to work to pull a double shift, but a blizzard is coming. There'll be no customers, so the boss sends you home. Traffic is already tied up on the interstate, so you decide to take a back road shortcut. The storm comes on faster than you expect, the conditions deteriorate rapidly and you skid off into a ditch and are knocked unconscious. When you come to, the snow is piled up around your car and you can't open the doors. You have no cell phone. Your family is not expecting you for hours, they have no idea about your shortcut, and you begin to realize that things are not looking good.

Tow-truck theology says that at this point, you say a prayer for God to rescue you. As you're a pretty good person, God responds by tickling the ear of a gas station attendant on the interstate. He gets a funny feeling that he should put some hot chicken soup in a Thermos, grab the keys to the tow truck and drive down a deserted back road in a blizzard for reasons that are unclear. Miraculously, he manages to make out your car buried in the snow, digs in, pulls you out, warms you up with chicken soup, and has you home in time for dinner. Although this may be the way many people understand prayer, it's not the way it works.

The faith we claim as Christians is not an insurance policy against tragedy and loss. Capon continues to explain that the Divine has a "covenant of presence" with us. God will be with us, no matter what. As hard as it is to fathom, when we find ourselves stuck in that blizzard with very little likelihood that a tow truck is miraculously on its way, God is with us, and stays with us — until we die.[3]

It is a common temptation among faithful Christians of all stripes to believe — deep down — that if we're good, God will protect us and rescue us from life's difficulties. But being in relationship with God does not create some sort of divine force field protecting us from harm. Being in relationship with God strengthens us for living life, come what may.

In difficult times when our most heartfelt petitions seem to go unanswered and we feel abandoned by the Divine, people often wonder what they've done to deserve such a fate. Even Jesus is said to have cried out from the cross, "My God, My God, why have you forsaken me?" (Matt. 27:46). The experience of faithful people over the ages suggests that God is not, in fact, in charge of dispatching tow trucks. Instead, the Spirit that gives us life longs to be recognized as an intimate companion on our life's journey. We are in covenant with the Spirit that remains with us whatever happens along life's journey.

IT'S A MATTER OF SEEING

Seldom, if ever, do two people have the same experience and perceive it in exactly the same way. On the journey of life, we accumulate filters through which we see the world. By changing the filter on the lens of a camera, the photographer doesn't change the scene but the interpretation of the scene. So it is with the spiritual life. Frederick and Mary

Ann Brussat suggest, "Just as photographers use filters on their lenses to remove haze from a scene or to enhance the brightness of a certain color, [spiritual] filters emphasize particular understandings of the sacred. Filters do not change the scene as much as they change the perception."[4]

Simply paying attention is the foundation of all spiritual practices. To that end, the Brussats encouraged readers to recognize the presence of the sacred in everyday experiences. The poet and doctor William Carlos Williams used to carry a notepad around with him in which he listed "Things I noticed today that I've missed until today."[5] Buddhist monk and author, Thich Nhat Han, advocates pursuing "mindfulness," a practice that includes paying attention to even the most mundane of activities.[6] Instead of rushing through life to get to something else, try concentrating intently on every aspect of brushing your teeth, climbing stairs, or washing dishes. Each activity has the potential to center a person in the moment and overcome the tendency to let the self-chatter of the mind drown out an awareness of the now.

Peace activist Rick Ufford-Chase finds prayer expressed in conversation, play, and other unexpected moments:

> I do most of my prayer in dialogue with other people. I feel most connected to God when I'm playing with new ideas with someone else about who God's calling us to be. I remember when I was in college I was part of InterVarsity and there was a lot of emphasis, of course, placed on daily reflection. And I just couldn't make it happen. Morning after morning, I'd get up and I'd try and make it happen. Then I'd try it at night and it didn't matter what time of day I tried it, I'd fall asleep every time. I just couldn't focus. I finally called my dad and said, "What do you do? You're a minister." And he said, "Well, I think I'm more like you. You know, for years I've gotten up at 5 o'clock in the morning, gotten you kids off to school, then I go into work by 7 A.M. Nobody else is around in the church. I'd pour myself a cup of coffee and I read the funny papers. And it's quiet time when nobody else bothers me and sometimes

moments of great insight happen—sometimes they don't—and that's prayer for me." It just kind of freed me to know that prayer's going to work differently for different people. My guess is it will work differently for me at different moments in my life. I'll have different ways of engaging God through prayer. Play is a huge way for me to engage God. I find that playing hard and laughing with friends and family makes my heart sing. And, every once in a while, I manage to go to Quaker meeting and have some kind of genuine insight in the midst of quiet and genuine contemplation.

Spiritual director and author William Martin tells the story of how we came to be so distracted:

Once upon a time, the heavenly host gathered in the celestial boardroom and Yahweh (Chair of the Board), asked what they thought of the whole "heaven and earth" project. The heavenly host sang out, "Holy, Holy, Holy, God. Heaven and Earth are full of your Glory!" Ha Satan, however, was heard to mutter, "Kiss-ups."

As Yahweh made a fuss over how grand the creation of male and female were, Ha Satan could not help but call attention to their tendency to disobey. Yahweh admitted that to be true, and promptly began praising their capacity for compassion. Aggravated, Ha Satan called attention to subparagraph 288 of the Cosmic Charter stating that disobedience must be punished. Yahweh agreed but pointed out that it also stated that compassion must be blessed.

Yahweh was so overwhelmed with the potential of male and female, the Creator poured out a spontaneous blessing on them that was unique among all the other inhabitants of heaven and earth. They alone would possess a distinctive capacity for memory that enabled them to recall and learn from the past. They would also be gifted with an unrivaled imagination that enabled them to envision the future and create wondrous things.

Following the pronouncement of the blessings, Yahweh began to dismiss the board. Ha Satan protested loudly, "I object to your having blessed the male and female when the regulations clearly state that you must punish them as well as bless them!" Yahweh replied, "I did."[7]

Although blessed with the gifts to remember the past and imagine the future, the same capacities also torment us. We wallow in despair, dwelling on the wounds of the past or cowering in anxiety over potential disasters concocted by our fertile imaginations. In so doing, we essentially spend the majority of our conscious time in the past or in the future—not present to the reality of the here and now.

It's been said that there are only two questions that really matter on the spiritual path. The first is: Where am I? The second is: What time is it? There is only one answer to each of these questions: Here and Now. The only time and place one can encounter the Divine is here and now—not in the past or in the future.

A FUTURE FOR PRAYER?

Rejoice in hope, be patient in suffering, persevere in prayer.

—Romans 12:12

Perhaps the future of prayer rests in our ability to liberate it from simply being an exercise in begging, asking, or informing God of anything. According to Winnie Varghese, the point of prayer is "to take us back to the silence of the deep knowing within ourselves of our own worthiness and unity with God." In an apocryphal story, Mother Teresa is asked by a reporter: "When you pray, what do you say?" She replies, "Nothing; I listen." "What do you hear?" asks the reporter. "Nothing. God listens." Seeing the puzzled look on the reporter's face, she assures him, "If I have to explain it to you, you won't understand." Deeper than a "conversation" with the Divine, perhaps prayer is best understood as simply being open to the Divine.

Being open to the Divine takes work and is not simply a matter of being trained in "Five Easy Steps to Intimacy with God." Those who seem to have the most profound relationships with the Spirit tend to practice what most people would call meditation. Disciplines like Tai Chi, Yoga, and Buddhist meditation practices have proven to be helpful for those seeking a deeper connection with the Divine.

In the Judeo-Christian tradition, Paul claims that the purpose of prayer is not to let God know what we need or want (Rom. 8:26). The purpose of prayer is to intentionally be in God's presence, to live lavishly in a relationship that Philosopher-Theologian Martin Buber called an "I-Thou" relationship. I-Thou relationships do not objectify other people (or the Divine) into "I-it" connections to be used for one's own selfish purposes. An I-Thou attitude acknowledges that where we are most clearly going to meet God is in the dynamic of relationships with other people. Maybe it's in a relationship that has been strained or broken. In even a brief shimmer of possible reconciliation, the awareness of the mystery of grace can be intoxicating. What is that other than the Holy?

To transform God's image from some sort of list-checking, gift-giving Santa Claus for adults is a tall order—and part of the change will come in redefining the purpose and practice of prayer. Prayer is not magic. Praying harder is not going to get you what you want or even what you think would be good for the world. Much of prayer's real power is in changing us. As Richard Rohr writes: "Prayer is not about changing God, but being willing to let God change us."[8] When we are changed, we may be able to see things in a new way or find the strength to live faithfully with what we cannot change. John B. Cobb Jr. brings a process theology perspective to prayer when he observes:

> The function of prayer is to open ourselves to God's gracious working in our lives and to seek to align our own intentions with God's call to us. This should be the total stance of our lives, not

limited to times of prayer. But surely prayer can be an occasion for focusing on this relationship and overcoming obstacles to it. As we live more in harmony with God's purposes, we will act or pray as we are led, believing that what we do matters to others and to God as well as to ourselves.[9]

When Paul tells the Thessalonians to "pray without ceasing" (1 Thess. 5:17), he's not advocating that they constantly pray for more stuff. Nor are they to pray to change the mind and the behavior of a controlling theistic deity. Instead, they—and we—are to seek an attitude toward life in which prayer is seamlessly integrated into our very being, where we can give thanks no matter what happens.

Like any pursuit of intimacy, prayer is intensely personal. In all its many forms, prayer defies analysis and superficial systems for implementation and success. Sometimes reduced to rummaging around for whatever gets us through the day, prayer is a lifelong courtship—testimony to humanity's striving toward a relationship with that unknowable yet inescapable sense of what Marcus Borg calls, "the More."

19

Compassion
The Heart of Jesus's Ministry

Considering the witness of the Gospels, you wouldn't be thought strange to claim that the essence of Jesus's ministry might be distilled down into one word: compassion. The three synoptic Gospels record Jesus identifying the most important commandment—and he was not the only one in his time to quote Deuteronomy in lifting up the priorities of loving "God with your whole heart, soul, strength, and mind, and to love your neighbor as you love yourself." Jesus made it clear throughout his ministry that the standard of behavior he expected of his followers was not only love of neighbor, but love of outcasts and enemies, as well—genuine love, acted upon even at a cost and risk to oneself.

To understand Jesus's commitment to the practice of compassion, it helps to know a little about the world into which he was born. Roman annexation of Palestine in 63 BCE created an unsettling mix of religious, political, and economic conflict. With the Roman presence affecting almost every aspect of life, the task of remaining a faithful Jew became increasingly challenging. The response of some Jews in Jesus's time was to commit themselves to the Torah's holiness code and submit to God's mandate to "...be holy, for I the Lord your God am holy" (Lev. 19:2).

Unfortunately, the concept of holiness carried with it the notion of achievable perfection. As a result, this particular group of Jews emphasized the portions of the Law that stressed separateness. Jewish life was polarized into clean and unclean, pure and defiling, sacred and profane. People, too, were divided into categories of clean or unclean, righteous or sinner.

Jewish movements like the Essenes, credited with being the copyists and creators of the Dead Sea Scrolls, are thought to be an extreme example of this philosophy. They formed an isolated, monastic-like community in the desert, completely separating themselves from others. Perhaps most familiar to readers of the New Testament as practitioners of the holiness code were the Pharisees. Although they are represented as his main opposition in the Gospels, Jesus identified with the Pharisees more than with the Sadducees. While the Sadducees were the literalist Priests bound to the temple, the Pharisees were out in the countryside doing their best to make Judaism doable for the people of the land. Jesus, however, pushed beyond even their comfort level in making Jewish practice and principles accessible. The stress on adherence to purity laws and refusing table fellowship with sinners by some Pharisees evidently created a large group of outcasts and set the stage for the Gospel writers to portray them as Jesus's villainous opposition.

Jesus stepped into this rigid, legalistic environment, flying in the face of the Pharisees' prime directive: separation from anything unclean. Although Jesus identified with the Pharisees who were trying to humanize the law, he still parted company with them on their interpretation of holiness and their strict adherence to separation. Jesus's modus operandi was healing on the Sabbath and dining with sinners and outcasts. He invited his disciples to look beyond the conventional attitudes of his day and see how the way we treat one another is more important than the way we adhere to a set of rigid rules.

Far from ignoring the law or possessing a lack of moral standards, such behavior would include giving up things like oppression, exploitation, coercion, and greed—not to mention the tyranny of having to believe what is correct. By putting behavior ahead of belief in a hierarchy of values, Jesus's disciples are held to a standard that transcends the rules. Followers of Jesus are duty-bound to treat their fellow human beings with kindness, respect, and mercy—no matter the circumstance. Our actions of love are more important than the expression of our beliefs or keeping of the law.

"Compassion was at the center of Jesus's ministry and life," says Ron Buford. "So often in the Gospels you get the sense that Jesus looked into people's eyes, into their hearts, and he saw something. He saw who they were. He saw what they needed. And no matter what law he had to break, if he had to break a law in order to make that person whole or to make their lives better, Jesus did it."

Sister Helen Prejean says:

The miracle stories, especially healing people, brought out the compassion of Jesus. I remember being touched by that story of the leper. Our religion teacher had really brought out how lepers had to live in camps outside, they had to shout, "Unclean!" when people came near and that they were all alone. They must have looked hideous. Jesus was coming along the road and this leper had ventured out and everybody must have been trying to hold him back but he goes, "Jesus, Jesus! If you will, you can make me clean!" And I remember Jesus's response was, "I will," and touched him. That impressed me, that he would touch him. Then gradually, as I studied the scriptures, [I learned] you were made unclean if you touched an unclean person in the holiness code. I learned all about that. But that was one of the stories that touched me when I was a little girl.

There are clearly political as well as personal dimensions to the stories of Jesus's healings. As Brian McLaren points out:

The fact that Jesus is drawn to sick people and sick people are drawn to Jesus tells us something. This isn't a trickle-down redemption, you know? Trickle-down redemption starts with the wealthiest and hopes grace makes its way down. For Jesus, grace is a grassroots, bottom-up work. God starts with those who are suffering, those at the bottom, and God works up from there. And the kinds of healings that are done are so fascinating. Obviously, healing blindness—that's a pretty obvious one; that says a lot about where we begin: without seeing the light, stuck in our own darkness. Then there's the whole category that is described in the New Testament as demon possession. It looks a lot more like what we would call mental illness but it goes even deeper. I think of one encounter Jesus has with this fellow and he says, "What's your name?" He calls out from him the name of what's disturbing him. And the name he gives would be like today somebody saying, "Platoon." He uses a military word, "Legion." What's driving you crazy? What's making you insane? "Platoon." The man is oppressed in spirit by this world that's so militarized, so violent, so full of occupation and oppression. "This is what's making me crazy," the man says. And Jesus restores this man to humanity and sanity by freeing him from the spirit of militarism, you might say. All of the miracles to me are astounding. One of my favorites is this: There's a guy in the synagogue and he has a withered hand, which suggests everything about our ability and our capacity, our ability to manage, to keep things "in hand." In the synagogue Jesus tells him, "Stretch out your hand. Open the hand." That image of calling people in the religious community to have an open hand. All of these miracles, to me, embody everything Jesus says in words. They put it into drama, and body, and action. They're like guerrilla theater, dramatizations of Jesus's liberating words.

NOT GUILTY BY REASON OF COMPASSION

On a certain Sabbath Jesus and his disciples were hungry. Since they happened to be passing through grain fields at the time, they plucked some heads of grain to eat along the way. Evidently, some Pharisees saw this and accused them of breaking the Sabbath (Matt. 12). Although work on the Sabbath was strictly prohibited by the holiness code, Jesus deflected their disapproval by reminding them of a familiar story in Jewish history illustrating how even David did what was unlawful when he and his companions were hungry (1 Sam. 21). Then Jesus quoted one of the most outspoken critics of religious legalism, Hosea, and declared, "If you had known what this means, 'I desire mercy and not sacrifice' you would not have condemned the guiltless" (Matt. 12:6–8).

Jesus continued on his way and came to a synagogue. The Pharisees followed him inside where the text says there was a man with a deformed hand. Once again, Matthew casts the Pharisees as heartless legalists, asking Jesus if it was lawful to heal the man on the Sabbath. Jesus replied, "Suppose one of you has only one sheep and it falls into a pit on the Sabbath; will you not lay hold of it and lift it out? How much more valuable is a human being than a sheep? So it is lawful to do good on the Sabbath" (Matt. 12:11–12).

Jesus's subsequent healing of the man on the Sabbath was another example of his transcending the holiness code with a higher law, the law of compassion. In effect, Jesus said to the self-righteous religious busybodies, "You can take your holiness codes, your strict observance of the law, your sense of righteousness and you can, well, you know what you can do with them!"

Although the Pharisees were quick to pronounce Jesus's guilt, a jury of Jesus's peers would likely have rendered a different verdict: not guilty by reason of compassion. The point of the law is not the law, but people. The law is a human attempt to express an orderliness in life—without which human life in community would be impossible. If the rules get in the way of a single healing, life-giving, compassionate act, they're not to be followed.

Does that mean you're only being compassionate if you're breaking some law or code? No, but it does mean wrestling with what's really important in life—and to know that putting people first is not without cost. Jesus's overturning of the tables in the temple was a passionate criticism of the Sadducees' legalistic temple operations and unethical economic practices. That along with his regular flaunting of the holiness codes were in no small part a contributing factor in his eventual arrest and execution.

THE FIRST SIGN OF CIVILIZATION

Jesus called the disciples to see beyond the conventional attitudes of his day that they might "be merciful just as your Father is merciful" (Luke 6:36). Matthew Fox and others have suggested a better translation as, "Be you compassionate as your Creator in heaven is compassionate." Jesus was not primarily a teacher of either correct beliefs or right morals but of authentic human relationships. Jesus demonstrated a way of life that led to the transformation of those whom he encountered. In fact, Fox reminds us, "For the Jew, compassion is the secret name for God." In striving to be compassionate, in demonstrating what it means to live an authentically *human* life, Jesus is calling us to our divinity.

To be compassionate, therefore, is to recognize our utter interdependence in God's world and to see other people, be they stranger or outcast, as sisters or brothers. Winnie Varghese believes that one of the great stories of Jesus's compassion is that of the Syrophoenician woman:

> At first he rejects her, calls her a dog and says, "How dare you take from me!" She responds, "Even the crumbs of the table are left for the dogs." And [then] it says he has compassion. Interestingly, it's a controversial text because it almost seems that Jesus changes his mind or opens up in some way. That's compassion. Compassion isn't a still thing that we have or we don't have. Compassion evolves. We generate it. It grows. It's a powerful enough story that it stays in the record. We have it. They didn't wipe it off

as a "Jesus mistake." It seems to make Jesus even more authentic to who he was supposed to be. Which is what compassion is. We are drawn out to the people and the situations and the experiences that we don't necessarily believe are our challenge or our struggle or, frankly, aren't our interest. You know, compassion is that we are made bigger, more compassionate, more empathetic, more in love than we have been before.

Compassion brings about transformation—for both the one suffering and for the oppressor. As Minerva Carcaño says:

Compassion toward someone who is hungry comes in one form. Compassion for one who is an oppressor comes in another form. For me the role of compassion varies from context to context, from situation to situation, from person to person. For the one who is hungry physically, I want to feed them and encourage others to do likewise, knowing that in that act of feeding it's not just giving, it's also receiving. For as we share we experience God's love, we experience the presence of Christ Jesus. I am very mindful of the fact that indeed, Christ walks among the poor. And so compassion in that situation is being open to seeing the face of Christ and receiving the blessing of being in communion with someone who hungers, but who probably knows God in very deep and profound ways. Compassion for one who is an oppressor comes in a very different form. It's challenging them to break away from their sin and be made well. It's encouraging them to leave behind that which is neither good for them or for others, and so it comes in a very different way. It's holding that person accountable in love, and yet it is compassion because it's yearning for their well-being, their spiritual well-being, and their wholeness completely in all of their life, just as much as being compassionate in the feeding of one who hungers for daily bread.

Our word *compassion* comes from the Latin and literally means "to bear or feel the suffering" of another—not just intellectually, but viscerally. Language scholars point out that the Hebrew and Aramaic root word for compassion (*racham*) is a plural form of the singular noun "womb." From the singular noun "womb" you move to the plural "compassion." Jesus makes the abstract notion of a plural womb concrete by modeling and teaching the nourishing, life-giving, all-embracing practice of compassion above all things. If laws, rules, or customs get in the way of acting with compassion, then away with them.

Writer Walter Wangerin shows us what Ezekiel's plea for a new heart and a new spirit (Ezek. 18:31) can look like today:

> Every time you meet another human being you have the opportunity. It's a chance at holiness. For you will do one of two things, then. Either you will build him up, or you will tear him down. Either you will acknowledge that he *is*, or you will make him sorry that he is—sorry, at least, that he is *there*, in front of you. You will create, or you will destroy. And the things you dignify or deny are God's own property. They are made, each one of them, in God's own image.... Turn your face truly to the human before you and let her, for one pure moment, shine. Think her important, and then she will suspect that she is fashioned of God.[1]

For this is one of the core values of the Hebrew tradition: beyond simply tolerating the unlovable, it's about breaking with legalistic conventions to be *especially* present to the needs of those who seem unlovable, needful, or who are excluded for whatever reason.

There's a popular story in which a student of anthropologist Margaret Mead asked her to describe the earliest sign of civilization in a given culture. Expecting a treatise on clay pots or crude axes or grinding stones, Dr. Mead's answer was simply "a healed femur," the human thighbone. She went on to explain that a healed femur indicated that someone cared. Someone had to do the injured person's hunting and gathering until the leg healed. The evidence of compassion, she said, is the first sign of civilization.

CHANGED IN AN INSTANT

The Bible is mostly suspicious of people with resources and power because the tendency is that once one has wealth and power, it's easy to forget and become insulated from people who are in need.

In one of his sermons, Harrell Beck quotes Albert Schweitzer, saying "'Concern for people is the beginning of hope.' And when I find somebody hopeless I conclude that they are not very much concerned about anybody. Isn't it funny that the great harbingers of hope in our time have been the Teresas, and the Kings, and the Romeros, and the Gandhis? Good heavens! Of all the people who had a right to resign from hope, maybe Schweitzer was right."[2]

Stephen Covey, author of the best seller, *The Seven Habits of Highly Effective People,* relates an encounter he had on a subway in New York one morning. People were sitting quietly, reading newspapers, lost in thought, or resting with their eyes closed. At the next station, a man and his children entered the subway car. The children were so loud and rambunctious that instantly the whole climate changed.

The man sat down next to Covey and closed his eyes, apparently oblivious to the situation. The children were yelling back and forth, throwing things, even grabbing people's papers. It was very disturbing, and yet the man next to Covey did nothing. It was difficult not to feel irritated. How could this man be so insensitive as to let his children run wild like that and do nothing about it, taking no responsibility at all? It was easy to see that everyone else on the subway felt irritated, too.

Finally, with as much patience and restraint as he could muster, Covey turned to the man and said, "Sir, your children are really disturb-

ing a lot of people. I wonder if you couldn't control them a little more?"
The man lifted his gaze as if to come to a consciousness of the situation
for the first time and said softly, "Oh, you're right. I guess I should do
something about it. We just came from the hospital where their mother
died about an hour ago. I don't know what to think, and I guess they
don't know how to handle it either." Covey was stunned.

"Can you image how I felt at that moment?" he asks. His understanding shifted. He relates, "Suddenly I saw things differently, and because I
saw differently, I thought differently, I felt differently, I behaved differently. My irritation vanished. My heart was filled with the man's pain.
Feelings of sympathy and compassion flowed freely. 'Your wife just died?
I'm so sorry. Can you tell me about it? What can I do to help?' Everything
changed in an instant."[3]

All of this is about the virtue that Marcus Borg says is the acid test for
our faith—the virtue of compassion.[4] The way of Christ—the way of
compassion—is creative, healing, and life-giving. To be compassionate
is to recognize our utter interdependence in God's world.

To see another person, even a stranger, as a sister or brother, is the
beginning of compassion and the embracing of what Jesus preached and
practiced as the primary quality of a life centered in God.

—∞—

JESUS: HOLY COMPASSION

Cumulus lover of all souls
Moved by agony's mountain
And those who live in the valley of despair.

Cloudlike drifter, grief stricken at a friend's tomb
Tear puddle in ancient sand.

Mindful of hidden potential, long concealed by choices
    and isolation,
Showering living water upon a life-parched woman.

Mist of restoration and hope
Even through the crowd's fear-induced fog,
Connecting with a woman's faith filled touch.

Weeping, raising wing formations over Jerusalem
Inviting fledglings to find their home.

Sprinkling mercy on thieves, cowards, the hard-hearted,
And those who execute an Empire agenda.

Bursting with care and prodding over Beth-zatha
Spraying a man poolside with healing invitation.

Sweet Jesus, rain on me
Drench my soul with your heart of compassion.

            —Cynthia Langston Kirk

20

Creative Transformation

Yesterday's faith and discipleship seem to have become
threadbare and impotent. There is an urgent need for
a fresh infusion of faith, new visions of redemptive
grace, and conceptions of discipleship equal
to the deep needs confronting us.[1]

—Lloyd M. Conyers

Creativity and innovation are valued and sought after qualities in virtually every human endeavor—except religion. In many faith traditions, it
is tradition itself that is worshipped, held up as the whole purpose of the
religious enterprise. Be it an infatuation with "smells and bells" or resistance to the use of inclusive language, many faithful people have confused defense of their understanding of right practice and right thinking
with what they call faith.

They insulate themselves from the unpredictable, demanding, transforming nature of the Spirit with a fierce, pious, unbending commitment to
the church. They practice what Richard Rohr has called a "cosmetic piety"
intended to look good on the surface, but lacking any real depth or complexity.[2] Defense of the changeless nature of their revealed truth becomes a
virtue to be aspired to, regardless of how lifeless and rote the practice itself

becomes. Yvetter Flunder has said, "We'd rather have a controlled dead God than a lively chaotic God. We have a funeral for Jesus every Sunday."[3]

To say that the purpose of many churches is the maintenance of the institution is perhaps too noble a sentiment. Many churches have more in common with hospice units, clergy more in common with chaplains than outposts and practitioners of the kingdom of God. It's not just comforting the human patients as they all slowly die off. It is clinging to the threadbare and dying theologies of the past that is at issue. The message itself is on life support. Some are convinced that if we only preached the "true gospel" with more vigor, there would be a great revival. Others have warped the message into an individualistic prosperity-oriented, victory-focused, self-help Kool-Aid. Many have found success by dressing up the message with catchy music, engaging videos, and lighthearted messages. But what needs creativity, what needs to be transformed, is not just the medium but also the core message.

A rapidly growing segment of the population is not involved in organized religion of any sort—and they are not just waiting to be invited. According to Christian pollster George Barna, they are "passionately disinterested" in the church.[4] Add to that the growing media presence of vocal and articulate atheists and the prospects for Christianity as we know it are looking grim. People are simply no longer moved by the notion that they are horrible sinners from birth, redeemed only by the sacrifice of an impossibly perfect man at the hands of a bloodthirsty, tribal God. People no longer see the church as the sole keeper of salvation. Seekers of spiritual integrity and members of the "Church Alumni/ae Association" are finding their own creative ways to fulfill the deepest longings of their souls, free from the perceived, and often very real, hypocrisy of the church.

DATING THE DATING SERVICE

And this is not a new phenomenon. Even back in the 1950s, Thomas Merton observed:

The great tragedy of our age is the fact that (if one dares to say it) there are so many godless Christians. Christians, that is, whose religion is a matter of pure conformity and expediency. Their "faith" is little more than a permanent evasion of reality; a compromise with their deepest life in order to avoid admitting the uncomfortable truth that they no longer have any real need for God or any real vital love for God. They conform to the outward conduct of others just like themselves, and they call this the Church. And these "believers" cling together offering one another an apparent justification for their lives that are essentially the same as their materialistic neighbors whose horizons are purely those of the world and its transient values.[5]

For many in our fast-paced, uncertain world, experiencing a sense of belonging and acceptance is the primary benefit of a faith community. Meaning, too, is often a motivating factor, as is forgiveness, healing, or the arrival of young adults' first children. In this era of church shopping, browsing spiritual consumers reject many a church before they discover one that supports their beliefs and perpetuates their preferences and prejudices most closely.

For the majority of western Christians, a close second to the priority of acceptance is that of community. As social beings, people long for community and fellowship along life's journey. Yet more often than not, as Merton asserts, community is used by many as insulation from the real world or any potential encounters with the Divine in favor of easy conformity and the justification of one's comfortable lifestyle.

Richard Rohr notes, "Belonging systems do not necessarily lead to transformation and in fact, they often become an inoculation against transformation or a total substitute for it. Just the fact that I am accepted or 'belong' according to the church rules, I can assume that I know God or have met God. I think we've confused the dating service with the date."[6]

In the short term, simply belonging often fulfills the need for which people are yearning. Otherwise thoughtful people tolerate remarkably bad theology and shallow spirituality because the belonging system itself is perceived as having more value than what the belonging system stands for or practices. People keep paying their dues to the dating service that not only doesn't connect them with their true love but actively works against revealing just how much love and grace is available to them. Women serve faithfully in churches that deny their authority to be in leadership. Parents of gays and lesbians silently tolerate hate speech from the pulpit that condemns their children. Progressively minded individuals endure clichéd prayers and liturgies that shore up spiritual ideas they have long since abandoned. While the criteria for choosing a faith community rarely includes a catalyst for personal and societal transformation, such criteria are precisely what are needed. Individuals, faith communities, relationships, dogmas, doctrines, conventional wisdom, and the world itself, are all in need of transformation.

METAMORPHOSIS

Do not be conformed to this world, but be transformed by
the renewing of your minds, so that you may discern what is
the will of God—what is good and acceptable and perfect.

—Romans 12:2

When Paul appeals to Christians in Rome to resist conforming with the world, he challenges them to first renew their minds. In so doing they will be so changed that they will be virtually unrecognizable. Paul uses the Greek word from which we also get the word "metamorphosis," a term more likely found in science books referring to caterpillars and butterflies, tadpoles and frogs. Yet for many in our culture, the idea of transformation has been wed to simplistic ideas of being "born again" or being "saved."

As we pointed out in Chapter One, the Greek text of John 3 has Jesus say that you have to be born "from above" (*anothen* in Greek), implying a journey, a process, or a way of life. When Jesus informs Nicodemus of this requirement, the literalist Nicodemus balks and asks, "How can anyone be born after having grown old?" In order to have Nicodemus's response make sense to readers, well-intentioned translators changed the Greek word attributed to Jesus that means "from above" into the English word "again." In so doing, the idea of being "born again" entered the Christian lexicon, suggesting that what Jesus was looking for was a one-time event rather than a lifelong relationship with the Spirit of Life. As important a concept as "born again" has become, it not only isn't in the text, it likely misrepresents the original intention of the storyteller.

Likewise, the requirement of being "saved," as it has come to be understood, is, at best, dubious. In light of studies of the origins of Christianity, theologians are rethinking the narrowness of the "savior" language popular among Christians today. The Greek word from which "save" comes is also the root of words meaning to heal, preserve, do well, or be made whole. According to gospels that have been discovered in only the last century, a number of early Christian communities thrived without savior language at all. The communities associated with the Gospel of Thomas and "Q" (from which Matthew and Luke get many of their stories) don't even have crucifixion and resurrection stories. The doctrinal savior language was really only brought to flower in the fourth-century creeds.

Both being "born again" and being "saved" suggest one-time, static achievements. But the first disciples were called the people on "the Way," suggesting just the opposite: transformation, transition, and change—a dynamic way of life. By understanding the broader definitions of what these concepts can mean, we open ourselves to deeper understandings of life and the possibility of metamorphosis.

REEXPERIENCING REALITY

Transformative spirituality is about the positive transformation of our lives, our relationships, and our way of being in the world. With life always moving and recreating itself around us, our need to handle change is unavoidable. Despite our efforts to limit unpleasant upheavals, the normalcy of life prevails. When people are wrenched out of the relationships or situations with which they've grown comfortable, people often wonder if they will be up to the task of putting their world back together again. Robert McAfee Brown calls these challenges moments of "creative dislocation." He writes how, in retrospect, the times with the most significant growth in his life were times of great upheaval, or creative dislocation. The very brokenness can transform us to be more than we ever thought we could be.[7] As Ken Wilbur says, "Transformative spirituality, authentic spirituality, is revolutionary. It does not legitimate the world, it breaks the world; it does not console the world, it shatters it. And it does not render the self content, it renders it undone."[8]

For most people, it's only when they've been "undone" that there is an opportunity for the mystery of grace to work its magic. Jesus was gifted at "undoing" people in order to transform their lives and their thinking. His use of parables leveraged his own experience of the presence of the Divine in such a way that it caused the hearers to creatively experience a new reality. Bernard Brandon Scott has said, "A parable is meant to allow you to imaginatively re-experience reality." The story transports hearers to a place of vulnerability, exposing them to a previously unimagined alternative view of life.

Megan McKenna, too, sees stories and parables as change agents:

A story is not interested in information or content. It's interested in shifting your perception of reality, your view of the world, what's really going on. In fact it's interested in unlearning you so that you can start someplace else. It's not interested in confirmation, it's interested in transformation, that it gives you enough wisdom that you will now change to be more in harmony, communion, connection with what is in the story. And it's not interested in telling you that you're okay and that you belong. It's interested in asking, "How are you messing up; how are you not in communion; how do you need to be changed?"

Jesus's creative use of parables to bring people to moments of disequilibrium is not a unique teaching method. Be it Nathan exposing King David's murder of Uriah in 2 Samuel or the Kôans of Zen Masters, story has been employed from time immemorial to transform people's self-perception, thoughts, and actions.

Music, dance, poetry, and the visual arts are likewise creative channels of transformation. Hildegard of Bingen declared that "Wisdom is found in all creative works"[9]—and she hadn't even heard Mahler's 2nd Symphony or John Coltrane playing "Naima." Matthew Fox says that, "Wisdom is found in *all* creative works, so we're bringing forth wisdom and that is the Christ when we bring forth our creativity."

Today, film has become perhaps the most profound medium ever available to storytellers. As modern-day parables, movies help us delve deeply into the most stirring, disturbing, and inspiring aspects of life. Bernard Brandon Scott writes, "Movies and television shows are our modern myths; through them we work out who we are and negotiate the problems of modern life."[10]

Frederic and Mary Ann Brussat speak of "befriending" films and suggest the viewing of movies as part of one's spiritual practice. The moment when the lights go down can be a "sacred interlude" of preparation. Being fully attentive to what is on the screen can offer an experience of "mindfulness." Along with a number of other practical suggestions, the Brussats urge moviegoers to see movies as a way to "explore the mythical overtones of drama that transcend the confines of our personal worlds and introduce us to the universality of human experience. Think of the film as a passport that gives you access to other cultures. Celebrate stories that take you to new places and break down the walls that all too often separate us from other peoples."[11]

CHANGED AND TRANSFORMED

As people expend their energies arguing over the vicissitudes of conservative or liberal principles, the spirituality many are seeking is not to the left or to the right, but deeper. Christianity is not about things we should or shouldn't do, or about just being nice. It is about reveling in the beauty of creation, about taking part in the wonderment of it all by living, loving, and being. It's about embracing the pain and suffering of the world and transforming it into new life. It's about harnessing the creative Spirit that is so much a part of defining what it means to be human and using that creativity to, as Aquinas said, "preserve things in the good." Matthew Fox is convinced that this is not a discipline reserved for monks or ascetics, but a defining attribute of what makes us truly human:

> When we integrate our passion for justice and for joy into our work—whether we be therapists or preachers or doctors or carpenters or repairers of car engines or growers of food or parents parenting—all this is creative. Creativity is something that flows through every human being, every day. We're creative at how we pay our bills, and balance our checkbooks, and instruct our children, and put the food on the table, and decorate the rooms of our houses. Think about it, this is who we are as a species. This is what distinguishes us from other species.

The path toward transformation is different for every traveler, but the need for transformation is an integral part of the human experience. In the words of that great theologian, Bob Dylan, "If you're not busy being born, you're busy dying."

As we pursue the growth we're called to seek in order to reach our full potential, it may be helpful to remember what Taoism teaches its adherents: so long as bamboo is alive and growing it is pliable and flexible. Once it dies, however, it becomes brittle and is easily snapped. Creativity and transformation are principles that stave off our tendency to become hard and brittle, and open us instead to the transformative power of God's unconditional love and grace.

—m—

O God, make me discontented with things the way they
    are in the world,
and in my own life.
Make me notice the stains when people get spilled on.
Make me care about the slum child downtown, the misfit
    at work,
the people crammed into the mental hospital,
the men, women and youth behind bars.
Jar my complacence, expose my excuses,
get me involved in the life of my city and world.
Give me integrity once more, O God,
as we seek to be changed and transformed,
with a new understanding and awareness of our common
    humanity.[12]

—Robert Raines

21

Embracing Mystery

Religion has always been about honoring mystery.
[But] we have created people who've been
afraid of ambiguity, mystery.[1]

—Richard Rohr

Professor Gordon D. Kaufman has said, "We may find a certain security in believing that 'our' way is the only way. This is a natural part of any cultic religious experience. Far greater faith is required, however, to seek and trust that which you accept as infinite, beyond your comprehension, and subject to change. Today, this just may be the challenge of an educated and thinking Christian—to retain a faith 'in face of the mystery.'"[2]

Many seekers today are discovering ancient spiritual insights for the first time, not through blind faith and certitude, but through a commitment to openness and flexibility. Those who leave room for spiritual uncertainty discover what mystics have always known: ambiguity is not something to be feared but recognized as an integral part of any spirituality that continues to develop and evolve. To acknowledge the wisdom of the unknowable. To celebrate the importance of the experiential. These are at the heart of the long-established spiritual practice reemerging in our day, that of embracing mystery.

The idea of mystery itself refers to that which is unexplainable or beyond comprehension. Its Greek root implies the closing of eyes and lips, suggesting that which is beyond our ability to see or even comprehend. Antiquity is rife with mystery cults and other rites, the meaning of which was known only to the initiated. Even in the early Christian movement, there were carefully guarded teachings referred to as "the mysteries."

Rudolph Otto is just one in a long line of thinkers who have tried to categorize the nonrational reaction experienced by those who are awestruck or full of wonder. When he published *The Idea of the Holy*, he described the source of that indescribable and awe-inspiring sacredness with the Latin words *numen* and *numinous* (literally meaning divine power or spirit). Otto's intent was to offer vocabulary that suggests the presence that is just beyond our ability to grasp or describe. But his efforts to describe the indescribable come up against the same challenge of anyone trying to quantify or categorize mystery. The truly holy is not something grasped in the intellectual realm, but firmly rooted in the experiential.

Ironically, while mystery has always been the source and core of what we call religion, those who fully embrace mystery are usually relegated to the fringes of religious systems. For the sake of institutional stability and corporate identity, right belief and certainty have been emphasized instead.

People have been programmed to be suspicious of ambiguity and are, in fact, expected to adopt predetermined belief systems, never mind the stifling spiritual effects it has on adherents.

"When you think about it, faith as belief is relatively impotent," says Marcus Borg.

You can believe all the right things and still be a jerk. And to soften that: you can believe all the right things and still be miserable, or still be in bondage, still be untransformed. So the emphasis upon belief is, I think, modern and mistaken. It's also very divisive—once people start thinking that being a Christian is about believing the right things, then anybody's list of what the right things are to believe becomes a kind of litmus test as to who's

really a good Christian and who's not. And in my own work (and
I think this is very ancient) I emphasize that being a Christian is
really about one's relationship with God. And that relationship
with God can go along with many different belief systems.[3]

Whatever comes next for Christianity, it will have to teach people
how to believe and live and not dwell simply on *what* to believe. Travelers with mystery will be grounded in the experiential that grows out of
the seeker's sense of inner authority. In the same way music, art, drama,
and poetry defy any one interpretation, those who embrace mystery are
free to interpret the Divine in new and fresh ways, bringing to the table
a variety of understandings. Concrete operational thinkers will find this
line of pursuit maddeningly counter-productive. Yet it is the very inde-
scribability of these insights, their fleeting nature, and the disequilibrium they create, that give them their value. From poetry to music to
gardening to making love, people open to the presence of this ineffable
mystery experience it each in their own way. The spirit fills in the rest.

—⚌—

MYSTICS AMONG US

I am being driven forward
Into an unknown land.
The pass grows steeper,
The air colder and sharper.
A wind from my unknown goal
Stirs the strings
Of expectation.

Still the question:
Shall I ever get there?

There where life resounds
A clear pure note
In the silence.[4]

—Dag Hammarskjöld

He concealed it for more than thirty years. The United Nations secretary-general was a modern mystic. Only after Dag Hammarskjöld was killed did it become widely known that his remarkable strength of will and passion for peace was driven by a closely guarded spiritual struggle and intense inner life. In his desk, friends discovered the manuscript of his journal and what was to become the spiritual classic, *Markings*.

Mystics can be found in every faith tradition. Christianity claims a number of the giants of mysticism over the centuries, including Hildegard of Bingen, Mechtild of Magdeburg, Thomas Aquinas, Thomas Merton, and Howard Thurman. But regardless of faith traditions or even cultural circumstances, mystics endeavor to experience the Divine in as direct a manner as possible. One of the common characteristics of a mystic is one who transcends any cultic or superficial constraints in experiencing the Divine. They have no need of any mediation from priests, books, or other interpreters. Matthew Fox reminds us that Meister Eckhart saw every creature as "a word of God and a book about God." Fox says, "The book about God is not just in human books—a Bible that's 2,500 years old—it's in the universe which is 14 billion years old. God has been writing the book of nature for 14 billion years..."

For more and more people, long-held ideas and seemingly core values of faith have simply outlived their usefulness. This tack resonates with a growing number of seekers convinced that the "More" is quite accessible, if only given a chance.

Abraham Heschel writes, "Normal consciousness is a state of stupor, in which the sensibility to the wholly real and responsiveness to the stimuli of the spirit are reduced. The mystics...endeavor to awake from the drowsiness and apathy and to regain the state of wakefulness for their enchanted souls."[5]

For those who acknowledge a comfort with ambiguity and aspire to the state of wakefulness, Heschel suggests, one requirement is universal: the need to break one's dependency on mediated, rote, and authoritarian religious experiences. Culver "Bill" Nelson has suggested a helpful starting place from which to begin the detox program: "The image of God as a person has to give way to the image of God as a presence." This essentially mystical idea is naturally going to be a challenge to people and institutions not inclined toward mysticism, which is just one of the reasons why the church has seen mystics as a threat.

Be it hard questions, nuanced insight, comfort with ambiguity, or a hunger for a direct experience of the Divine, those who embrace mystery as a spiritual discipline all have one more conviction in common: there is much to be learned. According to Jack Good, author of *The Dishonest Church*, "The church has pretended to know more about the Ultimate Mystery than it does. Once again it has confronted people with premature answers when questions are both more appropriate and more inviting."[6]

Whatever the mystery of the Divine is, the book is not closed. Another twentieth-century mystic, Quaker Rufus Jones, said it well in *TIME* magazine in 1948: "Vital religion cannot be maintained and preserved on the theory that God dealt with our human race only in the far past ages, and that the Bible is the only evidence we have that our God is a living, revealing, communicating God. If God ever spoke, [God] is still speaking...[God] is the Great I Am, not a Great I Was..."[7]

Embracing mystery involves unlearning that which has come to be accepted as conventional wisdom. It entails honoring that which can be sensed but not described, felt but not quantified. That said, there can be no doubt that there are indeed mystics among us. When we embrace mystery, strive to emulate Jesus's deep experience of the Divine, and live at peace with the unknowable, we may be among them.

MYSTERIOUS WAYS

I who am Divine am truly in you. I can never be sundered from you:
However far we be parted, never can we be separated.
I am in you and you are in Me.
We could not be any closer.
We two are fused into one, poured into a single mould.
Thus, unwearied, we shall remain forever.[8]

—Mechtild of Magdeburg,
thirteenth-century Rhineland Mystic

Maybe it's in a relationship that has been strained or alienated. A shimmer of grace in the moment of reconciliation offers a sensation that can only be described as intoxicating.

Perhaps it's in a beautiful sunset, a newborn baby, or being struck by some other facet of creation. Hildegard of Bingen wrote, "Creation reveals the hidden God just as clothes hint at the shape of a person's body."[9] And then there's music, art, and poetry. The artists having captured a sliver of the Divine in imagery, on canvas, or in song.

While our culture tends to compartmentalize the sacred and the secular, reserving special places and times as "holy" and others as hopelessly secular, the Divine has a way of sneaking into peoples' consciousness at the most unexpected times.

There is a Celtic saying that heaven and earth are only three feet apart, but in the "thin places" the distance becomes even smaller. A thin place is where the veil that separates the sacred from the pedestrian is so transparent that one is able to catch a glimpse of the mystery beyond. A thin place is anywhere our hearts are receptive to "the More," anywhere the distance we put between us and the Divine begins to evaporate.

Most people have had experiences where the artificial boundary between the secular and the sacred becomes very thin indeed. In one of these thin places there is an immediacy of experience where words alone become irrelevant. We feel like we are in the presence of something mysterious, of something holy. Mechtild of Magdeburg wrote, "The day of my spiritual awakening was the day I saw and knew I saw all things in God and God in all things."

In many spiritualities, the simplest of life's necessities are lifted up and permeated with something…more. For Christians, it involves even the most common of elements: bread, water, and wine. These everyday staples become the *sacra* (sacred)—the sacraments, the means of grace. Organized religion has always realized and taken advantage of how profoundly the Spirit can be at work in even the most mundane of circumstances.

And while there are those who seek to separate and isolate the sacred, there are others who have embraced the whole world and imbued it with mystery. The Quakers and Franciscans are just two examples of worldviews striving to see all of life as sacred. Whether it is described as a spark of the Divine within each of us or a commitment to living all of life as a sacrament, their practices express the belief that all of life can be used by God. Who are we to declare some things holy or not holy?

Culver "Bill" Nelson tells of an encounter he had with Abraham Joshua Heschel. One Sabbath evening, Rabbi Albert Plotkin invited Nelson and his wife, Dee, to his home for dinner with Rabbi Heschel. Expressing their shared frustration, Nelson recalls Heschel saying:

> People talk about the sacred and the secular. I don't understand it. Either God created the heavens and the earth or he didn't. And if he did, that's it. The sacred and secular, they don't exist. They blend into one another. On top of which, I want you to know that people talk about being spiritual. I don't understand that either. I mean spiritual and material—God was very material. He even created humans from the dust of ground. And everybody gets these mixed up: they are not separate from one another. There's just one reality—and that's the gift of God to us.

EMBRACING MYSTERY

*The most beautiful and profound emotion we can
experience is the sensation of the mystical. It is
the sower of all true science. He [or she] to
whom this emotion is a stranger, who can
no longer wonder and stand rapt
in awe, is as good as dead.*

—Albert Einstein

In today's world of expanding universes, black holes, dark matter, and multiple dimensions, it's hard to believe that we can know much of anything about anything. And while poverty, racism, war, injustice, and countless other issues continue to pose daunting challenges to the human race, the lure of mystery continues to haunt people. The possibility of the "more" offers people hope for a depth and breadth of life, not just for themselves, but also for all of creation, aching to be whole. The hunger for the holy, what Hildegard of Bingen called "the yearning for good," is a part of who we are. Our longing to be connected to mystery connects us to one another and the hope for a world renewed.

In her manifesto on mystery, "The Summer Day," poet Mary Oliver confesses that she doesn't know "exactly what prayer is," but she does know "how to pay attention."[10] Could it be that simple? By living the questions—and simply paying attention—we open ourselves to a perspective on life that prepares us to embrace mystery.

Awe at the beauty and complexity of creation gives us pause to consider—and perhaps compels a response: gratitude, a heightened consciousness, and constructive action. An awareness of our place in the universe and our responsibility toward creation is not only deeply biblical and practical, but increasingly critical—for both our present spiritual life and for our collective future.

Harrell Beck used to tell the story of the oldest living alumnus of the seminary returning to Boston University for homecoming. Much to the current students' chagrin, the man was invited to speak at the weekly chapel. The day came and they draped the elderly man over the pulpit. He gazed out at the students and said, "I would like to thank my alma mater for setting me free without setting me adrift." And he sat down.[11]

Isn't that what it's all about? When mystery is embraced, freedom is embraced. Openness is embraced. The journey is embraced. Far from being cast adrift, those who embrace mystery are set on a lifelong path of discovery, growth, and gratitude for the wonder of it all.

READER'S GUIDE

From its beginning, the Living the Questions curriculum has sought to expose participants to broad areas of thought around particular themes. While each chapter has a clearly stated focus, the goal is not necessarily to prove a point or make specific conclusions but to stir the pot and facilitate conversations.

Many of the topics in *Living the Questions: The Wisdom of Progressive Christianity* are in a transitional stage and are pointing toward something new. How these ideas and this emerging vision develop will be determined through the efforts of those willing to live with the questions and see what unfolds along the way.

CHAPTER 1   AN INVITATION TO JOURNEY

FOCUS: Faith is not a destination, but a journey.

1. How does Harrell Beck's statement "The beginning of true wisdom is asking the questions that have no answers" resonate with you?
2. Describe the advantages of being on a spiritual journey over "arriving" at the truth.
3. What are some of the defining characteristics of fundamentalism?
4. Where do you see fundamentalists of various faiths organizing themselves into political blocs?
5. How have "killing certainties" crippled the church's faithfulness to the gospel?
6. What role can ambiguity play in one's spiritual journey?
7. What are the implications of this chapter's theme for your personal spiritual journey? For your local faith community? For Christianity as a whole?

CHAPTER 2   TAKING THE BIBLE SERIOUSLY

FOCUS: The authority one places in the Bible plays a critical role in one's worldview and understanding of the Christian life.

1. What are the possible consequences of an unquestioning belief in the ideas of Biblical inerrancy and infallibility?

2. Marcus Borg suggests that a more historical and metaphorical approach to the Bible provides a way for non-literalists to be Christian. How does this sync with your experience?

3. How might looking at the Bible as the "fourth member of the Trinity" border on idolatry?

4. Describe Borg's stages of pre-critical naïveté, critical thinking, and post-critical naïveté.

5. Why does an awareness of the process by which the Bible came together matter?

6. What are the implications of this chapter's theme for your personal spiritual journey? For your local faith community? For Christianity as a whole?

CHAPTER 3   THINKING THEOLOGICALLY

FOCUS: While family, education, social class, and geography all contribute to how we think about God, our experiences and perceptions along life's journey also shape our thinking. Being comfortable with ambiguity, metaphor, and uncertainty help us get the Divine "out of the box" and rethink theological ideas that have become barriers to our further spiritual growth.

1. How might embracing the Bible's multiple theologies and various images of God facilitate one's thinking theologically?

2. According to Winnie Varghese, what is the benefit of "thinking theologically"?

3. John Dominic Crossan asks four questions of twenty-first century Christians: What is the character of your God? What is the content of your faith? What is the function of your church? What is the purpose of your worship? Describe how you might have answered these questions as a child or young person compared to your understanding today.

4. According to John B. Cobb Jr., omnipotence is an unbiblical concept that misrepresents the nature of the Divine. Describe the advantages of seeing God as a persuasive, relational power over the unbiblical notion of omnipotent, coercive power.

5. What advantages can you identify in using alternatives to the word "God" to describe the Divine?

6. Consider a theological concept or tenet of conventional wisdom and describe how and why your thoughts on it have evolved over the years.

7. What are the implications of this chapter's theme for your personal spiritual journey? For your local faith community? For Christianity as a whole?

CHAPTER 4   STORIES OF CREATION

FOCUS: How one perceives the creation stories is not only critical to the way one looks at the Bible, but how one understands the purpose of creation, the essence of human nature, and the attitude one takes toward the environment in which we live.

1. What are some of the purposes of creation stories in general?

2. What are some of the defining characteristics of the two creation stories in Genesis?

3. What are some of the ways a person's interpretation of the Genesis creation stories affects their worldview?

4. Barbara Rossing suggests that the false conflict between creation and evolution is distracting us from what we should really be spending our energies on. Discuss.

5. If the Genesis creation stories are about meaning, how might their literal interpretation compromise their intent?

6. What are the implications of this chapter's theme for your personal spiritual journey? For your local faith community? For Christianity as a whole?

CHAPTER 5   LIVES OF JESUS

FOCUS: From divergent opinions on Jesus's "program" to the reasons for his having been killed, the many portrayals of Jesus in the gospels, various other traditions, theologies, and the arts, amount to a Jesus who lived many different lives — each of which helps us in teasing out what it means to be a disciple of this mysterious and profoundly significant phenomenon called Jesus of Nazareth.

1. Why does the way Jesus is portrayed matter?

2. What are some ramifications of seeing the Gospels as part of "developing tradition"?

3. Describe some of the differences between the Synoptic Gospels and the Gospel of John.

4. How is it that our stories of Jesus are true — but not historical?

5. Describe some of the layers Yvette Flunder bemoans as obscuring the real Jesus.

6. Why would the alternative vision of Jesus's Kingdom be so treasonous or threatening?

7. What are the implications of this chapter's theme for your personal spiritual journey? For your local faith community? For Christianity as a whole?

CHAPTER 6   A PASSION FOR CHRIST

FOCUS: Little of what most people think of as Christianity has been untouched by the legacy of Paul's writing and influence. The many understandings of his interpretation of Christianity continue to be re-examined in the twenty-first century.

1. Discuss some of the ways Paul's life and message have influenced Christianity.

2. Why is it important to have an awareness of what is authentic Paul and what is not?

3. Describe the attributes and purpose of what Crossan calls the "three different Pauls."

4. The role of women is just one example of a teaching that is confused by later authors claiming Paul's authority. Explain.

5. Elaborate on how the concept of *pistis* being mistranslated as "faith *in* Jesus" (as opposed to the "faith *of* Jesus") has shaped Christianity as a whole.

6. In what ways can Paul's message ultimately be interpreted as one of hope?

7. What are the implications of this chapter's theme for your personal spiritual journey? For your local faith community? For Christianity as a whole?

CHAPTER 7   OUT INTO THE WORLD

FOCUS: There is a reformation afoot in Christianity—a re-visioning of the traditional understandings of Jesus, the virgin birth, substitutionary atonement, and the Christian life as a whole. Long-held ideas of divinity and of faith are changing and evolving to reflect twenty-first century thought and spirituality. Inspired by these fresh insights, progressive Christians can claim a distinctive voice by being in solidarity with the poor, countering the idolatry of wealth, practicing nonviolence, and by seeking justice and inclusivity in a culture dominated by fear.

1. Why is an embrace of the concepts of progress and change so vital to the future of Christianity?

2. How does your understanding of belief affect your spiritual journey?

3. What can you point to as core values of a progressive Christian message?

4. Discuss some of the possible consequences of recasting Christianity as a fluid and dynamic system of thought.

5. According to Brueggemann, what are the three definitive marks of the Church which have been kept "secret" and for which so many have been hungering?

6. What are some of the ways you imagine progressive Christianity "coming alive" in the twenty-first century?

7. What are the implications of this chapter's theme for your personal spiritual journey? For your local faith community? For Christianity as a whole?

CHAPTER 8   RESTORING RELATIONSHIPS

FOCUS: There are three biblical "macro-stories" that shape the whole of the biblical narrative: Bondage and Liberation, Exile and Return, and Sin and Forgiveness. Each representing a different facet of the human condition, they demonstrate what is necessary for the restoration of relationships on a variety of levels.

1. Describe some of the characteristics of the Exodus story and how it speaks to the human need for liberation from bondage.

2. List some of the cultural messages that subject us to bondage.

3. Where do you see the "isms" and the bondage from which Minerva Carcaño feels liberated still at work today?

4. "Promised Land Theology" can be problematic for Canaanites. Explain.

5. Describe some of the characteristics of the story of the Babylonian exile and how it speaks to the human need for a return from exile.

6. How do the "Priestly" story and temple sacrifice speak to the human need for forgiveness from sin?

7. In what ways might the dominance of the "Priestly" story and the doctrine of the atonement diminish the broader Biblical message?

8. Culver "Bill" Nelson claims that Jesus was against the sacrificial system of the temple cult in Jerusalem. Explain.

9. What are the implications of this chapter's theme for your personal spiritual journey? For your local faith community? For Christianity as a whole?

CHAPTER 9   THE PROPHETIC JESUS

FOCUS: Jesus was a troublemaker. He said and did things that were upsetting to agents of the political and religious domination systems that oppressed the weak and downtrodden. In this way, Jesus stood firmly in the tradition of the prophets of Hebrew Scripture—those who offered a clear and challenging "alternative script" to the status quo.

1. Describe some of the basic characteristics and passions expressed by the prophets of Hebrew scripture.

2. How do anger and righteous indignation play into the expression of a prophetic voice?

3. How are some of the characteristics of the "radical community" Jesus inaugurated still a threat today?

4. What are some of the ways Jesus's message threatens *your* status quo?

5. Compare and contrast the strategies of Clarence Jordan and Dorothy McRae-McMahon with that of the institutional church.

6. According to Yvette Flunder, it is essential for the "personal piety piece" and "justice work" to be brought together. Explain.

7. What are the implications of this chapter's theme for your personal spiritual journey? For your local faith community? For Christianity as a whole?

CHAPTER 10   EVIL, SUFFERING, AND A GOD OF LOVE

FOCUS: If God is all-powerful, all-loving, and all-good, how do you explain and respond to the existence of so much suffering and evil in the world?

1. Reflect on the Robert McAfee Brown quote, "Whatever the status of evil in the world, I know that the only God in whom I can believe will be a God found in the midst of evil rather than at a safe distance from it; suffering the evil rather than inflicting it."

2. What explanations have you heard offered through the years for the existence of evil?

3. How might the idea of the Divine participating with us—even in our suffering—affect our understanding of God?

4. Why are so many of the popular but unbiblical ideas of Satan and Hell so beloved by so many?

5. What do you think was at the core of the hoopla around Rob Bell's book *Love Wins*?

6. In the face of suffering and evil, what are our options?

7. What are the implications of this chapter's theme for your personal spiritual journey? For your local faith community? For Christianity as a whole?

CHAPTER 11   THE MYTH OF REDEMPTIVE VIOLENCE

FOCUS: The most potent religion in Western culture is not Christianity, but a belief in the redemptive power of violence. Although Jesus inaugurated a new order based on partnership, equality, compassion, and non-violence, his example and teachings have been eclipsed by an emphasis on a human unworthiness that demands and defends the need for Jesus's violent, suffering, atoning death.

1. Describe Walter Wink's notion of "The Myth of Redemptive Violence."

2. What are some of the ways you see violence integrated into our culture and popular Christianity?

3. The idea of Original Sin has spawned multiple theories of atonement. Discuss the theory that best describes your upbringing and where you are now.

4. What was Anselm's rationale for "coming up with" substitutionary atonement?

5. In what ways do ideas like Original Blessing and Satyagraha serve as a corrective to our confusing hodge-podge of atonement theories?

6. What are some of the thoughts Spong suggests as alternatives to the image of "Jesus, the Divine Invader" dying for our sins?

7. What options do twenty-first century Christians have in countering our collective infatuation with the myth of redemptive violence?

8. What are the implications of Christians actually practicing nonviolence?

9. What are the implications of this chapter's theme for your personal spiritual journey? For your local faith community? For Christianity as a whole?

CHAPTER 12   PRACTICING RESURRECTION

FOCUS: While much has been made of Jesus's literal and physical resurrection being the core historical event of Christianity, the biblical texts themselves present conflicting evidence. For many today, the resuscitation of Jesus's body is less important than the idea of resurrection as a credible and meaningful principle for living.

1. What evidence points to the physical resurrection of Jesus being a legendary, late-developing tradition?

2. What does the idea of resurrection have to do with life after death (if anything)?

3. When considering Jesus's death and resurrection, how might the notion of the spirit of Jesus dwelling in us strengthen us for new life in the here and now?

4. According to Winnie Varghese, how does the resurrection support the work God calls us to do?

5. How is "the expenditure of our life for the community" a form of the resurrected life?

6. What are the implications of this chapter's theme for your personal spiritual journey? For your local faith community? For Christianity as a whole?

CHAPTER 13   DEBUNKING THE RAPTURE

FOCUS: Failing to understand the message of hope offered in the Book of Revelation, many Christians have been misled by nineteenth-century doomsayers and modern-day apocalyptic preachers who proclaim their vengeful god's impending extermination of the apostate masses. Just what part of "love your enemies" doesn't their god understand?

1. What are some of the major ideas promoted by John Nelson Darby's theology and the Scofield Reference Bible?

2. Why is it important to counter the fictional biblical timelines of the rapture cult?

3. Theologically and psychologically, what does the rapture mentality foster?

4. How does the vision of violent apocalypse sync with the character and priorities of the Jesus represented in the Gospels?

5. Discuss John Dominic Crossan's claim regarding our "great Christian treason."

6. Of the possible elements of the "different story" Rossing sees a need for, what resonates with you?

7. If Jesus doesn't come to us through violence, death, war, and disaster, where will we find him?

8. What are the implications of this chapter's theme for your personal spiritual journey? For your local faith community? For Christianity as a whole?

CHAPTER 14   HONORING CREATION

FOCUS: While human beings have been gifted with a beautiful and complex world in which to live, its systems and resources are being stressed by our behaviors, lifestyles, and arrogance. Care for the environment is not only deeply biblical and practical, but increasingly critical—for both the present spiritual life and for our collective future.

1. In what ways might the expression "praying with open eyes" promote a deeper spirituality?

2. What are some of the consequences of "anthropocentric arrogance"?

3. What could our diet possibly have to do with the wider creation?

4. Reflect on the implications of so much environmental destruction occurring while Christian nations have been at the apex of control.

5. How does being "compassionate as God is compassionate" relate to creation?

6. What does Aquinas's definition of salvation have to do with your daily interaction with creation?

7. What are the implications of this chapter's theme for your personal spiritual journey? For your local faith community? For Christianity as a whole?

CHAPTER 15 A KINGDOM WITHOUT WALLS

FOCUS: The good news of the gospel tells of a radical hospitality where boundaries, barriers, and walls are overcome by a grace that knows no bounds.

1. In what ways are our prejudices and insecurities intertwined?
2. When you consider C.S. Lewis's sentiment: "Can you think of a type of person who might make you uncomfortable if they sat next to you? May that person come into your life soon," who comes to mind?
3. Besides the tax collector, the woman with the hemorrhage, the synagogue leader, and the woman at the dinner party, what other stories depict Jesus crossing barriers that separate people?
4. Share what role the practice of hospitality plays in your own life or the life of your faith community.
5. Describe the "humanity beyond our prejudices" to which we are called.
6. What are some of the rigid rules and theological walls that you've encountered in your spiritual journey?
7. At its 2012 General Conference, the United Methodist Church voted to retain discriminatory language against homosexuals in its *Book of Discipline*. Give other examples of entrenched systemic injustice and what rights groups have done/are doing to foster change.
8. What are the implications of this chapter's theme for your personal spiritual journey? For your local faith community? For Christianity as a whole?

CHAPTER 16 SOCIAL JUSTICE

FOCUS: Being a person of faith demands balancing spiritual pursuits with action. In a society which is often unjust, inequitable, and whose very structures are responsible for generating untold suffering and poverty, we are compelled to pursue social justice as an expression of hope in realizing a better world.

1. What are some of the characteristics of "prophetic theology"?
2. Compare and contrast personal/individual justice and systemic or structural justice.
3. What are the implications of people of faith being aware of the notion of "systemic justice"?
4. How does Jesus's call to liberation and justice conflict with the values of the dominant culture then and now?
5. How does fixating on the "virtue of individuals" legitimate the social structure?
6. What breaks your heart about your world or the system by which it's organized? Reflect on something you could do to create a first ripple.
7. What are the implications of this chapter's theme for your personal spiritual journey? For your local faith community? For Christianity as a whole?

CHAPTER 17   INCARNATION

FOCUS: The meaning of the incarnation has been debated since the beginning of Christianity. Although often associated with Jesus alone, the notion of incarnation can be understood most fully when it also includes Jesus's followers, called, like Jesus, to enflesh the Spirit in divinely human ways.

1. With whom does Jesus share the claim of miraculous birth? Why?
2. Why was the virgin birth story an honest mistake?
3. As the birth narratives in Matthew and Luke can't possibly be historical, what is their purpose?
4. In what ways do Brandon Scott, Robin Meyers, and Diana Butler Bass believe the creeds have distorted Christianity?
5. What are the implications for your faith of simply embracing Jesus as a human being?
6. How would re-imaging "God as the life power itself, the power of love itself" change our understanding of incarnation?
7. How does process theology make sense of the incarnation?
8. What are the implications of this chapter's theme for your personal spiritual journey? For your local faith community? For Christianity as a whole?

CHAPTER 18   PRAYER

FOCUS: The idea of prayer as the primary method of interaction with God is best thought of as a way of life rather than an activity reserved for specific times, places, and formulas.

1. Describe ways in which prayer can be distorted.
2. John Shelby Spong relates a story regarding prayer for his wife. What stands out for you in this story?
3. If prayer isn't a direct and effective way of influencing the Divine for our own benefit, what good is it?
4. How does Capon's "tow truck theology" and "covenant of presence" resonate with your experience?
5. Rick Ufford-Chase finds prayer expressed in conversation, play, and even reading the comics. What forms can you see prayer taking?
6. What place do words have when trying to "authentically listen" or achieve the silence of "deep knowing?"
7. What effect does the idea of prayer being legitimately different for people and changing over time have on your spiritual journey?
8. What are the implications of this chapter's theme for your personal spiritual journey? For your local faith community? For Christianity as a whole?

CHAPTER 19 COMPASSION

FOCUS: Jesus was not primarily a teacher of correct beliefs or right morals. He was a teacher of a way that transforms people from legalistic rule-followers into compassionate disciples who put people first.

1. How does the holiness code practiced in Jesus's day conflict with the notion of compassion?
2. What insights do Prejean and McLaren offer to your understanding of compassion?
3. Jesus a law-breaker? Explain.
4. Discuss the varying forms of compassion Minerva Carcaño describes.
5. How does the very definition of the word compassion deepen its meaning for you?
6. In *The Adventures of Huckleberry Finn*, Huck is presented a choice between turning in his best friend or continuing to aid and abet a runaway slave. In Twain's masterful scene Huck tears up the note he'd written to Jim's master (explaining the slave's whereabouts) and exclaims, "Alright then, I'll go to hell." What examples can you think of when you or others have been compelled to disobey a law in order to do the right thing?
7. What are the implications of this chapter's theme for your personal spiritual journey? For your local faith community? For Christianity as a whole?

CHAPTER 20 CREATIVE TRANSFORMATION

FOCUS: The essence of human nature is to take part in the dynamic and imaginative process of creation; transforming us, our relationships, our institutions, and our world.

1. What are some examples of "cosmetic piety" with which you've wrestled?
2. Discuss some of the barriers to transformation practiced by the institution.
3. Megan McKenna describes how storytelling is not for the conveying of information, for confirmation of what you know, or comfort in what you believe, but for "unlearning" and transformation. Explain.
4. Name some of the ways creative works and creativity itself are tied to wisdom.
5. How does the following ring true for you: "the spirituality many are seeking is not to the left or to the right, but deeper."
6. What are the implications of this chapter's theme for your personal spiritual journey? For your local faith community? For Christianity as a whole?

CHAPTER 21 EMBRACING MYSTERY

FOCUS: Christian practice is being re-visioned, re-tooled, and re-claimed by those who are living the questions of their faith. They're attentive to ancient ways, comfortable with ambiguity, and open to the unknowable and indescribable mystery of the Divine.

1. List some of the ways bringing back the sense of mystery can call us beyond our knowing into an exploration of the Holy.

2. How would acknowledging that "we dwell in mystery" affect one's day-to-day outlook on the world?

3. Culver "Bill" Nelson recounts Rabbi Heschel claiming that there's no distinction between the sacred and the secular. How have you found this to be true in your own experience?

4. In what ways do you see the embrace of mystery benefiting your spiritual journey?

5. What are the implications of this chapter's theme for your personal spiritual journey? For your local faith community? For Christianity as a whole?

ACKNOWLEDGMENTS

One of the first steps in any thought of acknowledgment has to be the acceptance that very little of what we've included here are new ideas. Nor is what we've attempted to set down in these pages definitive. The more we learn, the more we discover that not only have thinkers long past eloquently written what we've tried to say, but many of our contemporaries are exploring the same territory today in profound and meaningful ways. We hope that through the wisdom of our many contributors and with the help of those whom we acknowledge here (many of whom we've undoubtedly forgotten!), what we've brought together will be helpful to others who are with us on the journey. We are humbled by the opportunity.

As these chapters grew out of sermons in our local churches, we must confess: like clergy everywhere, we depend on "riffs," ideas, and snippets from other preachers, authors, writers, and thinkers to pull our messages together. While we've made every effort to acknowledge direct quotes and idea sources, some of the details on sources have long since been lost to the mists of time.

Other sources are not hard to recognize at all, especially the influence and inspiration of so many of our mentors and teachers, including professors Harrell Beck, John B. Cobb Jr., Bill Loader, Burton Mack; ministers Richard W. Cain, Larry Hinshaw, Jim Standiford, DeWane Zimmerman, and Rabbi Sam Siecol—with special thanks going to encourager and flatterer-in-chief Culver "Bill" Nelson and confidant Jack Spong.

For their encouragement and patience with us, we owe a huge debt of gratitude to the people of Asbury, Via de Cristo, and The Fountains United Methodist Churches in Phoenix, Scottsdale, and Fountain Hills, AZ, and we are grateful for our early faith experiences in the churches of our youth: Central and First United Methodist Churches in Phoenix.

In ways too numerous to list, we are indebted to those who have traveled and worked with us along the way: Penny Davis, Sandy Thron, and the Arizona Foundation for Contemporary Theology; Jim Burklo, Fred Plumer, and The Center for Progressive Christianity; Rex Hunt, Greg Jenks, Jeremy Greaves, Jason Davies-Kildea and Australia's The Progressive Christian Network of Victoria; Richard Titford, Dave and

ACKNOWLEDGMENTS

Pat Tomlinson, and the Progressive Christianity Network of Great Britain; Gretta Vosper and The Canadian Centre for Progressive Christianity; Graham Maule and the Wild Goose Resource Group/Iona Community; Yohann Anderson, Don Benjamin, Jim Bloom, Sean Buvala, Elizabeth Cabalka, Monica Corsaro, Chuck Currie, Eric Elnes, Paul Eppinger, Tyler Gingrich, Pat McMahon, Stephen Patterson, Barbara Wendland, and Hinckley G. Mitchell.

To all the industry gurus at HarperOne—especially Mickey Maudlin and Mark Tauber—along with everyone else behind the scenes supporting us along the way, we are grateful. Special thanks to Carla Barnhill, who tackled the first edit.

Living the Questions would not have been possible without the gracious participation of all of our Living the Questions contributors—especially Dom, Marcus, Jack and Christine, Diana, Tex and Peg, Brandon, and John Bell (who suggested we might better question the living than live the questions).

Likewise, *Living the Questions* wouldn't have seen the light of day or be able to continue without Director of Operations extraordinaire Jennifer Schwarz; Chris Bridges, Barb Catlin, Michelle Chambless-Ferguson, www.digitalcdr.com, Mark Ford, Scott Griessel of www.creatista.com, Craig Hedges, David Ice, Bob McBane, Anthony Rayl of www.noticedesign.com, www.rhinointernet.com, De De Rudolphy, Don Small, Roger Strom, and Brian Yee.

We offer our thanks to colleagues who've made our ministries more life-affirming: Mary Miller Bullis, Michael Eaton, Tom Kiracofe, Tim Lusk, William Martin, James Parkhurst, David Ragan, Rob Rynders, Dot Saunders-Perez, Buzz Stevens, Kathleen Stolz, Jane Tews, Dan Turner, and David Wilkinson—with special thanks to Cynthia Langston Kirk for her magnificent and inspired poetry (www.piecingstories.com).

For our gracious and patient spouses—Laura and Janice—we are truly thankful. We couldn't do what we do without their long-suffering and generous support, as well as the encouragement expressed by our parents, siblings, and extended families.

Finally, we'd like to thank everyone whom we will, after waking up in a cold sweat at 3:00 A.M., realize we forgot to include here.

The creation of this book has been enormously helpful to both of us. Our hope is that as it makes its way in the world, it might be of help to you, as well!

Gratitudo!

NOTES

EPIGRAPH

Harrell Beck, "Asking the Big Questions: Old Testament Wisdom as a Literature for Anxious Times," (lecture, Arrowhead Springs, CA, May 13, 1986).

PREFACE

1. Sam Keen, *Hymns to an Unknown God: Awakening the Spirit in Everyday Life,* (New York: Bantam Books, 1995), 4.

CHAPTER 1   AN INVITATION TO JOURNEY

1. Rainer Maria Rilke, *Letters to a Young Poet,* trans. by Stephen Mitchell (New York: Vintage Books, 1986), 34.
2. Maya Angelou, *Wouldn't Take Nothing for My Journey Now* (New York: Bantam Books, 1994), 73.
3. John Dominic Crossan, *The Power of Parable* (San Francisco: HarperOne, 2012), 247.
4. Center for Progressive Christianity, "About Us: The 8 Points," www .progressivechristianity.org/about/8points.cfm.

CHAPTER 2   TAKING THE BIBLE SERIOUSLY

1. N. T. Wright, "Surprised by Scripture: Translating, Understanding, and Obeying the Bible in King James's World and Ours," Socrates in the City lecture, New York, July 11, 2011. (New York: Socrates in the City, 2011), audio CD.
2. Marcus Borg, *Meeting Jesus Again for the First Time: The Historical Jesus and the Heart of Contemporary Faith* (San Francisco: HarperOne, 1994), 3.
3. Harrell Beck, "From Priestly Listener to Prophetic Witness: the Canon as the Church's Creation" (lecture, Arrowhead Springs, CA, May 13, 1986).
4. Beck, "Priestly Listener."

5. Frederick Buechner, *The Clown in the Belfry: Writings on Faith and Fiction* (San Francisco: HarperSanFrancisco, 1992), 31.
6. William Blake, "The Everlasting Gospel," *The Oxford Book of English Mystical Verse,* edited by D. H. S. Nicholson and A. H. E. Lee (Oxford: Clarendon Press, 1917), Lines 13–14.

CHAPTER 3   THINKING THEOLOGICALLY
1. Alice Walker, *The Color Purple* (New York: Harcourt Brace Jovanovich, 1982), 202–203.
2. Rolf P. Knierim, *The Task of Old Testament Theology: Methods and Cases* (Grand Rapids, MI: Wm. B. Eerdmans Publishing Company, 1995), 1.
3. Angelou, *Wouldn't Take Nothing,* 74–75.
4. Fosdick, H.E., *Dear Mr. Brown: Letters to a Person Perplexed About Religion* (New York: Harper & Bros, 1961), 27.

CHAPTER 4   STORIES OF CREATION
1. Sam Siecol, "Jewish Theology Through Humor and Story," (lecture, Scottsdale, AZ, March 5, 1990).
2. Charles Darwin, *The Life and Letters of Charles Darwin,* edited by Francis Darwin (London: John Murray, Albermarle Street, 1887), 307.

CHAPTER 5   LIVES OF JESUS
1. Kathleen Parker, "Makeover Gone Mad On Jesus," *Orlando Sentinel,* April 1, 2001.
2. Robert Funk, *The Five Gospels* (San Francisco: HarperSanFrancisco, 1996).
3. Etienne Charpentier, *How to Read the New Testament,* trans. John Bowden (New York: Crossroad Publishing Company, 1987).
4. Funk, *The Five Gospels,* 14.
5. John Dominic Crossan, *Jesus: A Revolutionary Biography* (San Francisco: HarperOne, 2009), 106.

CHAPTER 6   A PASSION FOR CHRIST
1. John Dominic Crossan, *The Greatest Prayer: Rediscovering the Revolutionary Message of the Lord's Prayer* (San Francisco: HarperOne, 2011), 111.

CHAPTER 7   OUT INTO THE WORLD
1. Harry Emerson Fosdick, *Christianity and Progress* (New York: Fleming H. Revell Co., 1922), 165.
2. Bertrand Russell, *An Outline of Intellectual Rubbish: A hilarious catalogue of organized and individual stupidity,* (Girard, KS: Haldeman-Julius Publications, 1943), 6–7.
3. Rilke, *Letters,* 34.
4. Harrell Beck, "The Heart of Biblical Faith: Being a Biblical People," (lecture, Arrowhead Springs, CA, May 13, 1986).

5. Harrell Beck, "From Priestly Listener to Prophetic Witness: the Canon as the Church's Creation," (lecture, Arrowhead Springs, CA, May 13, 1986).
6. Howard Thurman, quoted in Gil Bailie, *Violence Unveiled: Humanity at the Crossroads* (New York: Crossroad, 1995), xv.
7. Dag Hammarskjöld, *Markings,* translated from the Swedish by Leif Sjöberg and W. H. Auden with a Foreword by M. H. Auden (New York: Alfred A. Knopf, 1964), 205.

CHAPTER 8   RESTORING RELATIONSHIPS
1. Borg, *Meeting Jesus,* 120.
2. Richard Rohr, *Letting Go: A Spirituality of Subtraction,* Audio CDs (Cincinnati, OH: St. Anthony Messenger Press, 1987).
3. "A Native American Perspective: Canaanites, Cowboys, and Indians," in *Voices from the Margin: Interpreting the Bible in the Third World,* edited by R. H. Sugirtharajah (Maryknoll: Orbis Books, 1991).

CHAPTER 9   THE PROPHETIC JESUS
1. Crossan, *The Greatest Prayer.*
2. *Saving Jesus Redux* DVD series (Phoenix, AZ: livingthequestions.com, 2010).
3. *Saving Jesus Redux,* DVD.
4. John Dear, *Peace Behind Bars: A Peacemaking Priest's Journal from Jail* (Lanham MD: Sheed and Ward, 1995), 65.
5. James C. Howell, *Servants, Misfits and Martyrs: Saints and Their Stories* (Nashville, TN: Upper Room, 1999), 28.

CHAPTER 10   EVIL, SUFFERING, AND A GOD OF LOVE
1. Brown, "Jewish Contributions to a Christian Lent: The Impact of Elie Wiesel," in *A Journal of Reformed Thought: Perspectives* (Albany, NY: Reformed Church Press, Feb., 1986), 7.
2. Elie Wiesel, *Night* (New York: Hill and Wang, 1969), 75–76.
3. Abraham Joshua Heschel, *The Prophets* (New York: Harper and Row, 1962), 31.
4. Alfred North Whitehead, *Process and Reality: An Essay in Cosmology* [1929], edited by David Ray Griffin and Donald W. Sherburne, corrected ed. (New York: Free Press, 1978), 351.
5. Harold Kushner, *When Bad Things Happen to Good People* (New York: Avon, 1981).
6. William Sloane Coffin. "Eulogy for Alex," *NOW,* March 5, 2004, http://www.pbs.org/now/society/eulogy.html.
7. Glynn Hardy, "The Post-Tsunami God," *St. Matthew in the City,* January 30, 2005, http://www.stmatthews.org.nz/nav.php?sid=52&id=340&print.
8. Harold Kushner, *The Lord is My Shepherd: Healing Wisdom of the Twenty-Third Psalm* (New York: Anchor Books, 2003), 110.

9. *Frontline*, "Faith and Doubt at Ground Zero," PBS transcript: www.pbs .org/wgbh/pages/frontline/shows/faith/questions/911.html.

10. Kushner, *Lord is My Shepherd*, 91.

11. Steven Lee Myers, "Anthony Perkins, Star of 'Psycho' And All Its Sequels, Is Dead at 60," *New York Times*, September 14, 1992, www.nytimes. com/1992/09/14/obituaries/anthony-perkins-star-of-psycho-and-all-its-sequels-is-dead-at–60.html.

12. Aleksandr Solzhenitsyn, *The Gulag Archipelago* (New York: HarperCollins, 1976), 168.

CHAPTER 11 THE MYTH OF REDEMPTIVE VIOLENCE

1. Alfred Lord Tennyson, *In Memoriam A.H.H.*, canto 56.

2. Walter Wink, *Engaging the Powers: Discernment and Resistance in a World of Domination* (Minneapolis, MN: Augsburg Press, 1992), 15.

3. Wink, *Engaging the Powers*, 150.

4. *Patton*, directed by Franklin J. Schaffner (1970; Los Angeles, CA: Twentieth Century Fox).

5. Chris Hedges, *War is a Force that Gives us Meaning* (New York: Anchor Books, 2003).

6. Jerry Falwell, *The 700 Club* (Virginia Beach, VA: Christian Broadcasting Network), television broadcast, September 13, 2001.

7. Falwell, *The 700 Club*.

8. David Niewert, "Gospel of Hate: Arizona pastor Steve Anderson spews bile toward Obama, Frank, and gays," *Crooks and Liars*. Audio available at http://crooksandliars.com/david-neiwert/gospel-hate-arizona-pastor-steve-and.

9. Wink, *Engaging the Powers*, 22.

10. Eddie Izzard, *Dress to Kill*, directed by Lawrence Jordan (1999; New York, WEA Corp.), DVD.

11. Mahatma Gandhi, quoted at *Satyagrah*, www.gauravsinha.com/gandhi/ movement_satyagrah.html.

CHAPTER 12 PRACTICING RESURRECTION

1. C. S. Lewis, *The Abolition of Man* (New York: HarperCollins, 2001), 81.

2. Wendell Berry, "Manifesto: The Mad Farmer Liberation Front," *Reclaiming Politics*, Fall/Winter 1991, 62.

3. DeWane Zimmerman, sermon, First United Methodist Church, Phoenix, AZ, Easter Sunday, 1981.

4. *New York Times*, "Martin Buber, 87, Dies in Israel; Renowned Jewish Philosopher," www.nytimes.com/learning/general/onthisday/bday/0208.html.

CHAPTER 13 DEBUNKING THE RAPTURE

1. Barbara R. Rossing, *The Rapture Exposed: The Message of Hope in the Book of Revelation* (Boulder, CO: Westview Press, 2004), 1–2.

2. Rossing, *The Rapture Exposed*, 18.
3. Amanda Bower, Nancy Gibbs, Rita Healy, Marc Hequet, Tom Morton, Adam Pitluk, Matt Rees, Jeffrey Ressner, Melissa Sattley, and Daniel Terdiman, "Apocalypse Now," *TIME*, June 23, 2002.
4. Christopher Goffard, "Doomsday Prediction: Harold Camping is at the heart of the mediapocalypse over his Doomsday prediction," *Los Angeles Times*, May 21, 2011.
5. Rossing, *The Rapture Exposed*, 43.
6. Comments by Tony Campolo to the Cooperative Baptist Fellowship, June 26, 2003, www.bpnews.net/bpnews.asp?id=16205.
7. John Hagee, *From Daniel to Doomsday: The Countdown Has Begun* (Nashville, TN: Thomas Nelson, 1999), 104.
8. Robert Jewett, *Jesus Against the Rapture: Seven Unexpected Prophecies* (Louisville, KY: Westminster John Knox, 1979), 84.
9. Rossing, *The Rapture Exposed*, 170.
10. Ibid., 158.

CHAPTER 14   HONORING CREATION

1. Chief Seattle's Farewell Speech, 1854, http://firstpeoplesvoices.com/seattle.htm.
2. Katherine Paterson, *Read for Your Life #9* (New York: Houghton Mifflin Harcourt, 2011), Google eBook.
3. Emily Dickinson, *The Letters of Emily Dickinson*, ed. Thomas H. Johnson and Theodora Ward. (Cambridge, MA: Belknap Press, 1997), L 904.
4. J. Barrie Shepherd, *Whatever Happened to Delight?: Preaching the Gospel in Poetry and Parables* (Louisville, KY: Westminster John Knox Press, 2006), 14.
5. John Steinbeck, *The Log from the Sea of Cortez* (New York: Viking Press, 1941), 218.
6. Blue Man Group, *Earth to America*, www.youtube.com/watch?v=snPdEl0Duoo&feature=player_embedded.
7. "Species Act Provokes Heated Discussion At Ag Conference," *Livestock Weekly*, January 10, 2002.
8. "The Wisdom of Ann Coulter," *The Washington Monthly*, October 2001.
9. Henry David Thoreau, *Walden* (New York: Signet Classics, 1960), 146–147.
10. *Livestock's Long Shadow: Environmental Issues and Options*, Food and Agriculture Organization of the United States, 2006.
11. For an example of this line of reasoning, see "Bears Shed New Light on Noah's Ark," *Creation Revolution*, http://creationrevolution.com/2011/02/bears-shed-new-light-on-noah%E2%80%99s-ark.
12. John Sniegocki, "The Responsible Choice," *Commonweal*, September 14, 2007, http://commonwealmagazine.org.
13. Robert K. Musil, "Global Climate Change: Polar bears, penguins and people," sermon text available at http://firstucc.org/wp-content/uploads/2009/02/sermon-by-robert-k-musil.pdf.
14. Musil, "Global Climate Change."

CHAPTER 15   A KINGDOM WITHOUT WALLS

1. Stephanie Raha and Thomas J. McSweeney, eds. *Better to Light One Candle: The Christophers' Three Minutes a Day Millenial Edition* (New York, NY: Continuum Publishing Company, 2000), 357.
2. See "A Community Responds to Hatred," *Congregation Or Ami,* http://www.orami.org/Articles/index.cfm?id=3857; and "Not in Our Town," *Facing History and Ourselves,* www.facinghistory.org/explore/exhibit/stories/niot/read.
3. Center for Progressive Christianity, "About Us: 8 Points."
4. Sydney Carter, "Mother Teresa," unpublished poem.
5. Clergy for Justice, "Phoenix Declaration," *No Longer Silent,* www.nolonger silent.org/PhoenixDeclaration.html.
6. Jim Wallis, *God's Politics: Why the Right Gets it Wrong and the Left Doesn't Get It* (New York: HarperCollins, 2005), 217.
7. Eric Elnes, *The Phoenix Affirmations* (San Francisco: Jossey-Bass 2006), 51.
8. Elnes, *The Phoenix Affirmations,* 3.
9. Jerry Barlow, sermon, Via de Cristo United Methodist Church, Scottsdale, AZ, April 17, 2004.
10. Marcus Borg, *The Heart of Christianity* (San Francisco: HarperOne, 2004), 26.

CHAPTER 16   SOCIAL JUSTICE

1. Theodore Parker, *The Collected Works of Theodore Parker: Lessons from the World of Matter and the World of Man* (London: Trübner, 1872), 192.
2. Mose Allison, "Everybody's Cryin' Mercy," *The Best of Mose Allison,* 1975, Atlantic Records.
3. James A. Michener, *The Source* (New York: Fawcett Books, 1965), 158.
4. Harrell Beck, "From Priestly Listener to Prophetic Witness: the Canon as the Church's Creation," (lecture, Arrowhead Springs, CA, May 13, 1986).
5. Dawn Annette Mills, (lecture, Franciscan Renewal Center, Scottsdale, AZ, February 2007).
6. Mills, lecture.
7. Heschel, *The Prophets,* 1962, 3–5.
8. Robert F. Kennedy, Day of Affirmation Speech given at the University of Cape Town, South Africa, June 6, 1966.

CHAPTER 17   INCARNATION

1. Thomas Jefferson, Letter to John Adams, April 11, 1823, www.beliefnet.com/resourcelib/docs/53/Letter_from_Thomas_Jefferson_to_John_Adams_1.html.
2. Harry Emerson Fosdick, "Shall the Fundamentalists Win?" sermon given at First Presbyterian Church, New York City, 1922. Originally published in *Christian Work* 102 (June 10, 1922), 716–722.
3. Campbell, Joseph, *The Hero with a Thousand Faces* (Princeton: Princeton Univ. Press, 1972), 309.

4. Eusebius Pamphilus, *The Life of the Blessed Emperor Constantine: From 306 to AD 337* Christian Roman Empire Series, Vol. 8 (Merchantville, NJ: Evolution Publishing, 2009), 94.
5. John B. Cobb Jr., *The Process Perspective*, (St. Louis, MO: Chalice Press, 2003), 39.

CHAPTER 18 PRAYER

1. Harold Kushner, *Who Needs God* (New York: Touchstone, 2002), 33.
2. See Chapter 8 of Robert Farrar Capon's *Kingdom, Grace, Judgment: Paradox, Outrage, and Vindication in the Parables of Jesus* (Grand Rapids, MI: Wm. B. Eerdmans, 1985).
3. Robert Farrar Capon, unpublished lecture: Youth Specialties Conference. Permission to use granted by the author.
4. Frederick and Mary Ann Brussat, *Spiritual Literacy: Reading the Sacred in Everyday Life* (New York: Scribner, 1996), 36.
5. Frederick and Mary Ann Brussat, *Spiritual Rx: Prescriptions for Living a Meaningful Life* (New York: Hyperion, 2000), 33.
6. Thich Nhat Han, *The Miracle of Mindfulness* (Boston: Beacon Press, 1975).
7. William Martin, *A Path and a Practice: Using Lao Tzu's Tao Te Ching as a Guide to an Awakened Spiritual Life* (Cambridge, MA: Da Capo Press, 2004), 48.
8. Richard Rohr, *Breathing Under Water: Spirituality and the 12 Steps* (Cincinnati: Saint Anthony Messenger Press, 2005), 96.
9. Cobb, *The Process Perspective*, 105.

CHAPTER 19 COMPASSION

1. Walter Wangerin Jr., *Ragman and Other Cries of Faith* (San Francisco: HarperSanFrancisco, 1984), 129–130.
2. Harrell Beck, "The Joys of Liberation Preaching" (sermon, Arrowhead Springs, San Bernardino, CA, May 14, 1986).
3. Stephen Covey, *The Seven Habits of Highly Effective People* (New York: Fireside, 1989), 30–31.
4. Borg, *Meeting Jesus*, 60.

CHAPTER 20 CREATIVE TRANSFORMATION

1. Lloyd M. Conyers, *The Relevance of Revelation: The Conquest of Evil* (Little Rock: August House, 1988), 93.
2. Richard Rohr and Andreas Ebert, *The Enneagram: A Christian Perspective* (New York: Crossroad Publishing, 2001), xv.
3. Yvette Flunder, from a speech given at OutFront Arizona, Blessing All Our Families Conference, Phoenix, June 2, 2007.
4. George Barna, "Number of Unchurched Adults has Nearly Doubled Since 1991," *Barna Update*, May 4, 2004, www.barna.org/barna-update/article/

5-barna-update/140-number-of-unchurched-adults-has-nearly-doubled-since–1991.

5. Thomas Merton, *The Living Bread* (New York: Farrar, Straus and Giroux, 1956), xxii.

6. Richard Rohr, lecture recorded at Southwest Liturgical Conference, Anaheim, CA, 2001. Now available on: *Authentic Religion: Membership or Transformation?* Included in "Richard Rohr on Church" *Collected Talks: Volume Three,* available from Franciscan media: http://catalog.franciscan media.org.

7. Robert McAfee Brown, *Creative Dislocation* (Nashville: Abingdon, 1980).

8. Ken Wilbur, *One Taste: Daily Reflections on Integral Spirituality* (Boston: Shambhala, 2000), 28.

9. Matthew Fox, *The Coming of the Cosmic Christ* (San Francisco: HarperSan-Francisco, 1998), 21.

10. Bernard Scott, *Hollywood Dreams and Biblical Stories* (Minneapolis: Fortress Press, 2000), 4.

11. Frederic and Mary Ann Brussat, "Befriending Films," www.spiritualityand practice.com/films/features.php?id=10941.

12. Robert A. Raines, *Creative Brooding* (New York: MacMillan, 1968), 18.

CHAPTER 21 EMBRACING MYSTERY

1. Richard Rohr, "The Edge of Christianity," lecture at the Franciscan Renewal Center (The Casa): Paradise Valley, AZ, September 13, 2007.

2. Progressive Christianity, "The 8 Points: Point 2 – Study Guide," http://progressivechristianity.org/about/point2_study.cfm.

3. Marcus Borg, *Saving Jesus Redux,* DVD series published in 2010 by www.livingthequestions.com.

4. Hammarskjöld, *Markings,* 5.

5. Abraham Joshua Heschel, edited by Sylvia Heschel, *Moral Grandeur and Spiritual Audacity: Essays* (New York: Farrar, Straus and Giroux, 1996), 166.

6. Jack Good, *The Dishonest Church* (Santa Cruz, CA: Rising Star Press, 2003), 182.

7. Rufus Jones, "Mystics Among Us," *TIME,* October 11, 1948.

8. Quoted in Fox, *The Coming of the Cosmic Christ,* 118.

9. Barbara Newman, *Sisters of Wisdom: St. Hildegard's theology of the feminine* (Berkley: Univ. of California Press, 1989), 71.

10. Mary Oliver, *New and Selected Poems* (Boston: Beacon Press, 1992).

11. Harrell Beck, "Images of Hope, The Nails," (lecture, Rock Eagle, GA, March 8, 1985).

BIBLIOGRAPHY AND RECOMMENDED READING

Angelou, Maya. *Wouldn't Take Nothing for My Journey Now*. New York: Bantam Books, 1994.

Armstrong, Karen. *The Battle for God*. New York: Knopf, 2000.

Bass, Diana Butler. *Christianity After Religion: The End of the Church and the Birth of a New Spiritual Awakening*. San Francisco: HarperOne, 2012.

———. *Christianity for the Rest of Us*. New York: HarperCollins, 2006.

———. *A People's History of Christianity*. New York: HarperCollins, 2009.

Bass, Dorothy C. *Practicing Our Faith: A Way of Life for a Searching People*. San Francisco: Jossey-Bass, 1997.

Battle, Michael. *Ubuntu: I in You and You in Me*. New York: Seabury Books, 2009.

Bawer, Bruce. *Stealing Jesus: How Fundamentalism Betrays Christianity*. New York: Random House, 1997.

Bell, Rob. *Love Wins: A Book about Heaven, Hell, and the Fate of Every Person Who Ever Lived*. New York: HarperCollins, 2011.

Borg, Marcus. *The Heart of Christianity*. New York: HarperCollins, 2003.

———. *Jesus: Uncovering the Life, Teachings, and Relevance of a Religious Revolutionary*. New York: HarperCollins, 2006.

———. *Meeting Jesus Again for the First Time*. San Francisco: HarperSanFrancisco, 1994.

———. *Speaking Christian: Why Christian Words Have Lost Their Meaning and Power*. New York: HarperCollins, 2011.

Brown, Robert McAfee. *The Bible Speaks to You*. Philadelphia: Westminster John Knox Press, 1985.

———. *Creative Dislocation*. Nashville: Abingdon, 1980.

———. "Jewish Contributions to a Christian Lent: The Impact of Elie Wiesel." *A Journal of Reformed Thought: Perspectives*. (Feb. 1986). Albany, NY: Reformed Church Press.

Brussat, Frederic, and Mary Ann Brussat. *Spiritual Literacy: Reading the Sacred in Everyday Life*. New York: Scribner, 1996.

―――. *Spiritual RX: Prescriptions for Living a Meaningful Life*. New York: Hyperion, 2000.

Buber, Martin. *I and Thou*. New York: Charles Scribner's Sons, 1970.

Buechner, Frederick. *The Clown in the Belfry: Writings on Faith and Fiction*. San Francisco: HarperSanFrancisco, 1992.

Burklo, Jim. *Open Christianity: Home by Another Road*. Scotts Valley, CA: Rising Star Press, 2000.

Campbell, Joseph. *The Hero with a Thousand Faces*. Princeton, NJ: Princeton Univ. Press, 1972.

Cobb Jr., John B. *Becoming a Thinking Christian: If We Want Church Renewal, We Will Have to Renew Thinking in the Church*. Nashville: Abingdon Press, 1993.

―――. *The Process Perspective: Frequently Asked Questions About Process Theology*. St. Louis, MO: Chalice Press, 2003.

Cobb Jr., John B. and David Griffin. *Process Theology: An Introductory Exposition*. Philadelphia: Westminster Press, 1976.

Coffin, William Sloan. *A Passion for the Possible: A Message to US Churches*. Louisville, KY: Westminster/John Knox Press, 1993.

Conyers, Lloyd M. *The Relevance of Revelation: The Conquest of Evil: A Self Study Guide to the Scripture for the Laity*. Little Rock, AR: August House, 1988.

Cox, Harvey. *The Future of Faith*. New York: HarperCollins, 2009.

Crossan, John Dominic. *The Birth of Christianity: Discovering What Happened in the Years Immediately After the Execution of Jesus*. San Francisco: HarperSanFrancisco, 1998.

―――. *The Greatest Prayer: Rediscovering the Revolutionary Message of the Lord's Prayer*. New York: HarperCollins, 2010.

―――. *The Historical Jesus: The Life of a Mediterranean Jewish Peasant*. San Francisco: HarperSanFrancisco, 1992.

―――. *Jesus: A Revolutionary Biography*. San Francisco: HarperSanFrancisco, 1994.

―――. *The Power of Parable: How Fiction by Jesus Became Fiction about Jesus*. New York: HarperCollins, 2012.

Crossan, John Dominic, and Jonathan L. Reed, *Excavating Jesus*. San Francisco: HarperSanFrancisco, 2001.

―――. *In Search of Paul: How Jesus' Apostle Opposed Rome's Empire with God's Kingdom*. San Francisco: HarperSanFrancisco, 2004.

de Chardin, Pierre Teilhard. *Writings Selected with an Introduction by Ursula King*. Maryknoll, NY: Orbis Books, 1999.

Dillard, Annie. *Pilgrim at Tinker Creek*. New York: Harper and Row, 1974.

Dowd, Michael. *Thank God for Evolution: How the Marriage of Science and Religion will Transform Your Life and Our World*. Canada: Council Oak Books, 2007.

Ehrenreich, Barbara. *Nickel and Dimed*. New York: Henry Holt, 2001.

Ehrlich, Paul R., and Robert E. Ornstein. *Humanity on a Tightrope: Thoughts on Empathy, Family, and Big Changes for a Viable Future*. Lanham, MD: Rowman and Littlefield Publishers, 2010.

Fiorenza, Elisabeth Schussler. *In Memory of Her: A Feminist Theological Reconstruction of Christian Origins*. New York: Crossroad, 1994.

Fox, Matthew. *The Coming of the Cosmic Christ*. San Francisco: HarperSanFrancisco, 1998.

———. *Creation Spirituality: Liberating Gifts for the Peoples of the Earth*. New York: HarperCollins, 1991.

———. *Original Blessing: A Primer in Creation Spirituality*. Santa Fe: Bear, 1983.

Funk, Robert. *Honest to Jesus*. San Francisco: HarperSanFrancisco, 1996.

Funk, Robert, Roy Hoover, and the Jesus Seminar, eds., *The Five Gospels: What Did Jesus Really Say? The Search for the Authentic Words of Jesus*. New York: Macmillan, 1993.

Geering, Lloyd. *Christian Faith at the Crossroads: A Map of Modern Religious History*. Santa Rosa, CA: Polebridge Press, 2001.

———. *Tomorrow's God: How We Create Our Worlds*. Santa Rosa, CA: Polebridge Press, 2000.

Gomes, Peter. *The Good Book: Reading the Bible with Mind and Heart*. New York: William Morrow, 1996.

Good, Jack. *The Dishonest Church*. Scotts Valley, CA: Rising Star Press, 2003.

Hammarskjöld, Dag. *Markings*. Translated by W. H. Auden and Leif Sjoberg. London: Faber and Faber, 1964.

Hartshorne, Charles. *Omnipotence and Other Theological Mistakes*. New York: State Univ. of New York Press, Albany, 1984.

Hedges, Chris. *War Is a Force that Gives Us Meaning*. New York: Anchor Books, 2003.

Heschel, Abraham Joshua. *The Prophets*. New York: Harper and Row, 1962.

Horsley, Richard H., and Neil Asher Silberman. *The Message and the Kingdom: How Jesus and Paul Ignited a Revolution and Transformed the Ancient World*. Minneapolis: Augsburg Fortress, 1997.

Horsley, Richard H., and James Tracy. *Christmas Unwrapped: Consumerism, Christ, and Culture*. Harrisburg, PA: Trinity Press International, 2001.

Hugo, Victor. *Les Miserables*. New York: Penguin Classics, 1976.

Jenks, Gregory C. *The Once and Future Bible: An Introduction to the Bible for Religious Progressives*. Eugene, OR: Wipf and Stock, 2011.

Kelber, Werner. *Mark's Story of Jesus*. Minneapolis: Fortress, 1979.

Kingsolver, Barbara. *The Poisonwood Bible*. New York: HarperCollins, 1998.

Knierim, Rolf. *The Task of Old Testament Theology*. Grand Rapids: Wm. B. Eerdmans, 1995.

Koester, Helmut. *Ancient Christian Gospels: Their History and Development*. London: SCM Press, 1990.

Kornfield, Jack. *After the Ecstasy, the Laundry*. New York: Bantam, 2000.

Korten, David C. *The Great Turning: From Empire to Earth Community*. San Francisco: Berrett-Koehler Publishers, 2006.

Kushner, Harold. *The Lord is My Shepherd: Healing Wisdom of the Twenty-Third Psalm*. New York: Knopf, 2003.

———. *When Bad Things Happen to Good People*. New York: Avon, 1981.

Lamott, Anne. *Traveling Mercies*. New York: Random House, 1999.

Laughlin, Paul Alan, with Glenna S. Jackson. *Remedial Christianity: What Every*

Believer Should Know about the Faith, but Probably Doesn't. Santa Rosa, CA: Polebridge Press, 2000.

Levine, Amy-Jill. *The Misunderstood Jew: The Church and the Scandal of the Jewish Jesus.* New York: HarperCollins, 2006.

Levine, Stephen. *A Year to Live: How to Live This Year as if it Were Your Last.* New York: Bell Tower, 1997.

Living the Questions. *Countering Pharaoh's Production-Consumption Society* DVD. Phoenix, AZ: livingthequestions.com, 2007.

———. *Eclipsing Empire: Paul, Rome and the Kingdom of God* DVD Series. Phoenix, AZ: livingthequestions.com, 2008.

———. *First Light: Jesus and the Kingdom of God* DVD Series. Phoenix, AZ: living thequestions.com, 2009.

———. *Living the Questions 2.0: An Introduction to Progressive Christianity* DVD Series. Phoenix, AZ: livingthequestions.com, 2007.

———. *Matt and Lucy's Version Births: A Christmas Pageant* CD Rom. Phoenix, AZ: livingthequestions.com, 2009.

———. *Saving Jesus Redux* DVD Series. Phoenix, AZ: livingthequestions.com, 2010.

McFague, Sallie. *Models of God.* Minneapolis: Fortress Press, 1987.

Mack, Burton. *The Lost Gospel: The Book of Q and Christian Origins.* San Francisco: HarperSanFrancisco, 1993.

———. *A Myth of Innocence.* Minneapolis: Fortress Press, 1988.

———. *Who Wrote the New Testament? The Making of the Myth of Christianity.* San Francisco: HarperSanFrancisco, 1995.

Martin, William. *A Path and a Practice: Using Lao Tzu's Tao Te Ching as a Guide to an Awakened Spiritual Life.* New York: Da Capo, 2004.

Miller, Robert. *Born Divine: The Births of Jesus and Other Sons of God.* Santa Rosa, CA: Poleridge Press, 2003.

Mitchell, Stephen. *The Gospel According to Jesus.* New York: HarperCollins, 1991.

Nelson, G. Lynn. *Writing and Being.* Philadelphia: Innisfree Press, 1994.

O'Donohue, John. *Anam Cara: A Book of Celtic Wisdom.* New York: HarperCollins, 1997.

———. *Beauty.* New York: HarperCollins, 2004.

Oliver, Mary. *New and Selected Poems.* Boston: Beacon Press, 1992.

Pagels, Elaine. *Beyond Belief: The Secret Gospel of Thomas.* New York: Random House, 2003.

———. *The Gnostic Gospels.* New York: Random House, 1979.

Patterson, Stephen. *The Gospel of Thomas and Jesus.* Sonoma, CA: Poleridge Press, 1993.

Peterson, Eugene. *The Message.* Colorado Springs: Navpress, 2002.

Phillips, Jan. *No Ordinary Time: The Rise of Spiritual Intelligence and Evolutionary Creativity.* San Diego, CA: Livingkindness Foundation, 2011.

Progressive Christians Uniting. *Progressive Christians Speak: A Different Voice on Faith and Politics.* Edited by John B. Cobb Jr. Louisville, KY: Westminster John Knox Press, 2003.

Robinson, John A. T. *Honest to God*. Philadelphia: Westminster Press, 1963.

Rohr, Richard. *The Naked Now: Learning to See as the Mystics See*. New York: Crossroad, 2009.

Rossing, Barbara. *The Rapture Exposed: The Message of Hope in the Book of Revelation*. Boulder, CO: Westview Press, 2004.

Sandel, Michael. *Justice: What's the Right Thing to Do*. New York: Farrar, Straus and Giroux, 2009.

Schwartzentruber, Michael, ed. *The Emerging Christian Way: Thoughts, Stories, and Wisdom for a Faith of Transformation*. Kelowna, BC: CopperHouse, 2006.

Scott, Bernard Brandon. *Hear Then the Parable*. Minneapolis: Augsburg Fortress, 1989.

Shore, Bill. *The Cathedral Within: Transforming Your Life by Giving Something Back*. New York: Random House, 1999.

Shorto, Russell. *Gospel Truth: The New Image of Jesus Emerging from Science and History, and Why It Matters*. New York: Riverhead Books, 1997.

Smith, Huston. *Why Religion Matters: The Fate of the Human Spirit in an Age of Disbelief*. San Francisco: HarperSanFrancisco, 2001.

Smith, R. G. *Secular Christianity*. New York: Harper and Row, 1967.

Spong, John Shelby. *Living in Sin? A Bishop Rethinks Human Sexuality*. San Francisco: HarperSanFrancisco, 1988.

———. *A New Christianity for a New World: Why Traditional Faith is Dying and How a New Faith is Being Born*. San Francisco: HarperSanFrancisco, 2001.

———. *Reclaiming the Bible for a Non-Religious World*. New York: HarperCollins, 2011.

———. *Rescuing the Bible from Fundamentalism: A Bishop Rethinks the Meaning of Scripture*. San Francisco: HarperSanFrancisco, 1991.

———. *Why Christianity Must Change or Die: A Bishop Speaks to Believers in Exile*. San Francisco: HarperSanFrancisco, 1998.

Stark, Rodney. *The Rise of Christianity*. San Francisco: HarperSanFrancisco, 1996.

Steinbeck, John. *The Grapes of Wrath*. New York: Viking Press, 1939.

———. *The Log from the Sea of Cortez*. New York: Viking Press, 1941.

Stendahl, Krister. *Paul Among Jews and Gentiles*. Philadelphia: Fortress, 1976.

Taylor, Barbara Brown. *An Altar in the World: A Geography of Faith*. New York: HarperCollins, 2009.

———. *Leaving Church: A Memoir of Faith*. New York: HarperCollins, 2006.

Trible, Phyllis. *God and the Rhetoric of Sexuality*. Minneapolis: Fortress Press, 1984.

———. *Texts of Terror*. Minneapolis: Fortress Press, 1984.

Tutu, Desmond. *God is Not a Christian: Speaking Truth in Times of Crisis*. New York: HarperCollins, 2011.

Wiesel, Elie. *Night*. New York: Bantam, 1982.

Wink, Walter. *Facing the Myth of Redemptive Violence*. Chicago: Christian Peacemaker Teams, 2007.

———. *The Powers that Be*. New York: Doubleday, 1998.

INDEX

INDEX

Fosdick, Harry Emerson
  "Shall the Fundamentalists Win?," 15
  speaking of God, 24
  on stagnation in Christianity, 60
  on virgin birth, 177
  on vital faith, 66–67
Fox, Matthew
  on creation stories, 32–33
  on creativity, 218
  on modern myths, 217
  on Mother Earth as a metaphor for
    Jesus, 144
  Original Blessing , 112, 113
  on original sin, 108
  writings of, 138
Franciscans, 226
Freedom, 228
Fuller, Millard, 87
Fundamentalism, 6
Fundamentalist Christians, 15, 63,
    69–70, 129
Funk, Robert, 44

G
Galatians, 53
Galileo, 39
Gamaliel, 52
Gandhi, Mohandas (Mahatma),
    65–66, 113
Garden of Eden, 78, 141
Genesis
  1, 33, 34–35, 37, 137
  1:28, 139
  2, 35–36, 142
  2:4, 33
  2:4–25, 35
  7:2, 13
  7:14, 13
  9:3, 142
  18:2, 156
  flood stories in, 13, 18
  God of, 137
  Hebrew composition of, 31
  theme of exile and return in, 78

vegetarianism as the biblical ideal in,
    141–142
  versions of exodus, 18
Genocidal germ, 6
Gibson, Mel, 58
Glover, Mary, 158
God
  in all things and all things in, 138–139
  bad things and, 95–99
  character of, 168
  compassion and, 205
  different kind of, 167–168
  downtrodden as duty of the people,
    83
  evil and, 92–102
  indwelling in all of creation, 184–185
  justice of, 168
  language about, 24–26
  of love, 92–102
  love of, 152–153
  power of, 26–28
  as a presence, 224
  search for, 184
  thinking theologically and, 22–24
  walking humbly with, 171–174
  of wrath and vengeance, 107
Good, Jack, 224
Gospel of James. *See* Infancy Gospel of
    James
Gospel of Thomas, 47, 83, 215
Gospels (New Testament)
  characteristics of, 17–18, 42–43
  characteristics of writers, 44–45
  differences of, 44
  kingdom of God and, 50
  preciousness of life and, 124
  as source for knowledge of Jesus, 42
  synoptic problem of, 43
  Synoptics and John, 47
  two-source hypothesis, 46–47
Graham, Billy, 97
Graham, Franklin, 97
Grandjean, Philippe, 144
Ground of Being, 62, 185

INDEX

INDEX

ABOUT THE AUTHORS

DAVID M. FELTEN was trained at Boston University School of Theology and JEFF PROCTER-MURPHY at Claremont School of Theology.

David and Jeff have over forty years combined experience in local church ministry and currently serve as the pastors of United Methodist congregations in Arizona (David at The Fountains UMC in Fountain Hills and Jeff at Via de Cristo UMC in Scottsdale). They continue to collaborate on sermons and new resources for www .livingthequestions.com, providing DVD and internet-based curriculum to nearly 6,000 churches and other groups across the United States, Canada, the United Kingdom, Australia, and New Zealand in order to bring together, equip, and reeducate progressive Christians.